Ecomartyrdom in the Americas

ECOLOGY & JUSTICE SERIES

Ecomartyrdom in the Americas

*Living and Dying for
Our Common Home*

Elizabeth O'Donnell Gandolfo

ORBIS BOOKS
Maryknoll, New York 10545

Founded in 1970, Orbis Books endeavors to publish works that enlighten the mind, nourish the spirit, and challenge the conscience. The publishing arm of the Maryknoll Fathers and Brothers, Orbis seeks to explore the global dimensions of the Christian faith and mission, to invite dialogue with diverse cultures and religious traditions, and to serve the cause of reconciliation and peace. The books published reflect the views of their authors and do not represent the official position of the Maryknoll Society. To learn more about Maryknoll and Orbis Books, please visit our website at www.orbisbooks.com.

Library of Congress Cataloging-in-Publication Data

Names: Gandolfo, Elizabeth O'Donnell, author.
Title: Ecomartyrdom in the Americas : living and dying for our common home / Elizabeth O'Donnell Gandolfo.
Description: Maryknoll, NY : Orbis Books, 2022. | Series: Ecology & justice series | Includes bibliographical references and index. | Summary "A new assessment of the theological concept of martyrdom in light of those in Latin America who have given their lives while protecting the earth from those who threaten it"— Provided by publisher.
Identifiers: LCCN 2022038427 (print) | LCCN 2022038428 (ebook) | ISBN 9781626985124 (trade paperback) | ISBN 9781608339747 (epub)
Subjects: LCSH: Martyrdom—Latin America—History. | Martyrdom—Christianity —History. | Human ecology—Religious aspects—Christianity. | Environmental justice--Religious aspects—Christianity. | Persecution—Latin America. | Christian martyrs—Latin America.
Classification: LCC BL626.5 .G36 2022 (print) | LCC BL626.5 (ebook) | DDC 179/.1—dc23/eng20221107
LC record available at https://lccn.loc.gov/2022038427
LC ebook record available at https://lccn.loc.gov/2022038428

Yo, como tú,
amo el amor, la vida, el dulce encanto
de las cosas, el paisaje
celeste de los días de enero.

También mi sangre bulle
y río por los ojos
que han conocido el brote de las lágrimas.

Creo que el mundo es bello,
que la poesía es como el pan, de todos.

Y que mis venas no terminan en mí
sino en la sangre unánime
de los que luchan por la vida,
el amor,
las cosas,
el paisaje y el pan,
la poesía de todos.

—Roque Dalton

In memory of
Josimo, Chico, Alcides, Dorothy, Marcelo, Berta, and
"all the martyrs who have been slain
for defending the goods of the natural world."

Ustedes son lxs imprescindibles.
¡Que vivan!

Contents

Martyrs of Solidarity, Seeds of Hope

In October 2015, a group of pilgrims from El Salvador visited the Vatican to give thanks for the recent beatification of their beloved prophet, saint, and martyr, Archbishop Óscar Arnulfo Romero. Now canonized a saint in the Roman Catholic Church, Romero was assassinated on March 24, 1980, for his prophetic denunciation of economic injustice and political violence, especially the violence meted out against the Salvadoran people by the country's military government, which was backed by the United States and intent on preserving the wealth and power of the Salvadoran oligarchy. During a papal audience with the pilgrims, Pope Francis honored Romero's martyrdom with a message about the centrality of martyrdom for the Christian church: "From the beginning of the life of the Church, we Christians, persuaded by the words of Christ, who reminds us that 'unless a grain of wheat falls into the earth and dies, it remains alone' (Jn 12:24), have always maintained the conviction that the blood of martyrs is the seed of Christians." For the Salvadorans on pilgrimage that day, along with their companions at home and millions of others throughout the world, Archbishop Romero certainly is a seed of hope whose witness continues to bear fruit in what Francis called "an abundant harvest of holiness, of justice, reconciliation and love of God."[1] And yet Romero is not a traditional martyr, killed by non-Christians *in odium fidei*, out of hatred for the faith. Rather, he was killed by fellow Christians out of hatred for his insistence that the Christian faith demands solidarity with the poor and oppressed, active commitment to their liberation, and the creation of a just society in which the abundance of Creation might be shared by all.

Like Romero, thousands of other Christians and people of good will also laid down their lives for the sake of justice, liberation, and peace in late-twentieth-century Latin America. These "martyrs of solidarity," as Michael Lee aptly names them, have been recognized and remembered by their people as prophets, saints, and martyrs for decades, and in recent years, especially under the leadership of Pope Francis, the Roman Catholic Church has begun to officially recognize their witness as a form of martyrdom. Romero was officially named a martyr and beatified in 2015 and was canonized in 2018. His dear friend, Fr. Rutilio Grande, S.J., whose 1977 assassination was a turning point in the evolution of Romero's own ministry, was declared a martyr in 2020 and beatified in 2022, along with the two laypersons, Manuel Solórzano and Nelson Rutilio Lemus (just 16 years old) who were killed along with him. Rutilio, Manuel, and Nelson had been working to conscientize and organize the farmworkers of their parish according to the gospel dream of a world in which God invites all of humanity, but most especially the poor, to dine at the banquet table of Creation.[2] Another priest, Fray Cosme Spessotto, who was

---

[1] Pope Francis, "Address to the Pilgrimage from El Salvador," October 30, 2015, www.vatican.va.

[2] This image of the banquet table was invoked by Rutilio Grande and immortalized in the song "Vamos todos al banquete," which was composed by Guillermo Cuéllar as the entrance hymn to the "Salvadoran Popular Mass." See J. M. Vigil and A. Torrellas, *Misas Centroamericanas: Transcripción y comentario teológico* (Managua, Nicaragua: CAV-CEBES, 1988).

killed in 1980 for his denunciation of the abuses committed against the Salvadoran people by the ruling military junta, was beatified together with Rutilio, Manuel, and Nelson.

Pope Francis has also officially recognized the martyrdom of a number of other Christians who were killed for defending human rights and standing in solidarity with the poor and oppressed of Latin America during the worst years of state-sponsored violence and political repression in the late twentieth century. Bishop Enrique Angelelli, Fr. Carlos Murias, Fr. Gabriel Longueville, and lay catechist Wenceslao Pedernera were all killed in 1976 "because of their active efforts to promote Christian justice" during Argentina's "dirty wars," when "right-wing death squads kidnapped, tortured and assassinated anyone suspected of being a political or ideological threat."[3] When he was Archbishop of Buenos Aires, Jorge Bergoglio called these men martyrs during a memorial mass he celebrated for them in the Cathedral of La Rioja, and as Pope Francis he officially declared them to be martyrs in 2018. They were beatified in 2019. In Guatemala, several priests and laypersons have also been declared martyrs and beatified for their commitment to justice and peace in the face of state-sponsored genocide against the Indigenous people of the Quiché region between 1980 and 1991.[4]

Pope Francis's recognition of martyrs who were killed by fellow Christians out of hatred for solidarity, justice, and truth represents the culmination of a decades-long process. Over the past fifty years, the Latin American popular church, ecclesial base communities, and liberation theologians have been transforming the meaning of Christian martyrdom from within the liberation struggles of marginalized and oppressed peoples. Long before Jorge Bergoglio became Pope Francis, the popular church in Latin America recog-

---

[3] Seàn-Patrick Lovett, "Beatification of Four Modern Martyrs to the Faith in Argentina," April 27, 2019, www.vaticannews.va.

[4] "Ten Martyrs of Quiché Beatified in Guatemala," April 23, 2021, www.vaticannews.va.

nized and carried on the legacy of martyrs like Óscar Romero and Enrique Angelelli, along with the thousands of others who were also killed for their Christian commitment. It is only now, decades later, that this prophetic, grassroots recognition of martyrs of solidarity has finally made its way up through the ranks of the hierarchy to achieve institutional recognition. Granted, Pope Francis has also continued to officially recognize the martyrdom of Christians who have been killed around the world by non-Christians out of explicit hatred of the faith. But official recognition of this expanded understanding of martyrdom represents a significant development in the church's tradition and an institutional witness to the preferential option for the poor and oppressed as a central commitment of the Christian faith.

This official recognition for Latin American martyrs of solidarity is a welcome advance, especially given the history of Western Christian complicity with conquest, colonization, racism, and neocolonialism in the Americas and around the world. It indicates that the Catholic tradition is moving through a process of conversion a *metanoia*, or turning away from solidarity with the wealthy and powerful to solidarity with the colonized, poor, and oppressed. Yet there are ways in which this official process can also contribute to reinscribing patriarchal, racial, and clerical privilege in its preference for high-profile cases of martyrs who were lighter-skinned, male, and ordained priests or bishops in the Roman Catholic Church. And while the legacy of these martyrs should inspire us to carry on their work of solidarity in our own social contexts today, we run the risk of romanticizing and distancing ourselves from the historical realities in which martyrs of solidarity gave their lives if we do not recognize that marginalized communities, popular movements, and human rights defenders continue to risk their lives today for the sake of justice and peace.

The worst years of military dictatorships, death squads, and political disappearances have thankfully passed in most of Latin

America. But economic and political violence is not a thing of the past. Rather, the wealthy and powerful have found new ways and means of silencing the voices of those who seek liberation from unjust and oppressive systems. In fact, human rights defenders in Latin America have come under increasing attack in recent years. This is especially true for Afro-descendent, Indigenous, and queer folks seeking intersectional justice and liberation for their communities. Take, for example, the case of Marielle Franco, a Black queer woman who was born in a favela of Rio de Janeiro in 1979 and became a fierce opponent of racism, police brutality, and economic exploitation, fighting for the rights and dignity of Black and LGBT folks, first as an activist and then as a city councilwoman.[5] She was killed by hitmen in Rio de Janeiro on March 14, 2018, along with her driver, Anderson Gomes. Recent developments in Catholic theologies of martyrdom are at their best when they lift up the witness of contemporary human rights defenders who, like Marielle, persevere in the struggle against oppression and injustice in Latin America, and throughout the Americas as a whole. Benedictine monk Marcelo Barros makes this connection clear in his recognition of Marielle as one of the many martyrs who, whether Christian or not, challenge the church to stand in solidarity with the poor, marginalized, and oppressed, not as an "appendix to the faith," but as "the fundamental nucleus of what it means to follow Jesus."[6]

In recent decades, popular movements for human rights, justice, and liberation have come to recognize that environmental justice and ecological well-being are central to their struggles for

---

[5] See "Marielle and Monica: The LGBT Activists Resisting Bolsonaro's Brazil," documentary film, *The Guardian*, December 28, 2018, www.theguardian.com.

[6] Marcelo Barros, "Queremos nossos mártires vivos," Brasil de Fato Website, March 25, 2022, https://www.brasildefatope.com.br/2019/03/25/queremos-nossos-martires-vivos. All translations from original Spanish and Portuguese sources are mine unless otherwise noted.

the social, economic, and cultural well-being of marginalized and oppressed human communities. Indigenous peoples have recognized this connection between ecological and human well-being for millennia, and the retrieval of Indigenous identity and culture throughout Latin America has contributed to this ecological turn in the popular movements of the region. At the same time, under the reign of globalized neoliberal capitalism, extractivist industries have accelerated their pillage of the lands, forests, and waterways of the Americas in pursuit of limitless economic profit and at the service of insatiable consumer desire. When marginalized communities resist the invasion of extractivist projects in their territories, they are met with the violent tactics of international networks of power that stop at nothing to silence their protest. As a result, hundreds of land and environmental defenders are being killed each year for their commitment to environmental justice and ecological well-being. Like the twentieth-century martyrs of solidarity, these individuals are witnesses to the "cry of the poor," but they also hear the "cry of the earth," and they see both cries as intricately interconnected.[7]

Pope Francis's 2015 encyclical on the environment, *Laudato Si': On Care for Our Common Home*, offers an extended reflection on the interconnection of these cries, along with the interconnectedness at the heart of all Creation.[8] In this landmark document, Francis insists that human and ecological well-being cannot be separated or pitted against each other. Consequently, he invites his readers to undergo an ecological conversion such that we might come to embody what he calls "integral ecology" through recognition of our interconnection with the rest of Creation and through

---

[7] See Leonardo Boff, *Cry of the Earth, Cry of the Poor* (Maryknoll, NY: Orbis Books, 1997).

[8] Pope Francis, Encyclical Letter, *Laudato Si': On Care for Our Common Home*, May 24, 2015, www.vatican.va.

loving care for Creation as our "common home." Land and environmental defenders throughout the Americas, and around the world, embody this vision of interconnectedness and care for Creation, and far too many of them are paying for their social and ecological commitments with their lives. They are witnesses to solidarity with both the poor and the earth, with the oppressed and our common home, with marginalized communities and the natural goods on which they depend for sustenance and on which we all depend for a future in which our atmosphere and ecosystems can continue to support life on earth.

Martyrs of solidarity are assassinated for many reasons in our contemporary world of racism, patriarchy, economic exploitation, war, and other forms of violent conflict. This book is specifically dedicated to unveiling the martyrdom of environmental human rights defenders in the Americas, especially in Latin America, where the lion's share of documented murders of land and environmental defenders are taking place today. The United Nations defines environmental human rights defenders as "individuals and groups who, in their personal or professional capacity and in a peaceful manner, strive to protect and promote human rights relating to the environment, including water, air, land, flora and fauna." Individuals and communities who defend environmental human rights, which include land rights, are "highly vulnerable" and "under attack across the globe." In fact, according to the UN Environment Programme, "[w]orldwide, environmental defenders face growing assaults and murders—in conjunction with increasing intimidation, harassment, stigmatization and criminalization. At least three people a week are killed protecting our environmental rights—while many more are harassed, intimidated, criminalized and forced from their lands." Furthermore, John Knox, the first UN Special Rapporteur on Human Rights and the Environment, remarks that "[f]or their tireless work in empowering communities and protecting ecosystems, environmental defenders are killed in startling numbers. Murder is not the only way environmental defenders are persecuted; for every 1 killed, there are 20 to 100 others harassed, unlawfully and lawfully arrested, and sued for defamation, amongst other intimidations."[9]

This book uncovers the root causes and contextual circumstances of these murders, contemplates the stories of several "ecomartyrs," and offers ecotheological reflection on martyrdom in light of the dangerous praxis of defending land and environmental human rights.

The first three chapters of the book lay out the historical, political, and ecological contexts in which land and environmental defenders seek justice and liberation for their human communities in tandem with ecological integrity for the earth. Chapter 1, "The Pillage of Our Common Home: Ecomartyrdom and Extractivism in the Americas," seeks historical understanding of the colonial roots of extractivist violence in the Americas, analyzes the logic of extractivism today, and reflects on extractivism as a manifestation of structural sin fueled by an anti-social and anti-ecological imaginary. Chapter 2, "Fighting for Our Common Home: Extractivism and the Struggle for Environmental Justice in the Americas," details the contexts of extractivism and communal resistance in which land and environmental defenders carry out their struggles for justice and ecological well-being. Chapter 3, "Dying for Our Common Home: The Criminalization and Assassination of Environmental Defenders," describes both the processes leading to international recognition of environmental human rights and the right to defend the environment, on the one hand, and the ways in which land and environmental defenders are persecuted for the

---

[9]   "Who Are Environmental Defenders?" United Nations Environment Programme Website, www.unep.org.

work they do to protect their communities and the goods of the natural world, on the other.

It is important to note here that the persecution of land and environmental defenders also takes place in the United States and Canada, which are also marked by a colonial history of land theft, slavery, genocide, and ecocide, along with a contemporary landscape of settler colonialism, environmental injustice and racism, ecological degradation, and extractivist pillage of natural resources. Land and environmental defenders in this context—especially Indigenous, Black, Latinx, and poor white defenders—experience criminalization, defamation, arrest, and even death threats by those who seek to silence their voices. In this first part of the book, therefore, I attempt to tell the story of resistance to extractivism and environmental injustice in the Americas as a whole. However, for the most part, the rest of the book turns our attention to Latin America, where the murder of land and environmental defenders is a regular occurrence and where local communities often interpret these murders as a form of martyrdom.

In chapter 4, "Narrating the Witness: In Memory of Murdered Land and Environmental Defenders," I invite readers to contemplate the narratives of six ecomartyrs who have been assassinated in Latin America over the past forty years: Fr. Josimo Taveres, Chico Medes, Fr. Alcides Jiménez, Sr. Dorothy Stang, Marcelo Rivera, and Berta Cáceres. While these pages cannot do justice to their stories or the enormity of their sacrifice, my hope is that readers will come away from this chapter, which is really the heart of the book, with an appreciation for the depth of communal formation and personal commitment that led these individuals to accept the possibility of death as a consequence of their work for justice and ecological well-being. I end the chapter with a litany of other land and environmental defenders who have been assassinated in the last six years since Berta's murder. While this chapter lifts up the witness of high-profile ecomartyrs, I hope that it will also help readers understand that the individuals highlighted here were embedded within and formed by communities in which others have also suffered the same fate, and that these individuals represent thousands more slain environmental defenders in the Americas and throughout the world.

In chapters 5 and 6, I turn to theological reflection on the reality of ecomartyrdom, from an interreligious perspective and from the perspective of Christian theology. Chapter 5, "Wellsprings of the Witness: The Ecological Imaginations of Land and Environmental Defenders," seeks understanding of the spiritual, cultural, theological, and ecological inspiration for the commitments of land and environmental defenders. This chapter asks: Where does such great love and commitment come from? What are the wellsprings of such hope and courage in the face of the violent evils of extractivism? The wellsprings of the ecomartyrs' witness flow together and diverge in various ways, and while this chapter cannot do justice to their diversity and complexity, I hope that readers will come away with a sense of how deep these wellsprings run in the shared struggles for environmental justice in the Americas. In chapter 6, "Remembering the Witness: Ecomartyrdom in Christian Theological Perspective," I turn to theological reflection on ecomartyrdom in light of the Christian tradition and the aforementioned evolution that took place in Christian theologies of martyrdom in the twentieth century. Here I lay out the contours of that evolution in Latin American liberation theology, assess its claims from an ecotheological perspective, and uncover connections between twentieth-century martyrs of solidarity like Romero and those who have been and continue to be murdered for their defense of our common home.

Finally, I conclude with a consideration of how Christians and other people of good will might respond to the witness of ecomartyrs by honoring them with our own lived commitment to solidarity with environmental justice struggles in the Americas and around the world. A study guide is available at the end of the book to facilitate further understanding and personal and communal reflection on each chapter. There is also a companion website available to assist with these endeavors at www.ecomartyrdom.net.

In order to recognize the truly collaborative nature of all theological research projects, I would like to acknowledge those whose influence can be felt in these pages here, rather than in a separate acknowledgments section. Any errors or shortcomings in these pages are my own, of course, but this book would not have been possible without the support of many friends, family members, colleagues, students, and all those who have borne witness to the witness of ecomartyrs in writing, documentary films, online video tributes, music, artwork, and the continued struggle for environmental justice. First and foremost, I give thanks for my spouse, David, and our children, who have unconditionally supported my passion for this project. I also give thanks to Robert Ellsberg for his encouragement over the past few years and for seeing the promise of this particular project and its relevance to the mission of Orbis Books, which I have long admired.

Memory of martyrdom in Latin America takes on many rich and varied forms, including artistic expression. This book would not be complete without the artwork that graces both its cover and the pages of chapter 4. I therefore offer my deepest gratitude to Alexander Serpas, the Salvadoran artist who created the cover image, *"Ecomartirio: voz de la tierra, fuerza de vida"* (*"Ecomartyrdom: voice of the earth, life force"*). Many thanks also to Grace McMullen, my former student and Wake Forest University School of Divinity alum who crafted the prints of Josimo, Chico, Alicides, Dorothy, Marcelo, and Berta for chapter 4 with loving care and prayerful attention.

My colleagues at Wake Forest University School of Divinity have offered unwavering support for my research, and I am especially inspired by the work of my colleague Melanie Harris, whose ecowomanist wisdom graces some of these pages. Other Wake Forest colleagues who have been influential for this project and generous with their wisdom and insights include Miles Silman and John Knox, both of whom are far more knowledgeable than I am with regard to the realities of extractivism and the work of environmental defenders in Latin America and around the world. César Ascorra, the National Director of Wake Forest's Centro de Inovación Científica Amazónica in Peru, has also been generous with his expert knowledge and experience regarding the effects of gold mining in the Madre Dios region of the Amazon and beyond. Several Wake Forest students and alums have accompanied me on my journey through this book project as well. I offer my thanks to Joy Williams, Taína Díaz-Reyes, Jessica Rowe, and Liz Esquivel for their assistance, care, questions, and insights throughout my research and writing process. Many additional thanks to all of the students in both my Spring 2021 class, "Religion and Environmental Justice in Latin America," and my Fall 2021 class, "Contemporary Ecotheologies." Our conversations, contemplative moments, shared grief, and persistent questioning have contributed great insights and corrections to much of my thinking in this book. You all give me hope that a better world is not only possible, it is on its way.

Outside of Wake Forest, Daniel Castillo has been supportive of this project from the beginning, and his work on political ecology and liberation theology has been a helpful touchstone for my thinking in this project. Laurel Marshall Potter is also a kindred spirit and conversation partner whose questions, insights, and enthusiasm for this project have been an inspiration to me from the start. Martha Inés Romero, the Latin America regional

coordinator of Pax Christi, has been particularly helpful by gener-
ously sharing her insights and expert knowledge on extractivism
and violent conflict in Latin America, along with her experience
in community organizing and peacebuilding in the midst of these
conflicts. The good folks at the Hermano Mercedes Ruíz Foundation and in the Ecclesial Base Communities of El Salvador have
shown me what it means to embody the resurrection of martyrs like
Monseñor Romero and Berta Cáceres, and I would not come close
to understanding the memory of martyrdom without having had
the privilege of encountering their steadfast witness to its meaning
in the world today. Finally, I am grateful to the ecomartyrs themselves and to all those who keep their memory alive by carrying on
their cause. I have never even met most of these individuals but am
forever grateful for their witness and the challenge that they present
to my own personal journey, to the Christian church, and to all
people of good will. May the seeds of hope planted by the ecomartyrs bear much fruit in all of us who seek to live in solidarity with
one another and with the whole of Creation, our common home.

1

THE PILLAGE OF OUR COMMON HOME

Ecomartyrdom and Extractivism in the Americas

"Wake up! Wake up, humanity! We are out of time." These prophetic words were proclaimed in 2015 by Berta Cáceres in the speech that she gave when she accepted the internationally renowned Goldman Prize for her grassroots environmental activism in Honduras. At the time, Berta was organizing among her Lencan people to protect the sacred waters of the Gualcarque River and the surrounding communities from social, cultural, and ecological devastation by an internationally financed hydroelectric dam project. She ended her speech by dedicating the prize to all the rebels out there, including her mother, the Lenca people, the Río Blanco community, the people of her grassroots organization, and all the martyrs who have been slain for defending the goods of the natural world.[1] Less than one year later, Berta herself became one of those martyrs when she was shot to death by hired assassins in her home on March 2, 2016.

The martyrs to whom Berta dedicated her prize are not few in number. Nor was her assassination an isolated case, even in her own local context of western Honduras. Rather, she is one of just a handful of martyrs who have garnered international attention and renown. Since the turn of the twenty-first century alone,

---

[1] Berta Cáceres, "Goldman Environmental Prize Acceptance Speech," April 22, 2015, https://youtu.be/AR1kwx8b0ms.

though, thousands of land and environmental defenders around the world have been assassinated as a result of their work to protect the earth and its inhabitants from exploitation and destruction by profit-driven, extractive industries.[2] The activism and legacy of slain environmental defenders is intimately tied to local lands and peoples, but the social and environmental justice movements to which they belong form international networks of popular movements that are on the front lines of the global struggle against ecological destruction and climate breakdown. While no region of the globe has been entirely exempt from the phenomenon of these environmental killings, activists in the Global South are by far at greatest risk, and Latin America in particular has seen the lion's share of documented murders. Indigenous peoples are especially vulnerable.[3]

What are the root causes of these murders? Who exactly is being killed and why? How should ecologically conscious Christians and other people of faith and good will who are committed to environmental justice think about these killings and the lives that preceded them without romanticizing their suffering or justifying their early and unjust deaths? How might we remember and honor the witness of ecomartyrs in a way that carries on their work in the world and ensures that such work can be carried out safely and without risk of criminalization, defamation, and/or assassina-

---

[2] See Global Witness annual reports available at www.globalwitness.org and the extensive reporting done by Frontline Defenders at www.frontlinedefenders.org. While Latin America has the highest documented number of cases, both the Democratic Republic of Congo and the Philippines are also hotspots for the assassination of land and environmental defenders.

[3] Indigenous peoples throughout the Americas self-identify in many different ways, including and often preferably by specific tribal nations and communities. Preferred terminology for reference to pan-Indigenous identity varies geographically and generationally and includes the terms Indigenous, Native, American Indian, First Nations, and Original peoples. In this book, I make use of the three most general of these descriptors—Indigenous, Native, and Original—interchangeably.

tion? And finally, how might the martyrs' death for our common home inspire and empower the rest of us to dedicate our lives to the liberation, preservation, and well-being of our planetary home and all of its inhabitants?[4]

This book lifts up the witness of women and men in the Americas who have been murdered for their commitment to environmental justice and ecological liberation. We will begin in this present chapter with a historical and contemporary overview of and theological reflection on colonial and contemporary extractivism as the root cause and current driver of the ecological crisis. We will then proceed to consider the violent effects of extractivism, along with the ways in which local struggles for environmental justice are profoundly interrelated with the urgent global task of defending our common home from multiple ecological threats, especially the climate crisis. As we have already seen, individuals and communities on the front lines of this defense are under attack around the world, and the book proceeds to contemplate the stories of several environmental defenders who have been assassinated because of their commitments to social and ecological well-being. We will then turn to reflect theologically on the martyrdom of these individuals, in conversation with the cultural, spiritual, and theological wellsprings of their witness. Finally, the concluding claim of this book is that murdered land and environmental defenders can

---

[4] I often make use of the first-person plural pronouns "we," "us," and "our" throughout this book, in keeping with Nancy Pineda-Madrid's insight that such language "situates[s] the reader as active and responsible in the context of the argument that I am advancing." See Nancy Pineda-Madrid, *Suffering and Salvation in Ciudad Juárez* (Minneapolis: Fortress Press, 2011), 154n1. My own first-person context is that of a white, middle-class, cisgender, heterosexual, able-bodied academic woman with U.S. citizenship—an identity that grants me significant privileges granted by extractivist, neoliberal capitalism. I invite each reader of this book to reflect on their own intersections of identity, privilege, and oppression as they internalize and respond to the challenges presented by the realities of extractivism and ecomartyrdom in our world today.

and should be remembered and understood theologically by Christians as ecomartyrs. Therefore, their witness should challenge the church, especially in the Global North, to enter into solidarity with the ecological struggles of environmentally threatened communities not only in the Americas, but around the world. The book also includes a study guide with concrete suggestions for education and action to implement in classrooms, parishes, and other faith-based communities and grassroots organizations.

The phenomenon of ecomartyrdom in the Americas has five centuries of deep roots in European conquest and colonization of the continent, known to Indigenous peoples of these lands by many sacred names, including Turtle Island, Aztlán, and Abya Yala.[5] It is impossible to understand the murder of environmental defenders without contemplating this history. The present chapter therefore offers a brief introduction to the historical roots of extractivism, ecological destruction, and ecomartyrdom in the Americas, along with a theological analysis of the logic of extractivism as a sinful anti-social and anti-ecological imaginary that thrives on the crucifixion of both marginalized human communities and the more-than-human elements and inhabitants of the earth community, our common home.[6]

---

[5]   Néstor Medina explains that "Abya Yala is a term from the Kuna nation (they are located in the North region of Colombia and Southeast region of Panama) which means 'land in full maturity' or 'land of vital blood,' and which rejects ideas of the Americas as the 'New World.' Aztlán is the Nahua word used to identify the ancestral land of the Aztec people. Aztecah is the Nahua word that means 'people of Aztlán,' which refers to sections in the north of Mexico and the southwest of the United States of America. Turtle Island refers to the way the Ojibway and other First Nations of Canada speak about the creation of the world." See Néstor Medina, "Indigenous Decolonial Movements in Abya Yala, Aztlán, and Turtle Island: A Comparison," in *Decolonial Christianities: Latin American and Latinx Perspectives* (Cham, Switzerland: Palgrave Macmillan, 2019), 148n2.

[6]   I first encountered the phrase "more-than-human" in Robin Wall

Historical Roots of Environmental Injustice
and Ecomartyrdom in the Americas

The root causes of the murders of environmental defenders in the lands that European colonizers would name "the Americas" span back over 530 years to the beginning of the conquest and colonization of these lands by European powers and principalities. The Spanish, Portuguese, Dutch, British, and French empires that colonized the Americas brought with them not only the soldiers, weapons, settlers, and germs that destroyed up to 90 percent of the Indigenous human population. They brought with them an economic and ecological paradigm of colonial and capitalist extractivism that would progressively devastate lands, air, waters, and ecosystems throughout the hemisphere to this very day, all for the sake of wealth accumulation and Euro-American hegemony. While the historical progression of colonial and capitalist extractivism took on distinct features in Latin America as opposed to the United States and Canada, the entirety of the Americas is bound up in this same story of conquest, colonialism, and enslavement, along with the ecological impacts that such atrocities have wrought on the relationship between human beings and the land for centuries to come.

A Brief Account of Environmental History
in the Precolonial Americas

Indigenous peoples had made their home on the lands that many call Turtle Island or Abya Yala for anywhere from tens of thousands to over one hundred thousand years before the arrival of

Kimmerer's *Braiding Sweetgrass: Indigenous Wisdom, Scientific Knowledge, and the Teachings of Plants* (Minneapolis: Milkweed Editions, 2011). Ecologist and geophilosopher David Abram introduced the term to describe human immersion in a larger, sentient whole in *The Spell of the Sensuous: Perception and Language in a More-Than-Human World* (New York: Vintage Books, 1996).

Europeans.[7] In the Western cultural imagination, these lands were viewed not only as a "new world" to Europeans but as *terra nullius*," a pristine or virgin wilderness belonging to no one. But this myth was created precisely to serve the interests of conquering powers and settler colonists. Rather than a wilderness untouched by human intervention, the lands of the pre-Columbian Americas were skillfully tended and cultivated by Indigenous peoples for millennia via diverse and sophisticated systems of agriculture, forestry, transportation, trade, game management, and governance. In fact, Roxanne Dunbar-Ortiz points out that

> [a]s a birthplace of agriculture and the towns and cities that followed, America is ancient, not a "new world." Domestication of plants took place around the globe in seven locales during approximately the same period, around 8500 BC. Three of the seven were in the Americas, all based on corn: the Valley of Mexico and Central America (Mesoamerica); the South-Central Andes in South America; and eastern North America.[8]

Advising her readers to "follow the corn" and the accompanying movements of human migration, Dunbar-Ortiz illustrates the Indigenous landscape of the Americas at the time of European arrival as dynamic, widely and in some places densely populated, and supported by a diversity of complex civilizational forms.

From hunter-gatherer communities to semi-nomadic agricultural peoples to vast confederations and empires, pre-contact Native peoples sustained themselves by adapting to local landscapes and by adapting local landscapes to meet human needs.[9]

---

[7] See Paulette F.C. Steeves, *The Indigenous Paleolithic of the Western Hemisphere* (Lincoln, NE: University of Nebraska Press, 2021).

[8] Roxanne Dunbar-Ortiz, *An Indigenous Peoples' History of the United States* (Boston: Beacon Press, 2014), 15.

[9] Dunbar-Ortiz, 27.

With techniques such as controlled burning to manage forests, facilitate hunting, and rotate crops, Indigenous communities thrived in relative harmony with the natural world. Native cosmovisions, spiritualities, sacred stories, and ceremonial practices nurtured and reinforced the pursuit of such harmony through the cultivation of mutuality and reciprocity between human beings, the land, and more-than-human creatures.[10] Indigenous peoples of the Americas were and are fallible human beings, though, and as such were not and are not always perfectly attuned to harmonious relationships with Creation. Native scholars and activists warn against the romantic, yet dehumanizing, myth of the "noble savage." To be Indigenous to the land does not mean that Native peoples are essentially "closer to nature," nor does it mean that they have attained ecological perfection. Rather, Indigenous peoples developed ecological sensibilities and environmentally responsible practices through trial and error over many generations.[11] That process continues to this day, for example, as Native communities adapt to a changing climate.

Such caveats should remind us all of the dangers that romanticization and instrumentalization of traditional ecological knowledge pose to the cultural dignity and integrity of Native communities. Nevertheless, it remains true that while Indigenous lifeways affected the more-than-human environment in many ways, Indigenous cosmovisions discouraged objectification

---

[10] See, for example, George E. "Tink" Tinker, *American Indian Liberation: A Theology of Sovereignty* (Maryknoll, NY: Orbis Books, 2008), and Kimmerer, *Braiding Sweetgrass*.

[11] An entire body of research exists surrounding this process of Indigenous accumulation of "Traditional Ecological Knowledge" (TEK). Many thanks to Taína Díaz-Reyes, my former student at Wake Forest School of Divinity, for introducing me to this concept and body of work. For an excellent collection of essays on this topic, see Melissa K. Nelson and Dan Shilling, eds., *Traditional Ecological Knowledge: Learning from Indigenous Practices for Environmental Sustainability* (New York: Cambridge University Press, 2018).

and exploitation of nature, and practical safeguards were often in place to prevent abuses of the natural world—abuses that would eventually come back to haunt human communities in the form of ecological degradation that would ultimately harm the human ability to survive. Upon the arrival of Europeans in the Americas, though, these cosmovisions were demonized and these ecological safeguards were too often destroyed by the genocidal displacement of Native peoples from the lands to which they belonged. A population of anywhere between sixty million to over one hundred million people throughout the Americas was reduced by 90 percent in the century following the arrival of Christopher Columbus and the beginnings of the Spanish invasion of the region in 1492.[12] As other European powers began their own colonial campaigns, the death toll mounted.

Although the introduction of new diseases accounted for massive amounts of death, scholars have identified many other factors that impacted Native peoples' ability to survive: "war, massacres, enslavement, overwork, deportation, the loss of will to live or reproduce, malnutrition and starvation from the breakdown of trade networks, and the loss of subsistence food production due to land loss."[13] Each of these factors contains elements of environmental violence and ecological degradation that not only harmed the land but also the ability of Indigenous peoples to depend on the land for subsistence. As Dina Gilio-Whitaker puts it, "In one way or another these are all environmental factors that were rooted

---

[12] Researchers have actually identified a period of global cooling that followed this devastation of the Indigenous population of the Americas, due to such a drastic reduction in the practice of agriculture. See Alexander Koch et al., "Earth System Impacts of the European Arrival and Great Dying in the Americas after 1492," *Quarternary Science Reviews* 207 (March 2019): 13–36.

[13] Dina Gilio-Whitaker, *As Long as Grass Grows: The Indigenous Fight for Environmental Justice, from Colonization to Standing Rock* (Boston: Beacon Press, 2020), 40.

in settlers deliberately blocking Native peoples' access to resources necessary for maintaining an Indigenous way of life."[14] Because human beings are deeply interrelated and interdependent with the land and the more-than-human world, George Tinker points out that genocide and ecocide went hand in hand.[15]

The very first environmental defenders on these lands that we now call "America," therefore, were the Indigenous peoples who were slaughtered by Europeans for attempting to protect their lands and lifeways when faced with the twin terrors of genocide and ecocide. For example, in the Caribbean, the Taíno cacique Hatuey is remembered as one who valiantly resisted the Spanish invasion, prophetically denouncing the conquistadors' lust for gold. Communal memory of Hatuey's legacy recalls that, when organizing his people to revolt, he showed his warriors a basket full of gold and proclaimed: "This is the Lord of the Spanish. To have it, they bring us trouble. For it, they persecute us. Because of it, our fathers and brothers have been killed. Because of it, they abuse us."[16] Hatuey was burned at the stake, refusing baptism with the famous statement that he wanted nothing to do with a heaven where the Spanish would be present. With his death, the Taíno elders cried out to the sun, imploring "that the light of his body would not be extinguished, not with the wind of hurricanes nor with the sound of thunder, not with the rains that flood nor the passage of time."[17] As we will soon see, the stories of more recent and contemporary ecomartyrs attest that the process of violent conquest and the light of Indigenous and allied resistance continues to this very day.

---

[14] Gilio-Whitaker, 40.

[15] See Tinker, 57.

[16] Kintto Lucas, *Rebeliones Indígenas y Negras en América Latina: Entre viento y fuego* (Quincenario Tintají, 2004), 36.

[17] Lucas, 38.

Colonial and Capitalist Extractivism
in the Americas

In Latin America, the *nueva trova*—the "new troubadour" or "new song"—movement of the twentieth century was a cultural phenomenon of protest music that expressed the longings of the poor and oppressed for liberation from centuries of colonial and capitalist systems of exploitation. One song in particular illustrates how the extractivism of colonial and capitalist economics have resulted in the interlocking "cry of the earth and cry of the poor."[18] The song, written by the Uruguayan icon Atahualpa Yupanquí, is called "*Preguntitas sobre Dios*" ("Little Questions about God"),[19] and while the theological implications of the lyrics are profound, let us first learn from the analysis of reality that the song offers and save the theological insights for later chapters. The lyrics begin with the singer successively questioning his grandfather, his father, and his brother about their knowledge of God. In the first verse, his grandfather looks sad, perhaps because of the violent imposition of a Christian God, and he doesn't answer the question at all. The verse goes on to reveal that this *abuelo* died in the fields

> without a prayer or confession
> and the Indians buried him
> with a cane flute and drum.

---

[18] See Leonardo Boff, *Cry of the Earth, Cry of the Poor* (Maryknoll, NY: Orbis Books, 1999). Pope Francis uses this phrase, without referencing Boff, in his encyclical, *Laudato Si': On Care for Our Common Home*, May 24, 2015, www.vatican.va, § 49. Henceforth, *Laudato Si'* will be referenced as *LS*.

[19] Atahualpa Yupanquí, "Preguntitas Sobre Dios," Le Chant Du Monde recording house, 1951, available at https://youtu.be/MXBsGwwy7xE. This song has also been performed and recorded by other icons of the *nueva trova* movement, such as Victor Jara and Soledad Bravo.

In the second verse, the singer's father becomes very serious and doesn't answer the question either. This *padre*

> died in the mines
> without a doctor or protection

and Atahualpa Yupanquí laments that

> the color of miner's blood
> contains the gold of the master.

Finally in the third verse, the singer reveals that his brother

> lives in the hills
> and hasn't seen a flower
> sweat, malaria, and snakes
> that's the life of the woodcutter.

No one has ever asked this *hermano* about God, since no one that important has ever passed by his home.

The situations of each of these men represent the simultaneous exploitation of the earth and of human beings—in the cotton, sugarcane, banana, and indigo fields of intensive monoculture farming of colonial plantations and contemporary agribusiness; in the gold, silver, copper, and coal mines of colonial and contemporary mining operations; and in the widespread deforestation wrought by colonial and contemporary logging. In these three verses, Atahualpua Yupanquí sums up the existential despair, broken relationships with the land, and physical health consequences of extractivist economics with tragic realism. In his final verse, which raises powerful questions about God that we will consider later in this book, he insists that there is an ethical imperative in this world that is ultimately more important than God:

> *Y es que nadie escupa sangre*
> *pa' que otro viva major.*

Roughly translated, these lines state that no one should have to spit out blood so that others can live a more comfortable life. Without using technical or academic vocabulary, this line offers a poetic and prophetic analysis of how extractivist economics produces what political ecologists and environmental justice advocates call "environmental sacrifice zones," or places where the health and dignity of human beings, the land, and more-than-human creatures are sacrificed for the sake of a "greater good"—usually economic gain, political power, and/or the satisfaction of consumptive desire. Some people must "spit out blood" so that others can live a more comfortable life.

Conquest and domination, genocide and ecocide were carried out in the Americas with a purpose—that is, for the sake of the "greater goods" that are often characterized as God, Glory, and Gold. For now, let's focus on Gold and all that it literally and symbolically represents for the centrality of extractivist sacrifice in colonial and capitalist ventures. When Christopher Columbus and his men made landfall on the Caribbean islands now known as the Bahamas, one of his first concerns was finding gold.[20] On his first voyage alone, he also captured about two dozen Indigenous people to bring back to Spain to be sold, for gold, as slaves. Thousands were later captured and forced to labor for the invaders in their pursuit of gold and other natural resources. The entire process of conquest and colonization was a massive human and ecological sacrifice, not only of the Original peoples discussed above, but also of over twelve million enslaved Africans, who would also be forcibly displaced from their homelands, with millions dying along the middle passage and survivors being sold for profit and forced to extract further profit from the natural resources of the land stolen from the original inhabitants of the Americas. Enslaved Indig-

---

[20] See extracts from entries in Columbus' journal during his 1492 voyage at www.sourcebooks.fordham.edu.

enous and African women's bodies, like the land, were exploited for their labor and for the resources they could reproduce in the form of new generations of laborers to work the land. The profit derived from this extraction of land, lives, and labor shored up the power and wealth of conquerors and colonists, while sacrificing the flesh and blood of human beings and the more-than-human world at every turn. This was just as true, if not more so, after Latin American nation states gained independence in the 19th century and Euro-descendent creole elites were thereby free to enclose communal lands, accelerate extractivist endeavors, and harness the benefits of neocolonialism and economic liberalism for themselves and their foreign investors. In the words of Uruguayan writer Eduardo Galeano, Latin America has been "the region of open veins. Everything from the 'discovery' until our times has always been transmuted into European—or later, United States—capital, and as such has accumulated on distant centers of power. Everything: the soil, its fruits and its mineral-rich depths, the people and their capacity to work and to consume, natural resources and human resources."[21] While Galeano wrote these words in the early 1970s, with a primarily economic and geopolitical lens (that is, not an ecological lens), his imagery of "open veins" is an apt metaphor for how the extractivist model of relating to land and labor bleeds the earth and its inhabitants dry (sometimes quite literally).

A similar dynamic took place in the process of capital accumulation that was carried out in the conquest and colonization of the lands now known as the United States and Canada. British and French invasion of the continent was no less racist or cruel than that of Spanish and Portuguese counterparts, and the political independence achieved by settler colonists did nothing to hold off

---

[21] Eduardo Galeano, *Open Veins of Latin America: Five Centuries of the Pillage of a Continent*, 25th anniversary edition (New York: Monthly Review Press, 1997), 2.

the expansion of empire westward. Rather, the arrogance of American exceptionalism and the "Manifest Destiny" of the white race fueled the "civilizing" impulse to forcibly take and tame the land for the sake of resource extraction. Under settler colonialism in the United States and Canada, Indigenous peoples were violently removed from their lands even more extensively than in Latin America. White settlers who took their place employed extractivist techniques for eking a living, and perhaps even some wealth, out of the soil. Enslaved labor was necessary for profitable resource extraction, especially in the United States, repeating and refining the dynamic of human sacrifice carried out further south. Cheap labor extracted from poor whites—known as waste-people—added to the accumulation of capital by those in power, especially in the coal mines of Appalachia and in the sweatshops of the northeastern United States, where natural resources extracted from the land were transformed by exploited workers into products for sale. After emancipation, sharecropping and prison labor replaced the plantation system of chattel slavery, but what continued unabated was extraction of profitable resources from the land and from Black bodies compelled to perform that extraction by unjust economic circumstances and a racist legal system. Poor whites and "ethnic" European immigrants (from Ireland and Southern and Eastern Europe) continued to work for poverty wages and under inhumane conditions in the mines and factories. After the Great Migration of African Americans from the Southeast to the Northeast, Midwest, and West in the early twentieth century, and as poor and ethnic Europeans successfully "became white" and the majority entered the middle and upper classes, the United States began extracting cheap, exploitable migrant labor from Latin America.

All the while, powerful individuals and corporations became wealthier and more powerful, especially those who were able to expand their extractivist endeavors into Latin America with lucrative investments in banana and rubber plantations, railroads and logging campaigns, and mining and petroleum projects. North American businessmen built their corporate empires on the resources that these extractivist industries provided. While Latin American elites were beholden to and dependent on these North American investors, they enjoyed the wealth and power that the neocolonialism of laissez-faire capitalism afforded them, and they stopped at nothing to defend their shared interest with extractivist global capital. The dirty wars and counterinsurgency tactics of the late twentieth century produced an entire generation of martyrs—tortured, murdered, and disappeared by state-sponsored and U.S.-trained forces for their commitment to undoing these violent and oppressive systems of land ownership and worker exploitation. The revolutionary struggles of the late twentieth century were directed at redistributing land, political power, and economic resources more equitably and implementing more humane labor practices, whereas we will soon see that the more recent struggles of environmental justice movements challenge the foundations of an extractivist economy altogether.

The Logic of Extractivism Today

Extractivism has only accelerated under the advance of neoliberalism in the late twentieth and early twenty-first centuries. Neoliberal economics operates not only according to the imperative of capitalist accumulation but also according to the logic of absolute liberty to privatize, extract, and deregulate trade in labor and goods for sale in a now thoroughly globalized marketplace. In the neoliberal extractivist model, human beings (or more specifically, human beings at the top of economic, racial, and gender hierarchies) are entitled to tap into and remove for their own economic and geopolitical benefit what Berta Cáceres called "*la sangre de la tierra*" ("the blood of the earth"). The authors of a report on extractivism and conflict in Latin America titled "Pacha: Defending the Land" define extractivism more specifically as "a model of appropriation of natural resources that includes diverse sectors such as mining, oil exploration, and agriculture." Other sectors implicated here include logging, cattle ranching, and the construction of hydroelectric dams. The report's definition continues: "The appropriation of these resources happens through intensive practices and with the objective of exporting raw materials to the global markets. Therefore, the limits of resources are not calculated nor [are] the consequences that the extractive processes cause on the lives of the people and the territories affected."[22] Depending on the specific industry, such consequences include displacement of human beings and other creatures from their homelands; deforestation, prolonged droughts, and accelerated desertification; toxic contamination of water and soil, leading to effects such as cadmium and mercury poisoning; severe weather events due to climate change; and much more.

While this discussion emphasizes the economic and ecological dimensions of extractivism, the Pacha report also highlights, and Berta Cáceres was insistent in her analysis and her activism, that the extractivist model at the heart of capitalism is racist and patriarchal to its core. The human beings harmed by extractivism are disproportionately nonwhite and female. The coloniality of knowledge, being, and power that is at work in this model designates women, Indigenous, and Afro-descendent peoples, along with other racialized rural *campesinos*, as ontologically equivalent to the "natural" resources that are rightfully exploited by ruling white males (and others who cooperate with them) for the sake of capitalist production and reproduction.

Networks of power that perpetrate and benefit from this arrangement include a number of actors at different levels,

---

[22] Group of International Relations and Global South (GRISUL/UNIRIO), "Pacha: Defending the Land" (Rio de Janeiro: Federal University of the State of Rio de Janeiro, 2018), 3. This report can be accessed online at www.grisulunirio.com.

including large and small transnational corporations; international financial institutions such as the World Bank and private banks with an international reach; narcotraffickers, organized crime networks, and other industries operating illegally in sectors such as gold mining and poaching; Latin American nation-states and political authorities acting both legally and illegally; and governments of wealthy and powerful countries such as the United States, Canada, and China. Economic and political structures are in place that guarantee the interest of these actors, and even when legal norms are in place to protect the environmental human rights of vulnerable populations, those norms are often unenforceable due to a lack of political will and/or structural support.

While it is important to unmask these powerful economic and political forces at work in this model, we would be remiss if we were to overlook the role of consumer demand in the extractivist equation. In a course that I taught on this topic at Wake Forest in Spring 2021, a guest speaker reminded our class of the consumer factor in a particularly powerful way. Our guest, César Ascorra, is a Peruvian ecologist who once worked for Caritas and is now the national director of Wake Forest's Center for Amazonian Scientific Innovation in the Madre de Dios region of the Peruvian Amazon, where deforestation is rampant due to logging and gold mining. When a student in the class asked César about whether the problem of corruption in the Peruvian government has precipitated the surge in illegal mining activity, he replied that she was asking the wrong question and that the real problem does not begin in Peru. The origins of the problem lie in the global market demand for products that are extracted from Peru. He said that when mahogany was in high demand, deforestation skyrocketed. Similarly, deforestation is even more of a problem now that gold is in high demand due to its widespread use in technology for personal electronic devices like laptops and smartphones. The violence of extractivism is a structural problem shored up by powerful individuals and political

and economic institutions, to be sure. But the destruction of the
Amazon is also fueled by *our* demand as consumers for products
that make our lives more comfortable, convenient, and entertaining.
In *Open Veins of Latin America*, Galeano remarks that "in this world
of ours, a world of powerful centers and subjugated outposts, there
is no wealth that must not be held in some suspicion."[23] Similarly, I
would add that, on the consumer side of things, there is no product
that must not be held in some suspicion, no purchase that is not
suspect, no consumer whose hands are clean. We are all complicit.

Extractivism as Structural Sin: An Anti-Social and Anti-Ecological Imaginary

The extractivist paradigm described in this chapter metes out violence
and death for human beings and the ecosystems in which we make
our home, sacrificing the lives of people and the planet alike. Some
human communities and some parts of the earth must "spit out
blood" so that others can live a more comfortable life. The Christian
tradition employs the theological language of sin and evil to name
such violent and death-dealing realities. I have reflected elsewhere on
the problematic aspects of sin language in the Christian tradition;[24]
but as a Christian theologian, it is difficult to acknowledge the twin
terrors of extractivism—genocide and ecocide—without resorting to
this language. In the Christian tradition, sin is often understood as
a rupture in the relationship between human beings and our divine
Creator. However, Pope Francis reminds us that the creation narratives in Genesis account for sin as a rupture in "three fundamental
and closely intertwined relationships: with God, with our neighbor
and with the earth itself."[25] Francis avers that today, the ruptures of sin

---

[23] Galeano, 267.
[24] See Elizabeth O'Donnell Gandolfo, *The Power and Vulnerability of
Love: A Theological Anthropology* (Minneapolis: Fortress Press, 2015).
[25] *LS*, § 66.

"are manifest in all [their] destructive power in wars, the various forms of violence and abuse, the abandonment of the most vulnerable, and attacks on nature."[26] Each of these sinful realities is characteristic of the extractivist paradigm, which wages war on marginalized human beings and the natural world in pursuit of maximal profit. Each of these ruptures represents the crucifixion of reality—of marginalized and oppressed human beings, of the earth, and of the incarnate God who stands in solidarity with all of crucified reality.[27]

Individuals perpetrate these evils in their extractivist endeavors and in the violence that they commit to silence dissent, but liberation theologies and the Catholic social tradition have also deepened our understanding of sin and evil to account for the structural, systemic, and institutional nature of these ruptures in our fundamental relationships with our human neighbors, with other inhabitants and elements of the earth community, and with the divine source of all Creation. The extractivist paradigm has been constructed and is perpetuated by human beings—individual and communal agents of economic exploitation and ecological harm. However, the actions of individuals have accumulated over time to coalesce in a political and economic world system that depends on extractivism for its perpetuation. This system normalizes extractivism as an engine of progress that facilitates longevity and quality of life for those who benefit from it, and it offers false

---

[26] *LS*, § 66.

[27] Here I draw on and extend the language of the "crucified people" to include the "crucified earth." Ignacio Ellacuría was the first to develop this language, though it has deeper roots in the biblical tradition, the early church, and the history of Latin American Christianity. Jon Sobrino has applied this concept most extensively in Latin American liberation theology, and James Cone has found the same insights to be present in African American religion and culture. For an extensive list of sources on the crucified people in Latin American theology, see chapter 6, note 14. For Cone's identification of the cross with anti-Black violence, see *The Cross and the Lynching Tree* (Maryknoll, NY: Orbis Books, 2011).

promises of these goods to those whom it exploits or discards as worthless to its aims of profit and prosperity.

Furthermore, this system also forms human beings in an extractivist mind-set—a social and ecological imaginary, if you will—in which our relationships with the divine, the earth, and other human beings are ruptured, not only materially but cognitively, emotionally, culturally, and spiritually. Drawing on the work of Charles Taylor, Emilie Townes, and Octavio Paz, Nancy Pineda-Madrid defines a "social imaginary" as a way of viewing the moral order of society that "assigns particular characteristics to the world and to divine action within it such that a given set of moral norms appears right, merits our pursuit, and is at least partially realizable."[28] Pineda-Madrid employs this framework as a heuristic device for exploring the dimensions of sin and evil at work in the phenomenon of feminicide in Ciudad Juárez, and it can also be helpful here for conceptualizing the complex and multilayered worldview in which extractivism and its accompanying violences "make sense." However, since the language of "social imaginary" denotes a pro-social disposition, I opt to call the extractivist imaginary "anti-social." Furthermore, I posit that social imaginaries always include implicit ecological dimensions—that is, assumed understandings of and attitudes toward the relationship between human beings and the natural world. I therefore suggest that we name the implicit ecological dimension of the extractivist imaginary explicitly as "anti-ecological."

In the extractivist imaginary, the social nature of human life is violently ruptured. While the human person cannot be reduced to or subsumed within the social dimension of our existence, we would not exist without our inherent sociality. Our very being is dependent on intra-human relationships of interdependence, relationality, and cooperation in pursuit of shared well-being. In the

---

[28] Pineda-Madrid, 41.

language of the southern African concept of *ubuntu*, "I am because we are." The human species would not have evolved to become *homo sapiens* without cooperation, communal resource sharing, and reciprocal relationships of compassion and care. In theological language, our very identity as creatures made in the *imago Dei*—the image of perfect Trinitarian Love—is grounded in the relationality of the divine, in whose creative and redemptive work we are called to participate. Extractivism violates the sociality and sacred calling of our species by pitting the wealth, power, comforts, and luxuries of some human beings against the health, dignity, and survival of others. It is an anti-social imaginary that relies on the zero-sum logic of scarcity thinking and divides humanity into those who are worthy of the privilege of existence and those who are exploitable and disposable once their capacity to produce privileges for the powerful is no longer needed or has run dry. Extractivism is therefore an anti-social imaginary.

Furthermore, extractivism violates the ecological nature of all created existence. Human sociality—indeed, our very existence—is embedded within the larger, interconnected whole of cosmic and planetary existence. We are part of, not separate from, this larger whole. As we will see that Afro-Indigenous cosmovisions profess, human beings are the younger siblings of the rest of Creation. We have emerged from the material elements and more-than-human biological ancestors that came before us, and we depend on the other elements and creatures of Creation for our existence, sustenance, and well-being. Our relationality with one another and the rest of the natural world makes us vulnerable to harm, to be sure, but without these relationships, we would not exist at all. Extractivism violates the ecological nature of human and more-than-human existence by setting some humans apart from the rest of the earth community and granting them the power to dominate, objectify, commodify, fence in, poison, and bleed dry the goods of the natural world for the sake of shoring up their own comfort, wealth, and power. The vulnerability of life in this world is mitigated for those of us who benefit from this system, but so too is the fundamental truth of interdependency and the beauty of interrelationship, compassion, and care in our fragile and fleeting world. In this anti-ecological imaginary, the ideal human existence is far removed from the vulnerabilities and inconveniences of life on this messy but beautiful planet. The human heart is thus numbed to the pain of existence, but also to the joys and hopes of a truly human life.

To borrow the language of biblical scholar Walter Brueggemann, the anti-social and anti-ecological imaginary of extractivism parallels the "royal consciousness" of Pharaoh, of the Solomonic kingship of ancient Israel, of the Roman Empire, and of all extractivist empires that suck the bodies of the oppressed and the earth dry for the sake of power and privilege. For Brueggemann, the royal consciousness is characterized by (a) affluence for the ruling elite at the cost of poverty for the masses (and I would add here, degradation of the earth); (b) oppressive social policies, including forced labor; and (c) static religion in which access to the divine is controlled by those with power. The royal consciousness also numbs its beneficiaries to the pain that it causes, and it violently silences all dissent.[29] Extractivism operates according to these same principles, including attempted control of people's access to the sacred, since the appropriation of sacred lands and landmarks is an effective tactic of spiritual control, and since the free market itself has taken on pseudo-sacred qualities under the globalized reign of neoliberal capitalism. In the face of the royal consciousness—arguably an anti-social and anti-ecological imaginary—Brueggemann argues that what is needed (and what the prophetic biblical tradition offers) is a "prophetic imagination," which offers both critique

---

[29] See Walter Brueggemann, *The Prophetic Imagination*, 2nd ed. (Minneapolis: Fortress Press, 2001).

of the royal consciousness (in this case, the extractivist imaginary) and a hope-filled, energizing vision of an alternative world. This prophetic imagination counters the apathy and numbness of the royal consciousness with pathos and compassion for suffering, and with a sacred vision of life lived in relationships of justice, harmony, and abundance. The land and environmental defenders featured in this book embody this prophetic imagination in their own social and ecological visions of an-other world—a world in which many worlds are free to coexist,[30] a world named in theological language as *el reino de Dios*—the reign or "kin-dom" of God.[31] The forces of extractivism are arrayed against this vision, with their *anti-reino* imaginaries, bulldozers, pistols, and tanks aimed at anyone who seeks justice and righteousness. And yet those whom we will name in this book as ecomartyrs refuse to be silenced, even in death.

This chapter has introduced the logic of extractivism as a sinful and anti-social, anti-ecological imaginary, and has uncovered the

---

[30] This is the language used by the Zapatistas of Chiapas, Mexico, to describe the world that they envisioned in their 1994 uprising and continue to embody in their construction of an autonomous Indigenous homeland and a world in which all people are free to fully exist. "The world that we desire is one in which many worlds fit. The Homeland that we are building is one in which all peoples and their languages fit, that is traversed by all paths, that all may enjoy, that is made to dawn by all." Comité Clandestino Revolucionario Indígena-Comandancia General del Ejército Zapatista de Liberación Nacional, "Cuarta Declaración de la Selva Lacandona," January 1, 1996, enlacezapatista. ezln.org.mx.

[31] See Ada María Isasi-Díaz's use of "kin-dom" language for the reign of God in "Solidarity: Love of Neighbors in the 1980s," in *Lift Every Voice: Constructing Christian Theologies from the Underside*, ed. Susan Brooks Thistlethwaite and Mary Potter Engel (San Francisco, CA: Harper & Row, 1990), 34. See also Isasi-Díaz, *En La Lucha: Elaborating a Mujerista Theology*, 10th Anniversary Edition (Minneapolis, MN: Fortress Press, 2004), and *Mujerista Theology: A Theology for the Twenty-First Century* (Maryknoll, NY: Orbis Books, 1996).

social and ecological threats that it poses. In chapter 2, we will take a closer look at how several extractivist industries operate, along with how grassroots environmental justice movements resist the violence of extractivism and embody alternative modes of social and ecological existence. In chapter 3, we will survey the violent tactics employed by the agents and beneficiaries of extractivism to repress the resistance and alternatives offered by these movements. Taken together, these first three chapters lay out the historical, social, economic, political, and environmental contexts and structures of sin in which environmental defenders are being criminalized, defamed, assaulted, and assassinated.

2

Fighting for Our Common Home

*Extractivism and the Struggle for
Environmental Justice in the Americas*

On New Year's Day of 1994, in the southern Mexican state of
Chiapas, a coalition of Indigenous people who call themselves the
Zapatista National Liberation Army rose up against neoliberal
globalization and the extractivist violence it metes out on the physical and cultural integrity of human beings, the political autonomy
of Indigenous peoples, and the ecological well-being of local lands
and the planet as a whole. Unlike many other revolutionary movements in late-twentieth-century Latin America, the Zapatistas did
not intend to replace the governing powers of the Mexican nation-
state. Rather, they sought political and cultural recognition, along
with the autonomy that would allow them to govern their communities and ecosystems in egalitarian ways that honor the dignity and
participation of each person, that protect local ecosystems from
extractivist industries, and that manage agricultural land use collectively and sustainably. Nearly thirty years after their initial uprising,
Zapatista communities embody their hope that *"otro mundo es
possible"* ["an-other world is possible"].[1]

---

[1] See chapter 1, note 29, for an explanation of the origins of this phrase in
the Zapatista uprising.

The land and environmental defenders whose stories form the centerpiece of this book also embody the hope of an-other possible world, as do the communities and ecosystems that they loved and cared for to the very end. When petroleum pipelines, gold mining, a hydroelectric dam, or monoculture soy farming threatens local communities and ecosystems in the Americas, socially and ecologically conscious movements like the Zapatistas and grassroots organizations like Berta Cáceres's Civic Council of Popular and Indigenous Organizations (COPINH) resist, coming together to defend their people and their common home. Popular (and by that I mean "people's") organizations and local communities raise awareness through educational initiatives and cultural productions like theater and song-writing; they attempt negotiation or legal mediation with the human sources of the extractivist threat; they mount protests and blockades aimed at preventing the extractivist action in question; they petition local and national governments for protection; they network and coordinate with local, national, regional, and international partners to bring visibility to their cause; and they ground their resistance in a vision and praxis of an-other world in which human communities and the more-than-human world are free to coexist in reciprocal relationships of justice, dignity, and life abundant. As we will soon see in chapter 3, these prophetic activities place environmental defenders at risk of defamation, criminalization, imprisonment, torture, and even assassination. The movements that land and environmental defenders birth and cultivate offer a paradigm for human existence that contrasts sharply with the extractivist model detailed above. Here in this chapter we will survey how various communities across the Americas embody alternative worlds in resistance to the profit-driven, extractive industries of fossil fuels, metallic mining, hydroelectric dam construction, logging, ranching, and big agriculture. We will conclude with a brief consideration of how these industries and the logic of extractivism more generally are deeply complicit in both gender-based violence and the climate crisis. Frontline defenders of environmental human rights are thus fighting not only against local expressions of extractivist violence, but against a much broader, interlocking system of oppression and death.

Identifying and Resisting Extractivism, Embodying Alternatives

Fossil Fuels

Two Indigenous prophecies frame the story of resistance to fossil fuel extraction in the Americas. A Lakota prophecy tells of a black snake that would rise up to devour the people and destroy the earth. Indigenous water protectors, especially in their resistance to the Dakota Access, Keystone XL, and other Tar Sands pipelines, have identified this black snake as the highways, oil trains, and pipelines that carry fossil fuels across the land to be refined and burned in order to satiate the insatiable American demand for energy.[2] Millions of pipelines crisscross the Americas to transport oil and natural gas, making possible the modern comforts of heating, cooling, cooking, computing, and traveling for those of us who can afford them. But these pipelines, along with the oil tankers and the refineries to which they are connected, come with immense environmental costs, especially to poor, Black, Latinx, and Indigenous communities. Most

---

[2] One Standing Rock Sioux historian, LaDonna Brave Bull Allard, recalls this prophecy from her childhood: "LaDonna remembered as a child hearing about a black snake that would come to destroy the earth. She had been taught that when eagle and condor—the Indigenous people from North and South America—came together, they could heal the world, that the seventh generation would stand up, and that when the black snake came to devour the earth, they would stop it. She decided that the prophecies were alive. The black snake was the pipeline, and the broader darkness or sickness, a disconnect in American life." See Katherine Wiltenburg Todrys, *Black Snake: Standing Rock, the Dakota Access Pipeline, and Environmental Justice* (Lincoln: University of Nebraska Press, 2021), 118.

significantly, "Spills, both small and large, are common, and they leave behind land and water that are poisoned and slick with oil. Since 2010 the federal Pipeline and Hazardous Materials Safety Administration has reported more than 6,900 incidents including spills at oil and gas pipelines."[3] Furthermore, fossil fuel refineries are often located in or near marginalized and disproportionately Black and Brown residential areas where health effects range from childhood asthma to respiratory illness to increased rates of cancer. Coal mining via mountaintop removal and hydraulic fracking for natural gas are similarly disastrous for local ecosystems and their human inhabitants alike. Finally, when we add to these hazards the devastating present and future effects of climate change, which is caused primarily by burning fossil fuels, it does indeed appear that the black snake has arisen to devour the earth.

Yet another Native prophecy offers some hope in the face of this bleak narrative. The documentary film *The Condor and the Eagle* highlights ancient Native prophecies that "when the Eagle of the North and the Condor of the South fly together, Indigenous peoples will unite the human family. Indigenous knowledge keepers will come together with world leaders to define a path of healing for all the humans and the planet—mother earth."[4] The film portrays Indigenous communities in Canada, the United States, the Andes, and the Amazon coming together to unite forces, to build one another up in solidarity, and to issue an urgent call to the non-Indigenous world that we must all learn from and form

[3] See Todrys. In January 2022, an oil spill off the coast of Peru that was triggered by a volcanic eruption in Tonga resulted in 6,000 barrels of oil contaminating the Peruvian coastline. The spill decimated the flora and fauna of a famously biodiverse region and fishermen in poor coastal districts were left without work. See Mitra Taj, "Oil Spill Triggered by Tsunami Devastates Coast of Peru," *New York Times*, January 21, 2022.

[4] *The Condor and The Eagle*. Documentary film directed by Sophie Guerra and Clément Guerra (2019).

alliances with Native peoples for the sake of human and planetary survival. While many environmental injustices plague the communities that appear in this film, the common threads that tie most of their narratives together are protection of water sources, declaring that "*agua es vida*, water is life," and resistance to fossil fuel extraction, demanding that we "keep it in the ground."

Because of the fundamental threat that fossil fuel extraction poses to groundwater, wetlands, lakes, streams, and rivers, Indigenous water protectors and their allies have formed a movement that refuses to compromise the quality of life of local peoples and ecosystems for the sake of corporate profit or consumer demand. Because burning fossil fuels contributes to climate breakdown—the effects of which are already being felt by vulnerable communities today and will jeopardize the future of our planet as a whole—these movements seek out both clean energy alternatives, such as solar and wind power, and structural changes that would dramatically reduce energy consumption. The condor and the eagle are indeed flying together to guide the rest of humanity toward a more just, equitable, and ecologically sound future.

Metallic Mining

When Christopher Columbus arrived in the Americas, one of his top priorities was finding gold. Likewise, one of the first extractive industries implemented with the conquest and colonization of Latin America was mining for gold and other precious metals, such as silver. As such, the first chapter of Galeano's *Open Veins of Latin America*, "Lust for Gold, Lust for Silver," details the horrific lengths to which European invaders went to enslave human beings for the sake of extracting wealth from the land, and Atahualpa Yupanquí sings of miners who "spit out blood" so that others can have a more comfortable life. In addition to the deleterious effects of mining on those who were forced to labor in this industry during colonial times and on those who eke their livelihood out of it today, let us consider the devastating and long-lasting effects that metallic mining has on local landscapes, ecosystems, and water sources.

Global extraction of metal ores has more than doubled over the past two decades, particularly in areas of the world that are vulnerable to species loss and water scarcity. One study, which does not even include informal or illegal mining, found that "79% of global metal ore extraction in 2019 originated from five of the six most species-rich biomes, with mining volumes doubling since 2000 in tropical moist forest ecosystems." The study also found that "half of global metal ore extraction took place at 20 km or less from protected territories." And finally, "90% of all considered extraction sites correspond to below-average relative water availability, with particularly copper and gold mining occurring in areas with significant *water scarcity*."[5] The effects of metallic mining in these predominantly vulnerable regions include deforestation, which leads to species loss and desertification, along with depletion and toxic contamination of water sources. In turn, these ecological effects are felt in local human communities that depend on the natural resources of the affected ecosystems to survive. Human communities are losing access to these resources as they disappear, and they are being poisoned by the resources that remain. As usual, poor, Indigenous, and Afro-descendent communities are most affected by these environmental impacts.

For example, in the Madre de Dios region of Peru, gold mining has not only led to unprecedented deforestation of nearly 100,000 hectares in the past forty years, it has released into the air dangerous levels of mercury, which is toxic, but which then

---

[5]   Sebastian Luckeneder et al., "Surge in Global Metal Mining Threatens Vulnerable Ecosystems," *Global Environmental Change* 69 (2021). Emphasis in the original.

becomes most dangerous to human beings and other living creatures when it bonds with carbon and converts into highly toxic methylmercury.[6] Methylmercury accumulates in the food chain and, when chronically ingested, leads to a range of symptoms, including vision and hearing loss and impairment of speech and bodily movement. According to the Environmental Protection Agency, prenatal mercury poisoning in the womb can affect the growing brain and nervous system of the fetus, leading to impacts in children's "cognitive thinking, memory, attention, language, fine motor skills, and visual spatial skills."[7] Other toxic metals such as lead, arsenic, and cadmium are similarly dumped into the environment in the process of mining many other precious, industrial, and rare earth metals around the world. From the mining of gold in the Amazon, to uranium and copper on Native American lands in the Southwestern United States, to lithium in Bolivia, Argentina, and Chile—the social and environmental impacts of metallic mining are devastating to people and the planet alike.

Another danger that mining industries pose to local communities and ecosystems lies in the construction of "tailings dams," which are structures designed to permanently store solid, liquid, and/or slurry by-products of metallic and mineral mining. These by-products are often toxic and can even be radioactive. Thousands of such structures have been built around the world, and, even with a minimal failure rate, the results of a dam breaking are catastrophic. In just the past decade alone, Brazil has experienced two of the most extensive failures of tailings dams in the world, both associated with iron ore mining operations owned by the Brazilian multinational corporation Vale S.A. In November 2015, the Mariana dam in Minas Gerais failed, releasing 90 million tons

---

[6]   Catrin Einhorn, "Alarming Levels of Mercury Are Found in Old Growth Amazon Forest," *New York Times*, January 28, 2022.

[7]   EPA Website, "Health Effects of Exposure to Mercury," https://www.epa.gov/mercury/health-effects-exposures-mercury.

of tailings that rose to a wave of 10 meters high, killed fourteen workers and five residents, and destroyed the homes of 600 families in the immediate locale. The tailings also resulted in the loss of 10,000 jobs and the contamination of land and waterways, key sources of sustenance and income for communities in the region.[8] Just over three years later, in January 2019, disaster struck Minas Gerais even more extensively in nearby Brumadinho. Although the Brumadinho dam released far fewer tons of tailings, the wave of waste buried buildings and other infrastructure 1 kilometer downstream, resulting in the death of 270 people.

Although some artisanal forms of mining can be conducted more safely, given the many environmental injustices, health effects, and dangers of metallic mining, Dom Vicente Fereirra, bishop of Brumadinho, prophetically tells the world that "[t]here is no responsible mining. Well, responsible, yes, for crimes. Responsible, yes, for many deaths. Responsible, yes, for the contamination of lakes and rivers. For the destruction of lives. There is no mining that can be called responsible in Latin America."[9] Communities across the Americas have organized and risen up to demand an end to these dangerous mining practices that are devastating human communities and their surrounding ecosystems. Local groups of affected families and communities have come together to protest new mining projects, to petition for the termination or at least greater regulation of existing operations, and to demand restitution for damages incurred by contamination and disasters such as those at Mariana and Brumadinho.

---

   [8]   Mario Parreiras de Faria, "Mariana and Brumadinho: Repercussions of Mining Disasters on Environmental Health," *Revista Brasileira de Medicina do Trabalho* 17, no. 1 (July 15, 2019).

   [9]   Divest in Mining Campaign, Facebook post, March 23, 2022, https://www.facebook.com/DivestInMining/photos/pcb.501317511714576/501317 055047955.

In Latin America, churches and faith-based organizations have become increasingly involved in anti-mining movements, and regional coordination between them has been facilitated by groups like Pax Christi International and the Red Iglesias y Minería [Churches and Mining Network]. In particular, the Churches and Mining Network describes itself as

> an ecumenical space, made up of Christian communities, pastoral teams, religious congregations, theological reflection groups, lay people, bishops, and pastors who seek to respond to the challenges of the impacts and violations of socio-environmental rights that are provoked by mining activities in the territories where we live and work.
>
> We are united and inspired by faith and hope in God the creator of life and of mother nature; a God who calls us to build a world in which all people can live with the dignity of children of God, in perfect harmony with mother Earth and all of creation.
>
> We accompany the faith, hope, and work of persons, institutions, and faith communities that every day defend harmonious coexistence amongst human beings and mother Earth, in the face of projects and lifestyles that impact them as expressions of inordinate interests that are external to and distant from their communities.[10]

The Churches and Mining Network also builds networks of international solidarity, particularly in its divestment campaign. In early 2022, the network took their campaign to Europe on a "Latin American Caravan for Integral Ecology in Extractive Times." Community leaders, pastoral agents, activists, and researchers from Brazil, Honduras, Colombia, and Ecuador brought this testimony to

---

[10] "Quienes Somos," Red Iglesias y Minería Website, https://iglesia symineria.org/quienes-somos/.

European churches and faith-based organizations: "There are thousands of us in organized resistance, demanding justice, demanding an end to colonial impositions, demanding respect for our right to make decisions and live in peace. We demand that the violence stop and that those responsible for the pain, devastation, and deaths due to these socio-environmental crimes must pay."[11] Like the movements against fossil fuel extraction mentioned above, the anti-mining movement professes that "water is life" and that, when it comes to metals and minerals, we should do everything in our power to "keep them in the ground."

Hydroelectric Dams

When Berta Cáceres was murdered in 2016, she and the Civic Council of Popular and Indigenous Organizations of Honduras (COPINH), were fighting to halt construction of the Agua Zarca hydroelectric dam on the Gualcarque River. Tens of thousands of dams exist throughout the Americas for the purposes of creating reservoirs for domestic and industrial water use, as well as irrigation for agriculture. Furthermore, hydroelectric dams have been hailed as significant sources of "clean energy" and catalysts for economic development, replacing billions of tons of carbon emissions each year and providing jobs and electricity for both domestic and industrial sectors.

While hydroelectric dams may seem like a panacea for "developing" countries and the climate crisis, they come with hidden costs that have been documented and denounced by communities affected by them for decades. These costs include increased

---

[11] "Comunidades latinoamericanas martirizadas por la minería denuncian en Europa su situación y proponen el cuidado de la Casa Común," Red Iglesias y Minería Website, March 17, 2022, https://iglesiasymineria.org/2022/03/17/comunidades-latinoamericanas-martirizadas-por-la-mineria-denuncian-en-europa-su-situacion-y-proponen-el-cuidado-de-la-casa-comun/.

incidence of parasitic and infectious diseases like malaria and schistosomiasis, a parasite that is carried by snails whose natural predators are disrupted by changes in their aquatic ecosystems due to dam construction. The effects of these diseases are especially devastating for children. The construction of hydroelectric dams also displaces local communities and wildlife, disturbs local ecosystems, and even destroys cultural heritage sites, especially sites of historical and sacred importance to Indigenous peoples. Furthermore, hydroelectric dams cause serious disruption to downstream water supplies and are also known to affect water quality, particularly when chemical defoliants are used to clear vegetation from the site of the flooded area.[12] As with the tailings dams involved in metallic mining, hydroelectric dams can fail, often with fatal consequences for affected communities.

Indigenous peoples are disproportionately affected by these negative consequences of mega-projects that harness the natural power of waterways as an energy source. Forced displacement due to dam construction is especially traumatizing, particularly for Indigenous and Afro-descendent communities who have been sustained by local ecosystems for generations, or even millennia.[13] Rivers and watersheds are sacred entities in the cosmovisions of many of these communities, and the consequences of damming a river can be as spiritually and culturally damaging as it is materially and ecologically so.

Communities standing in opposition to dams have come together to organize and protest the effects of existing dams and protest the construction of new ones. In Brazil, the historic popular organization Vía Campesina has mobilized around the construction of both tailings and hydroelectric dams since the 1980s. The

---

[12] See Pete S. Michaels and Steven F. Napolitano, "This Hidden Costs of Hydroelectric Dams," *Cultural Survival Quarterly* 12, no. 2 (June 1988).

[13] Michaels and Napolitano.

Movement of People Affected by Dams (MAB) describes their organization as

> the result of a long work of collective construction. Because we do not accept injustice, the destruction of nature, and because we are sure that we can live in a better way, we organize and fight, with great sacrifice, facing powerful enemies that only exploit us, oppress us, and expel us from our communities.
>
> We organize ourselves to defend the interests of the populations affected by the system of electricity generation, distribution and sale. Our practice is guided by principles and values that find in the pedagogy of example and in solidarity among peoples the best way to convince others. Our struggle is nourished by the deep feeling of love for the people and love for life.

While protest and denunciation of the environmental injustices wrought by hydroelectric dam projects is a driving force behind this movement, MAB also seeks to overturn the capitalist commodification of water and energy through popular energy projects:

> We want the use of water and energy resources with sovereignty, distribution of wealth and popular control—this is the synthesis of the energy policy project that we defend. Until the early 1990s, the national electricity sector was state-owned under a monopoly regime: a single state-owned company produced, transported and distributed energy. After this period, public services were transferred to the private property regime, through a wave of privatizations. The new electric energy policy, under neoliberalism, became guided by market rules.
>
> The Brazilian territory has one of the largest water potentials in the world; therefore, we generate our electricity

via hydroelectric plants, a source with an extremely cheap production cost. Even so, Brazil ranks among the 10 countries that pay the most expensive energy tariffs. Our knowledge of this reality reveals that our struggle cannot be reduced only to changing the technological matrix and choosing the best source of renewable generation. Resistance to capitalist projects is of enormous importance.[14]

Alternative hydroelectric energy production by the people and for the people stands in stark contrast to the commodification of water as a resource to extract for the sake of capital accumulation.

Logging, Ranching, and Big Agriculture

When the Zapatistas rose up in 1994, the Lacandon Forest of Chiapas had already been the site of extensive deforestation for timber, as well as large farming operations for centuries. Two more immediate factors gave impulse to the uprising. First, in 1992, the Mexican government altered its constitution to allow for communal farmers to sell their communal lands, called *ejidos*, driving small Indigenous and Ladino farmers out of their territories to make way for "more productive agriculture [farming and ranching] through more efficient production on larger land holdings."[15] Second, the North American Free Trade Agreement was to take effect on January 1, 1994, the day of the uprising, which was strategically chosen by the EZLN to make a clear and direct statement about the "death certificate" that the agreement's reduction of tariffs on corn imports from the United States would impose on Indigenous farmers.[16]

---

[14] "Lutas," Movimento dos Antingidos por Barragens Website, https://mab.org.br/lutas/.

[15] James Nations, "The Ecology of the Zapatista Revolt," *Cultural Survival Quarterly* (March 1994).

[16] Nations, quoting Subcomandante Marcos.

With no market for their crops and ever scarcer access to land, the Zapatistas insisted that autonomous control of Indigenous territory would facilitate both protection of what remained of the Lacandon Forest and the kind of cooperatively owned and operated farming that would allow their communities to survive.

Similar struggles against the destruction of forests for lumber and agricultural use have been waged across the Americas for centuries. In recent years, global market demands have increased both legally sanctioned and illegal enterprises in logging, ranching, and large-scale monoculture farming. Such enterprises not only destroy forests and usurp small farm holdings that rural peoples depend on for subsistence, they pollute and deplete the water supply. And even if they operate legally, they invite the presence of drug cartels seeking extortion money and work as mercenaries. Faced with the land-grabbing invasions that accompany these market trends, communities have the same choices that the Zapatistas had in the 1990s: to emigrate to a town or city, or further north to the U.S.; to stay and work for large landholders in the logging, ranching, and farming industries; or to rise up and resist with nonviolent tactics and/or armed self-defense of the communities' territories. It is no wonder that many communities are choosing organized resistance.

For example, Purépecha women in Cherán—a town in Michoacán, Mexico—rose up in 2011 to protect their territory from the violence that accompanied the incursion of illegal logging. Their movement sparked a fire in the Purépecha people of Cherán, who declared their autonomy and formed their own government to defend their lands from not only logging but large-scale monocrop farming of avocados. The market demand for avocados, especially in the United States, has made this cash crop very lucrative, even for smaller-scale farmers. But the social and environmental costs of avocado production are high, including draining local water supplies and attracting cartels eager to cash in on this industry by extorting growers and/or serving as armed guards or mercenaries for them when resistance arises. Avocados are often referred to as "green gold," but community leader David Ramos refers to them as "gold stained with the blood of Mother Earth." Therefore, the people of Cherán have prohibited growing avocados on lands within their territory, other than for family consumption. They are reclaiming their ancestors' insistence that they care for the earth, for the land and water and the forests, because these gifts are life itself.[17]

Although Indigenous peoples are disproportionately vulnerable to the threats of land-grabbing and deforestation in Latin America, Afro-descendent communities are also at high risk of displacement by these phenomena. In Brazil, enslaved Africans who escaped from their bondage fled to the forests and mountains to form isolated communities called "*quilombos*." In many cases, Africans integrated with Indigenous peoples, and while enslaved Africans brought their own Indigenous wisdom about living in harmony with nature from their motherland, they also learned from the original peoples of the Americas about the specificities of living from the abundance of these particular forests and soils. Inhabited by the descendants of the original *quilombolas*, many *quilombos* exist in Brazil to this day, as do maroon communities in other parts of Latin America. But their claims to their ancestral territories have been continuously threatened by migrants, settlers, and corporations attempting to clear forests and seize farmlands for construction of railroads and highways, for logging enterprises, for

---

[17] For the story of how the women of Cherán gave birth to this movement, see *Mujeres de Fuego* [Women of Fire] podcast, November 4, 2021, Audible.com. See also Mark Stevenson, "Mexican Town Protects Forest from Avocado Growers, Cartels," AP News, January 27, 2022, https://apnews.com/article/business-world-news-mountains-mexico-caribbean-32a4508534bffb-00cf341119de733d5d, and "Mexicans Defend Forest from Gangs, Avocados," AP News YouTube channel, January 27, 2022, https://youtu.be/2aWZtU4fJ9g.

large-scale ranching and farming, and even for tourism purposes. For centuries *quilombolas* had no means of defending a legal claim to their lands, but Brazil's 1988 constitution enshrined the rights of *quilombolas* to their ancestral lands, and the Brazilian government has officially recognized nearly 3,000 of these communities, mostly within the Amazon region.[18] Nevertheless, only a couple of hundred land titles have been granted to *quilombolas* by the government, and mounting pressures for land place *quilombola* land squarely in the sights of extractive industries. One *quilombo* in the Atlantic Forest, whose community had struggled for twelve long years to receive recognition, remarks that "[i]t's a paradise here. A paradise where we can fly like a bird flying in the air. In free air." His particular community produces small-scale organic crops like bananas in a way that is environmentally friendly and sustainable for the community. The community relies on the forest to care for their needs, with over 300 species in their communal knowledge, which they use for human sustenance and healing without depleting the forest of its ability to survive. Other *quilombos* also rely on a combination of traditional knowledge, agro-forestry techniques, and eco-tourism to generate a robust and sustainable livelihood for their communities.[19]

Ladino, mestizo, and other *campesino* communities in many parts of Latin America also face harassment and displacement due

---

[18] "Freedom—Quilombo Land Title Struggle in Brazil," If Not Us Then Who YouTube Channel, August 9, 2016, https://youtu.be/evVzfNhSFLw. See also Sue Branford and Maurício Torres, "Brazilian Supreme Court Ruling Protects Quilombola Land Rights for Now," Mongabay Website, February 13, 2018, https://news.mongabay.com/2018/02/brazilian-supreme-court-ruling-protects-quilombola-land-rights-for-now/.

[19] See Waverli Maia Matarazzo Neuberger, "Back to the Future: Quilombos and Their Potential to Protect Brazil's Atlantic Forest," Landscapes for People, Food, and Nature Website, May 8, 2015, https://peoplefoodandnature.org/blog/back-to-the-future-quilombos-and-their-potential-to-protect-brazils-atlantic-forest/.

to the incursion of extractive logging, ranching, and agricultural projects. *Raising Resistance* is a documentary film that recounts the struggle of small farmers in Paraguay to resist the land-grabbing tactics of larger-scale Brazilian settlers who lay claim to communally farmed *campesino* land in order to implement monocrop farming of genetically modified soybeans.[20] Soy is a protein-rich crop in high demand globally due to its utility as animal feed and its prevalence in many processed foods. It requires high application of potent herbicides, such as Roundup (glyphosate), which kill off surrounding subsistence farmers' crops that are not genetically modified to withstand such harsh chemicals. Furthermore, exposure to such herbicides also places workers and surrounding community members at high risk of health effects such as eye and skin irritation, along with increased risk of cancer, kidney disease, celiac disease, endocrine disruption, autism, and more.[21] Other agricultural workers throughout the Americas are similarly at risk due to herbicide and pesticide exposure. For example, an epidemic of kidney disease is plaguing sugarcane workers in Central America. Scientists have posited that the increased incidence of this condition in certain low-lying regions is tied to higher temperatures and scarcity of potable water, indicating that climate change is playing a role in exacerbating the problem.[22] But,

---

[20] *Raising Resistance*. Documentary film directed by David Bernet and Bettina Borgfeld (Javia Films, 2013).

[21] While the U.S. Environmental Protection Agency has determined that current use of glyphosate is not hazardous to human health, the World Health Organization has indicated that it is a probable carcinogen, and scientists have expressed concern for its health effects and widespread presence in many food products, especially soy. Some of these risks do not derive from glyphosate alone, but in combination with other environmental toxins. See J. P. Myers et al., "Concerns over Use of Glyphosate-Based Herbicides and Risks Associated with Exposures: A Consensus Statement," *Environmental Health* 15, no. 19 (2016).

[22] Rosa De Ferrari, "The Silent Massacre: Chronic Kidney Disease in

again, many small farmers and agricultural workers are fighting back and embodying alternative means of sustaining their families and communities.

Extractivism, Gender Justice, and Climate Justice

Each of these extractive industries operates according to a sinful, anti-social and anti-ecological logic of violent exploitation that harms both human communities and the lands, waters, and ecosystems on which they depend to survive. Before we conclude this chapter, it is important that we take a moment to consider how the logic of extractivism and each of the examples of extractivism detailed above are also deeply implicated both in violence against women and LGBTQ+ folks and in the environmental racism that characterizes the climate crisis. And yet here too many environmental resistance movements embody alternative paradigms of communal governance and ecological lifeways.

Racialized Violence against Women and LGBTQ+ People

When illegal loggers came to invade Cherán, backed by the violence of organized crime and the complicity of local politicians and law enforcement, they told the townspeople that they were going to finish up with the forests, then come for the animals, and then they would take the women.[23] As we have already discussed, the logic of extractivism is intricately intertwined with the logic of patriarchy. Ecofeminists have been arguing this point for decades: it is the same

---

Central America's Sugarcane Workers," University of Pittsburgh Panoramas: Scholarly Platform Website, November 14, 2017, https://www.panoramas.pitt. edu/health-and-society/silent-massacre-chronic-kidney-disease-central-americas-sugarcane-workers.

[23] *Mujeres del Fuego* podcast.

logic of domination that sets the extractivist sights of powerful men on the natural resources of "Mother Earth" that also sets their sights on the sexual and reproductive resources of women. Furthermore, the patriarchal violence of capitalism treats both the earth and women's bodies as expendable sacrifice zones, not worthy of agency, health, dignity, respect, or even life itself. Indeed, when extraction from the earth or the bodies of women is no longer pleasurable or profitable, they become entirely disposable, marked for death.

These violent realities are especially true for women of color, who have historically been and continue to be objectified and commodified for their sexual and reproductive capacities. Ecowomanist ethicist Melanie Harris identifies this as the central claim of ecowomanism:

> Pointing to parallel oppressions suffered by enslaved African women whose bodies were raped and violated for the purpose of breeding slaves during the history of American slavery, and the similar ways in which the body of the earth, including mountains, rivers, and farming fields, have been used and overused for economic gain and resource, ecowomanism claims that the same logic of domination that functioned as a theoretical underpinning for the transatlantic slave trade (and other forms of systemic oppression) is the same logic of domination at work in cases of ecological violence and control.[24]

Ecowomanist analysis and praxis, therefore, goes deeper than ecofeminism to diagnose the patriarchal *and* white supremacist nature of the ecologically destructive world order that emerges with

---

[24] Melanie L. Harris, *Ecowomanism: African American Women and Earth-Honoring Faiths* (Maryknoll, NY: Orbis Books, 2017). See also Melanie L. Harris, "Ecowomanism: An Introduction," in *Worldviews: Global Religions, Culture, and Ecology* 20, no. 1 (2016): 5–14.

the advent of colonialism and slavery. Extractivism is not only sexist; it is racist to its core.[25]

How does this play out in concrete contexts of contemporary extractivism? Three illustrative examples are worth considering:

Under chattel slavery in the Americas, it was the labor of Black bodies, especially the bodies of Black women, that was extracted for the sake of extracting agricultural products and raw materials such as cotton, sugarcane, lumber, and gold from the land. As Harris points out, Black women were further exploited for their sexual and reproductive capacities under sharecropping and the evolution of these forms of anti-Black exploitation continue to this day throughout the Americas, especially in the prison industrial complex of the United States. In the realm of extractivist big agriculture today, the exploitation of women's labor and sexuality is taking place in the context of migrant farm labor, which in the United States is mostly performed by immigrants from Latin America, most of whom identify as Indigenous or are of predominantly Indigenous ancestry. Nichole M. Flores's work in Catholic social ethics highlights not only the injustices perpetrated against migrant workers in general, but the sexual violence against migrant women, who face harassment and sexual assault in the fields.[26] In this case, the extraction of a cheap and plentiful food supply relies on a system of worker exploitation that seamlessly integrates with sexual violence against women. The rape of the earth by big agriculture is interconnected with the literal rape of migrant women.

---

[25] Cedric Robinson makes the argument that even the development of early capitalism in Europe depended on categories of racialization. See *Black Marxism: The Making of the Black Radical Tradition* (London: Zed Press, 1983, reprinted Chapel Hill: University of North Carolina Press, 2000).

[26] See Nichole M. Flores, "Trinity and Justice: A Theological Response to the Sexual Assault of Migrant Women," *Journal of Religion and Society* 16, no. 1 (2018): 39–51.

A second example relates to the phenomenon of "boom-towns," which are "usually rural areas experiencing population explosion because of industrial-scale extraction projects that require temporary labor." Not only has history shown that boomtowns are "susceptible to deep depressions that can be fatal to the local economy when the extraction period ends," the male laborers recruited into the extractive industry form "mancamps" that are connected with an increase in violent crimes, especially against women, such as human trafficking, physical and sexual assault, and murder. Even in areas where Indigenous women make up the smallest demographic, they are disproportionately affected by this violence. In the United States and Canada alone, more than 50 percent of Indigenous women have been sexually assaulted, more than 30 percent report rape, and Indigenous women are ten times more likely to be murdered than any demographic group.[27] In these boomtowns, Native women are just one more "natural resource" to exploit and leave for dead in the wake of violent extraction.

Finally, a third example similarly relates to the ways in which extractivism's effect on migration patterns leads to a myriad of social problems, including violence against women. As we have seen, extractive projects in Latin America often displace people from their rural communities, which are relatively more sparsely populated, forcing their internal migration to larger, more densely populated towns and cities, or to the United States. More densely populated towns and cities lack the resources to accommodate dramatic increases in the population, and while the resulting poverty is a violence in and of itself, women are often targeted for violence as workers in *maquilas* (factories) or in their daily lives. For example, since the neoliberal extractivist logic of NAFTA was implemented in the 1990s, an epidemic of feminicide has claimed

---

[27] *LN3: Seven Lessons of the Anishinaabe in Resistance*, Documentary Study Guide, https://www.stopline3.org/the-study-guide.

the lives of thousands of women in towns and cities along the U.S.-Mexico border, where *maquilas* rapidly proliferated under the new trade agreement. Rural people, who were being displaced from their homes due to the sale of communal lands or the way in which North American corn flooded the Mexican market, flocked to these sources of employment, and women were especially recruited to work in the maquilas. They were then targeted for violence, especially by local sectors of organized crime and even law enforcement.[28] For women who make the journey north to the United States, similar dangers await them along the way. Many women who migrate are even said to obtain birth control pills to prevent pregnancy from the sexual assaults that are commonly known to occur along their journey north.

It is important to note that extractivism also adversely affects women in unique ways due to their traditional roles as caregivers for their families. It is often women who are charged with the tasks of providing food and water for their households. Therefore, when extractivist industries pollute the soil, contaminate and deplete water sources, destroy the forest, and displace communities from their lands, it is often women who are forced to scramble for the resources needed to survive. Men are often the first to migrate from their homes in order to send income back to their families and women are the ones left behind to do the day to day work of keeping their children, the sick, and the elderly, alive.

It should also be noted that the patriarchal logic of extractivism contributes to the construction of gender identity and sexual orientation as normatively cisgender and heterosexual, because it is only within these confines that patriarchal extraction of women's sexual and reproductive capacities is possible. Therefore, anyone who transgresses these binary norms of gender and sexuality is

---

[28] See Nancy Pineda-Madrid, *Suffering and Salvation in Ciudad Juarez* (Minneapolis: Fortress Press, 2011).

considered despicable, disposable, and marked for death. Prior to European contact, many Indigenous communities of the Americas and Africa had more expansive, nonbinary conceptions of gender and sexuality, and some even saw great spiritual wisdom in "two-spirit" persons, who did not conform to male or female gender identity or sexual expression.[29] However, the combination of the patriarchal structures and misogynist sexual mores of European Christianity with the patriarchal and misogynist nature of colonial and capitalist extractivism has brought about over five hundred years of widespread demonization of and violence against gender nonconforming people in the Americas.[30]

Because of how ideologically and materially implicated race, gender, and sexuality are with the injustices of extractivism and ecological degradation, many of the organizations and movements resisting extractivism are led by women and insist on the leadership capacity of women, especially women of color, along with the need for racial justice, gender justice, and women's empowerment to be integrated with the struggle for environmental justice. Furthermore, cultural and political changes in recent years have led to the creation of greater space for the inclusion, leadership, and celebration of LGBTQ+ folks in this struggle as well.[31] While progress

---

[29] See the argument advanced by decolonial feminist scholar María Lugones. See María Lugones, "Heterosexualism and the Colonial/Modern Gender System," *Hypatia* 22, no. 1 (Winter 2007).

[30] See Melissa Pagán, "Extractive Zones and the Nexus of the Coloniality of Being/Coloniality of Gender: Towards a Decolonial Feminist Integral Ecology," *Journal of Hispanic/Latino Theology* 22, no. 1 (Spring 2020).

[31] One powerful example of this is Berta Cáceres's empowerment of Gaspar Sánchez, an Indigenous activist with COPINH who advances sexual diversity education. See Bryan Rogers, "Honduran Indigenous Activist Battles Colonialism, Patriarchy, and Militarism with Sexual Diversity Education," Upside Down World Website, November 22, 2017, https://upsidedownworld.org/archives/honduras/honduran-indigenous-activist-battles-colonialism-patriarchy-militarism-sexual-diversity-education/.

still needs to be made in this area on many fronts, it is becoming
ever more common for environmental justice advocates to apply
intersectional analyses to the challenges of extractivism—naming
and denouncing the ways in which economic exploitation, racial
oppression, and heteropatriarchal violence are all interconnected
with the degradation of the earth.

Extractivism and Climate Justice

All the extractivist industries detailed above not only inflict immediate harm to local communities and ecosystems, they also all
contribute in one way or another to the acceleration of the climate
crisis on a global scale. The planet is warming, ice caps are melting,
and sea levels are rising at an alarming rate. Severe weather events,
erratic weather patterns, droughts, and wildfires are all already taking
place and affecting vulnerable communities around the world, especially in the Global South and especially in poor and marginalized
communities, the global majority of which are composed of people
of color. For the people already affected by these phenomena, apoca-
lypse is happening *now*! Those of us protected by privilege may stave
off these effects in our own lives for another few decades, but we
too will eventually suffer the consequences. For these reasons, Berta
Cáceres's Goldman Prize acceptance speech implores humanity:
"Wake up! We are out of time!"

Fossil fuel extraction is the most obvious industry driving
climate change, since burning fossil fuels is the primary source of
the global carbon emissions that cause the greenhouse effect and
resultant warming of the planet. However, the environmental
impacts of mining, logging, ranching, big agriculture, and hydroelectric dams contribute both to the destruction of forests that
absorb carbon and to the release of additional carbon and methane
into the atmosphere. Even hydroelectric dams are implicated here,

although they do replace the burning of billions of tons of fossil fuels each year and are considered a significant source of renewable energy around the world. In addition to the deleterious social and environmental impacts of hydroelectric dams for local communities that we have already considered, these dams actually produce far more greenhouse gas emissions than is commonly assumed. Dams require the burning of fossil fuel during their construction, of course, and while emissions vary from dam to dam and over time, the decay of organic material in the flooded areas (water reservoirs) created by hydroelectric dams releases both carbon and methane into the atmosphere.[32] These emissions are not currently counted in global greenhouse gas inventories, despite the presence of tens of thousands of dams around the world.[33] Furthermore, hydroelectric dams are constructed in developing countries not for the sake of electricity access for local communities, but rather

---

[32] See Matt Weiser, "The Hydropower Paradox: Is This Energy as Clean as It Seems?" *The Guardian*, November 6, 2016, https://www.theguardian.com/sustainable-business/2016/nov/06/hydropower-hydroelectricity-methane-clean-climate-change-study. For studies supporting these claims, see Ilissa B. Ocko and Steven P. Hamburg, "Climate Impacts of Hydropower: Enormous Differences among Facilities and over Time," *Environmental Science and Technology* 53, no. 23 (2019): 14070–14082; Laura Scherer and Stephen Pfister, "Hydropower's Biogenic Carbon Footprint," *PLOS One* 11, no. 9 (2016): e0161947; and Bridgit R. Deemer et al., "Greenhouse Gas Emissions from Reservoir Water Surfaces: A New Global Synthesis," *BioScience* 66, no. 11 (November 2016): 949–964.

[33] See Alice Tianbo Zhang et al., "Power of the River: Introducing the Global Dam Tracker (GDAT)" at Columbia University Center on Global Energy Policy Website, November 2018, https://www.energypolicy.columbia.edu/sites/default/files/pictures/GlobalDams_CGEP_2018.pdf. See also Perry Wheeler, "Over One Hundred Twenty-Five Groups Petition EPA to Report GHG Emissions from Dams and Reservoirs," Earthjustice Website, March 22, 2022, https://earthjustice.org/news/press/2022/over-one-hundred-twenty-five-groups-petition-epa-to-report-ghg-emissions-from-hydropower-dams-reservoirs.

for the sake of fueling the development of mining and manufacturing industries and providing irrigation for large monocrop farming enterprises. The global network of unsustainable production and consumption in which these industries are implicated drives climate change due to their reliance on other extractivist projects for raw materials, their need for international transportation to export commodities, and their contribution to the release of greenhouse gasses from landfills that hold the garbage produced by industrial and consumer waste.

While renewable and clean energy production is absolutely essential to mitigating the climate crisis, this crisis cannot be fully addressed without a dramatic reduction in the habits of human consumption, especially in high-wealth countries (with the United States as the biggest culprit).[34] New hydropower dam projects represent our commitment to continue consuming at the same level and in the same patterns that we have been doing at alarmingly exponential rates over the past century or so. Climate justice advocates across the Americas therefore insist that we need a structurally effective paradigm shift in not only energy production but in how we consume both energy and other goods whose production harms human beings and the planet in both the short term/ local context and the long term/global context.

Local water protectors and other environmental defenders also insist that their work at the local level is not just for themselves and their own communities alone, but for the good of humanity and the planet as a whole. As Imelda, one of the Purépecha *abuelas* from Cherán, states:

> Cherán has always fought for the good of not just our community or our culture, but the whole world.... I do what I do for the moon and the sun, for the four

---

[34] See Hope Jahren, *The Story of More: How We Got to Climate Change and Where to Go from Here* (New York: Vintage Books, 2020).

seasons to do their own work, for the water so that there is enough water in its season, for the sun to do what it's supposed to do, and for the earth to do what it's supposed to do to bear fruit.[35]

From the Tar Sands to Standing Rock, from Chiapas to Cherán, from the Andes to the Amazon—the work of resisting the violence of extractivism at the local level is interconnected with global efforts to demand environmental justice, slow down rising temperatures, and seek sustainable means of adapting to the changing climate. As with resistance to extractive industries, those who are most affected by the injustice and violence of the climate crisis are at the forefront of local, regional, and international movements for climate action that takes into account a wholistic and realistic picture of how local struggles for environmental justice are related to global efforts to seek climate justice.[36]

Violence upon Violence

In this chapter, we have surveyed the environmental violence and racism suffered by marginalized and vulnerable peoples across the Americas whose local communities and ecosystems are under attack by extractivist industries. We have also caught a glimpse of the witness to hope that is embodied by communities and popular movements that stand up to protect their lands, forests, and waterways and that seek alternative paradigms for organizing their existence

---

[35] *Mujeres de Fuego* podcast.

[36] Take, for example, the work of the Movement of Victims Affected by Climate Change and Corporations (MOVIAC) in Central America (http://moviaces.blogspot.com/). An excellent resource that features many North American women from vulnerable communities who are leaders in local and/or global movements for climate justice is Ayana Elizabeth Johnson and Katherine K. Wilkinson, *All We Can Save: Truth, Courage, and Solutions for the Climate Crisis* (New York: One World Books, 2020).

in equilibrium with one another and the more-than-human world. In the Americas, organized communities and movements of poor, Indigenous, Black, and Brown communities are fighting for our common home, in the hopes of creating an-other world in which we can all live in relationships of justice and peace with one another and in a relationship of equilibrium with the rest of the natural world.

Unfortunately, when local communities resist extractivist projects, the agents and beneficiaries of those projects are well prepared to fight back with multiple violent tactics, from criminalization to defamation, assault, and assassination. The violence of extractivism is compounded by campaigns of terror against local communities, along with smear campaigns, incarceration, death threats, and murder of community leaders. In the chapter that follows, we will examine the general contours of these human rights violations prior to highlighting the stories of land and environmental defenders whose lives were ultimately stolen from them as a result of their work for environmental justice. What these murdered defenders unveil here is violence upon violence, destruction of life upon destruction of life. And yet their witness points their communities and the rest of us toward active hope for an-other world in which many worlds—human and more-than-human—are free to coexist.

3

DYING FOR OUR COMMON HOME

The Criminalization and Assassination of Environmental Defenders

Human beings depend on the natural elements of water, air, earth, and fire for our existence and our continued survival. Environmental defenders throughout the Americas therefore profess: water is life. *Agua es vida. Água é vida. Yaku kawsay. Mní wičóni.*[1] Water is life. So too, the air that we breathe is life. The soil from which we harvest our sustenance is life. And fire is also life, not only when it protects us from the cold and helps us to prepare our food, but also when it burns in our hearts as we protect our common home and fight for justice and peace for the earth and its inhabitants. These elements, and the many creatures and ecosystems that they coalesce to form, are foundational building blocks for a common home that provides us with opportunities for not only life, but health, dignity, cultural integrity, creativity, and more.

When the Purépecha women of Cherán rose up against criminal violence, illegal logging, and avocado plantations in 2011, they were fighting to defend the natural elements that make life possible. Soon after the women's uprising, the whole community

---

[1]   Each of these sentences translates the phrase "water is life" into Spanish, Portuguese, Quechua, and Lakota, respectively.

came together to organize their town in a more egalitarian and participatory fashion that would restore ancestral practices and protect their territory from the cartels, loggers, politicians, and police who were responsible for the destruction of their sacred forests and water sources. In the early days of this struggle, community members came out into the streets day and night to remain vigilant and prevent loggers from passing through. On each street corner, the women built a fire to keep warm and to prepare food for the community. As they built and tended these fires of resistance, the community of Cherán, like countless other communities in the Americas and around the world, were defending their right to live a sovereign and dignified life supported by their own cultural values and by access to the natural elements that give them spiritual and material sustenance.

Unfortunately, when land and environmental defenders organize to protect themselves and the earth from the violence of extractivist industries, the agents and beneficiaries of those industries are well prepared to strike back with both generalized and targeted violence. The loggers who invaded Cherán were backed by cartels that unleashed a campaign of terror on the once relatively peaceful community and that targeted specific defenders in an attempt to silence their voices and make "examples" of them as a warning to others. This chapter uncovers how land and environmental defenders are often persecuted for their commitment to protecting both the earth and their communities' fundamental right to enjoy access to the goods of the earth within a safe, healthy, and sustainable environment.

We will proceed in two parts. First, we will lay a foundation for understanding that environmental defenders are exercising a fundamental human right in their activities to protect the environment, with reference to how this right has been progressively articulated in international legal norms. Second, we will offer a general overview of how this right to defend the environment is being violated throughout the Americas in a multitude of ways, from criminalization to defamation, torture, assault, and assassination. Chapter 4 is then dedicated to contemplating the stories of several land and environmental defenders who have been murdered for their lived commitment to human and ecological well-being in Latin America. Familiarizing ourselves with their lives and the conditions that led to their deaths will prepare us for reflecting theologically on their witness, as ecomartyrs, to the urgency of integrating social and environmental justice in our world today.

The Right to Defend the Environment

For human beings to enjoy fundamental human rights and dignity, we need access to the natural resources that sustain life, and our environment must be a place that is safe and healthy for us to live, rather than a place that is depleted of resources and contaminated by various forms of toxic waste and pollution. While many land and environmental defenders throughout the Americas are fighting for the inherent sacredness and worth of the natural world as such, they are also fighting for the basic human rights that the natural world makes possible for human communities to enjoy. The office of the United Nations' Special Rapporteur on Human Rights and the Environment frames the question of environmental human rights this way:

> All human beings depend on the environment in which we live. A safe, clean, healthy and sustainable environment is integral to the full enjoyment of a wide range of human rights, including the rights to life, health, food, water and sanitation.
>
> Without a healthy environment, we are unable to fulfill our aspirations. We may not have access to even the minimum standards of human dignity.[2]

---

2 "About Human Rights and the Environment," United Nations Office of

The UN appointed its first special rapporteur with a mandate to explore and promote human rights obligations relating to the enjoyment of a safe, clean, healthy, and sustainable environment in 2012.[3] But looking back even further, the United Nations has made slow but steady progress over the past three decades in establishing international norms to support environmental human rights and the specific right of environmental activists to defend these rights.

This process took a giant leap forward in 1992, when the United Nations brought together government and civil society leaders from 179 countries for an international Conference on Environment and Development in Rio de Janeiro. The purpose of the conference, also known as the "Earth Summit," was to study the impact of human activities on the environment and to produce a broad agenda for sustainable development in the twenty-first century, the results of which are recorded in the 27 principles of the Rio Declaration. The conference stressed the importance of local, national, and regional participation of all relevant parties in environmental decision-making processes. Principle 10 of the Rio Declaration thus states that "[e]nviron-mental issues are best handled with participation of all concerned citizens, at the relevant level" and sets forth three fundamental

---

the High Commissioner on Human Rights Website, https://www.ohchr.org/en/special-procedures/sr-environment/about-human-rights-and-environment.

[3] "Special Rapporteur on Human Rights and the Environment," United Nations Office of the High Commissioner on Human Rights Website, https://www.ohchr.org/en/special-procedures/sr-environment. My colleague at Wake Forest University, John Knox, was the UN's first Special Rapporteur on human rights and the environment, and I am grateful for the insights and resources that he provided, both as a guest speaker in my Spring 2021 class, "Religion and Environmental Justice in Latin America," and as a conversation partner when I began conducting my research for this book. Any errors or oversights within this chapter, however, are my own.

rights of people who are affected by environmental issues: the right to access to information about environmental issues affecting their community; the right to participation in decision-making about environmental issues affecting their community; and the right to environmental justice, including redress and remedy in the case of environmental harm.[4]

In 1998, the United Nations commemorated the fiftieth anniversary of the Universal Declaration of Human Rights with a declaration on human rights defenders that laid out the "right and responsibility of individuals, groups and organs of society to promote and protect universally recognized human rights and fundamental freedoms."[5] Put quite simply, in other words, human beings have the right to defend human rights. It would take time for the category of "human rights defenders" to include environmental defenders, but another advance came about in 2007, when the General Assembly of the United Nations adopted the "Declaration on the Rights of Indigenous Peoples," which, like the Rio Declaration, included affirmation of the rights of local peoples, in this case Indigenous peoples, to prior consultation and participation when it comes to the decisions on environmental issues affecting their communities. Building on the International Labour Organization's Indigenous and Tribal People's Convention (ILO 169),[6] Article 26 of the 2007 declaration affirms the right of Indigenous peoples to

[4] "Principle 10," United Nations Environment Programme Website, https://www.unep.org/civil-society-engagement/partnerships/principle-10.

[5] "Declaration on Human Rights Defenders," United Nations Office of the High Commissioner of Human Rights Website, https://www.ohchr.org/en/special-procedures/sr-human-rights-defenders/declaration-human-rights-defenders.

[6] International Labour Organization, "Indigenous and Tribal People's Convention, 1989 (No. 169)," https://www.ilo.org/dyn/normlex/en/f?p=NORMLEXPUB:55:0::NO::P55_TYPE,P55_LANG,P55_DOCUMENT,P55_NODE:REV,en,C169,/Document.

sovereignty on the lands that they have traditionally occupied, and Article 32 of the declaration states the following:

1. Indigenous peoples have the right to determine and develop priorities and strategies for the development or use of their lands or territories and other resources.

2. States shall consult and cooperate in good faith with the Indigenous peoples concerned through their own representative institutions in order to obtain their free and informed consent prior to the approval of any project affecting their lands or territories and other resources, particularly in connection with the development, utilization or exploitation of mineral, water or other resources.

3. States shall provide effective mechanisms for just and fair redress for any such activities, and appropriate measures shall be taken to mitigate adverse environmental, economic, social, cultural or spiritual impact.[7]

The Declaration on the Rights of Indigenous Peoples explicitly affirms spiritual and cultural rights here, including provisions for how these rights pertain to a spiritual relationship with Indigenous lands, territories, waterways, and seas, along with other natural goods. When Indigenous peoples defend ecological, social, and spiritual well-being in their territories, they are defending their right to exist as a people in relationship with the more-than-human world.

More broadly, the UN Special Rapporteur on human rights defenders has offered explicit support for including all environmental defenders in the category of human rights defenders, thus affirming the right and responsibility to protect fundamental

---

[7] United Nations General Assembly, "Declaration on the Rights of Indigenous Peoples," Article 32, September 13, 2007, https://www.un.org/development/desa/indigenouspeoples/wp-content/uploads/sites/19/2018/11/UNDRIP_E_web.pdf.

human rights and freedoms. In a 2016 report to the General Assembly, then Special Rapporteur Michel Forst highlighted the particular situation of environmental defenders around the world and raised the alarm about increasing violence against them, which he identifies as a violation of their right to defend environmental human rights. The report specifically defines "environmental human rights defenders" as "individuals and groups who, in their personal or professional capacity and in a peaceful manner, strive to protect and promote human rights relating to the environment, including water, air, land, flora and fauna."[8] In the report, the Special Rapporteur stresses that "it is the responsibility of the international community and of States to empower and protect environmental human rights defenders" and expresses a reminder that "empowering environmental human rights defenders is crucial to the protection of our environment and all other related human rights."[9]

While these declarations and reports affirm environmental human rights and the rights of environmental defenders to promote and protect these rights, they are not legally binding and have little more than symbolic authority. Even the Inter-American Commission on Human Rights (IACHR) and the UN Human Rights Council (HRC) have limited ability to protect the right to defend environmental human rights.[10] However, in 2018, over two dozen

---

[8]   Note that the report also affirms that "land and environmental rights are interlinked and are often inseparable. As a result, the two broad categories of defenders advocating for the environment and for land rights are often characterized as 'land and environmental rights defenders,' 'environmental rights defenders,' or just 'environmental activists.'" See United Nations General Assembly, "Report of the Special Rapporteur on the Situation of Human Rights Defenders," August 3, 2016, https://documents-dds-ny.un.org/doc/UNDOC/GEN/N16/247/09/PDF/N1624709.pdf?OpenElement.

[9]   United Nations General Assembly, "Report of the Special Rapporteur on the Situation of Human Rights Defenders."

[10] See Trish Glazebrook and Emmanuela Opoku, "Defending the

countries from Latin America and the Caribbean signed the legally binding "Regional Agreement on Access to Information, Public Participation and Justice in Environmental Matters in Latin America and the Caribbean." Also known as the Escazú Agreement, this "is the first legally binding instrument in the world to include provisions on environmental human rights defenders (EHRDs) and is also the first environmental agreement adopted in Latin America and the Caribbean."[11] The agreement, which came into force in 2021 after receiving the sufficient number of ratifications, recognizes the right to a healthy environment and offers legal norms for guaranteeing the environmental rights to information and participation in decision-making that are detailed above. Furthermore, the agreement "requires signatory States to prevent and investigate attacks against those who protect and defend environmental rights. The agreement acknowledges the significance of the work carried out by EHRDs and obliges States to establish guidelines on appropriate and effective measures to ensure their safety."[12] Unfortunately, only twelve countries have ratified the agreement to date, and it remains to be seen how legal implementation of it will affect the work of land and environmental defenders on the ground. Nevertheless, this is a tremendous advance for the protection of environmental human rights and those who defend them.

Most recently, in 2021, the United Nations Human Rights Council officially recognized for the first time that human beings

---

Defenders: Environmental Protectors, Climate Change and Human Rights," *Ethics and the Environment* 23, no. 2 (2018): 83–109.

[11] Zaineb Ali, "The Escazú Agreement: A Landmark Regional Treaty for Environmental Defenders," Universal Rights Group Website, February 10, 2021, https://www.universal-rights.org/contemporary-and-emerging-human-rights-issues/the-escazu-agreement-a-landmark-regional-treaty-for-environmental-defenders.

[12] Ali, "The Escazú Agreement." The agreement itself and further information about its implementation can be found at https://www.cepal.org/en/escazuagreement.

have the right to a safe, clean, healthy, and sustainable environment.[13] This issue will now be brought to the General Assembly for member states to consider implementing a similar resolution. Like earlier declarations and reports, and unlike the Escazú Agreement, this advance is not legally binding, but it does represent a growing international consensus around environmental human rights and the rights of environmental defenders. Unfortunately, this international consensus has grown alongside of and in response to widespread violations of these rights, especially in the case of environmental defenders who endure all manner of personal risk when they carry out their work in defense of their communities and the goods of the natural world on which we all depend.

Violations of the Rights of Environmental Defenders

In chapters 1 and 2, we surveyed several contexts in which extractivist industries commit various forms of violence against human communities and the environment throughout the Americas. Widespread violations of environmental human rights are being committed in contexts of fossil fuel extraction, transport, and refining; metallic and mineral mining; hydroelectric dam construction; and logging, ranching, and big agriculture. Indigenous and Afro-descendent peoples, along with other impoverished rural communities, are disproportionately affected by these violations, and these industries contribute to the disparate effects of the climate crisis each in its own way. In turn, we caught glimpses of how affected communities and their allies have been standing up to extractivist industries to defend their rights to a safe environment, ancestral lands, cultural integrity,

---

[13] "Landmark UN Resolution Confirms Healthy Environment Is a Human Right," UN Environment Programme Website, December 6, 2021, https://www.unep.org/news-and-stories/story/landmark-un-resolution-confirms-healthy-environment-human-right. Note: As of April 2022, the United Nations General Assembly has not yet adopted this resolution.

and life itself. Unfortunately, the courage of these defenders is met with a wide range of violent tactics designed to defame, criminalize, eliminate, and otherwise silence the voices and movements of individuals and communities committed to action for social justice and ecological well-being. Thousands of land and environmental defenders throughout the Americas have been and continue to be subject to smear campaigns, police brutality, imprisonment, death threats, violent assault, torture, and assassination due to these practical commitments. Prior to lifting up the stories of several individual defenders who have been assassinated, it is important to first recognize that their murders are the culmination of a longer process and are embedded in larger systems that defend the violence of extractivism with a broader spectrum of violent actions.

Historically, the United States and Canada have been regions of the world where the violence of settler colonialism and its extractivist industries displaced, dehumanized, murdered, and massacred Native people in general and active resisters in particular. As the brief survey of environmental history in the Americas in chapter 1 attests, much Indigenous blood has been spilled for the sake of colonial, capitalist, and white settler access to wealth-generating natural resources. Furthermore, for generations during and after Reconstruction, African Americans were driven from their lands and lynched for defending their freedom and right to cultivate the soil for their families' and communities' sustenance and dignity. Environmental and land defenders are no longer as likely to be killed in the United States as Native peoples were during colonization and Westward expansion, or as African American farmers were under Jim Crow. However, environmental defenders in the United States and Canada are under other forms of attack by corporations and their hired security forces, as well as local, state, and federal government, and law enforcement.

Responses to the mobilization against the Dakota Access Pipeline at Standing Rock are illustrative of this phenomenon. A report on Indigenous resistance to carbon by the Indigenous Environmental Network and Oil Change International identifies several dimensions of the violent backlash against the mobilization. First of all, the company building the pipeline, Energy Transfer Partners, hired the private security firm TigerSwan to subdue the efforts of water protectors. According to a series of reports by *The Intercept* based on internal company documents,

> TigerSwan communications described the peaceful gathering as "jihadist" and "terrorist," and the private contractor used military-grade weapons and tactics to undercut, discredit, and punish the defenders. Tactics included infiltration, provocation, disruption of communications, aerial surveillance, and radio eavesdropping. Intimidation involved the use of large and visible forces of heavily armed personnel and personnel carriers, as well as drones and air surveillance. The "task force" arrayed against the defenders included agents from the U.S. Federal Bureau of Investigation, U.S. Department of Homeland Security, U.S. Justice Department and Marshals Service, and U.S. Bureau of Indian Affairs, as well as state and local law enforcement and police. TigerSwan transmitted daily reports "from the battlefield" to Energy Transfer Partners.[14]

Perhaps the most visible instances of these tactics were on display when local law enforcement repeatedly harassed and arrested water protectors, using attack dogs and water cannons, despite freezing temperatures.

---

[14] Indigenous Environmental Network and Oil Change International, "Indigenous Resistance Against Carbon," August 2021, https://www.ienearth.org/wp-content/uploads/2021/09/Indigenous-Resistance-Against-Carbon-2021.pdf.

Lasting effects of these attacks persist to this day: "One young white supporter had to have her arm amputated, and two Indigenous women lost eyes due to tear gas canisters. Hundreds were left with arrests on their records and files at the Federal Bureau of Investigation and Department of Homeland Security, with gratuitous charges including trespassing despite being arrested on public roads."[15] Other lasting effects of this situation persist in legislative changes across the country. Civilian protests against social and environmental injustices have been increasingly criminalized in the years following the mobilization of the Standing Rock water protectors. For example, in the years since the climate justice and Indigenous rights movements gained momentum at Standing Rock, dozens of laws have been passed in more than thirty states that criminalize opposition to pipelines.[16] As one report puts it, "After Standing Rock, protesting pipelines can get you a decade in prison and $100K in fines."[17] These laws restrict U.S. constitutional

---

[15] Indigenous Environmental Network and Oil Change International, "Indigenous Resistance Against Carbon." The UN Special Rapporteur on the rights of Indigenous peoples reported to the Human Rights Council in 2018 that "while Sioux leaders advocated for protests to remain peaceful, State law enforcement officials, private security companies and the North Dakota National Guard employed a militarized response to protests. More than 400 people were allegedly arrested, about 90 percent of them from the Standing Rock Sioux tribe, including Chairman Dave Archambault II. Civil society organizations reported the use of excessive violence and humiliation during the arrests." UN Human Rights Council, "Report of the Special Rapporteur on the Rights of Indigenous Peoples," August 10, 2018, https://www.ohchr.org/sites/default/files/Documents/Issues/IPeoples/SR/A.HRC.39.17.pdf.

[16] See Nicholas Kusnetz, "How Energy Companies and Allies Are Turning the Law Against Protesters," Inside Climate News Website, August 22, 2018, https://insideclimatenews.org/news/22082018/pipeline-protest-laws-felony-free-speech-arrests-first-amendment-oklahoma-iowa-louisiana/. See also the "Protest Law Tracker," International Center for Not-for-Profit Law, https://www.icnl.org/usprotestlawtracker/?location=&status=pending&issue=6&date=&type=.

[17] Naveena Sadasivam, "After Standing Rock, Protesting Pipelines Can

rights to peaceful assembly and contradict the United Nations' progress in affirming the rights of environmental defenders to promote and protect environmental human rights.

In a 2018 report to the UN Human Rights Council, the UN Special Rapporteur on the rights of Indigenous peoples connected the treatment of leaders at Standing Rock to the situation of Indigenous peoples around the world who are targets of criminalization, defamation, and assassination for their defense of the land and of Indigenous and environmental human rights. Such attacks against Indigenous and other environmental defenders include "specific instances of heavy-handed intimidation through militarization, including illegal surveillance, disappearances, forced evictions, judicial harassment, arbitrary arrests and detention, limits on freedom of expression and assembly, stigmatization, travel bans, and sexual harassment."[18] Targeted assassination is an all too frequent addition to this list, as evidenced by the murders of defenders featured in this book. The COVID-19 pandemic only exacerbated these trends, as defenders and their allies were confined to their homes, governments increased state control over civic spaces, and what little protections were in place fell away.

One contemporary example of how counter-resistance tactics coalesce to endanger water and land protectors takes us to the Bajo Aguán region of northern Honduras, where iron ore mines introduced in and around a protected national park in the early 2010s have been contaminating the rivers and the local water supply. In some communities, the mining company used violent intimidation to force local residents to sell their lands. When community members established a "Camp Dignity" in the community of

---

Get You a Decade in Prison and $100K in Fines," *The Grist* Website, May 14, 2019, https://grist.org/article/after-standing-rock-protesting-pipelines-can-get-you-a-decade-in-prison-and-100k-in-fines/.

[18] Indigenous Environmental Network and Oil Change International, "Indigenous Resistance Against Carbon."

Guapinol to protest the illegal concessions and the mine, a "Security and Vigilance Committee" was formed by the few local residents who supported the mine to organize an intimidation and media campaign against the water protectors and their supporters. Some community members also report a collaboration between the Security and Vigilance Committee and local organized crime hitmen who provided the security backing to the illegal clearing of lands for cattle ranching. Lands in the region have also been illegally seized for palm oil plantations and, between 2010 and 2014, over 100 community leaders and members of agricultural cooperatives were killed for demanding a return of stolen lands.

In late 2018, a combination of police, security guards, other armed actors, and military forces evicted the protectors at Camp Dignity, even following protectors to their homes and using excessive tear gas and gunfire. Two military officers were killed, and one armed civilian backing the mine was injured in these raids, but many speculate that the armed security for the mine opened fire to delegitimize and criminalize protesters. Thirteen of the Guapinol community leaders and human rights defenders learned of warrants for their arrests and turned themselves in to local authorities. They were accused not only of blocking the road during the eviction from Camp Dignity, but also of arson, illicit association, and other crimes.[19] Of the eight who were finally tried in February 2022, six were convicted and two acquitted of crimes against the politically well-connected mining company Inversiones Los Pinares.[20] Thankfully, the Honduran Supreme Court turned over the conviction

---

[19] "More Background on the Guapinól 13," SHARE Foundation Website, http://www.share-elsalvador.org/uploads/1/0/8/1/108170557/background_on_the_guapin%C3%B3l_13.pdf.

[20] "Honduras: Amnesty International Condemns Conviction of Six of the 'Guapinol Eight,'" Amnesty International Website, February 9, 2022, https://www.amnesty.org/en/latest/news/2022/02/honduras-amnesty-international-condemns-conviction-six-guapinol-eight/.

less than one day later, and all eight of the Guapinol environmental defenders were released after nearly two-and-a-half years of wrongful imprisonment.[21]

Nearly all of the violent tactics of intimidation, criminalization, and assassination are woven together in this one story that has involved hundreds of land and environmental defenders in this one small region of one relatively small Latin American country. Similarly, these forms of violence are all implicated in the stories of the murdered defenders to which we will soon turn. For defenders who identify as women, these violations often also include sexual harassment, gendered forms of torture, sexual violence, and rape. Indeed, targeted assassination is too often the culmination of multiple violations of environmental defenders' human rights in the years, months, weeks, and days leading up to their murders. Since 2002 alone, Global Witness has documented over 2,200 environmental defenders who have been assassinated for the work to protect their communities and the earth from degradation, mostly by the extractivist industries detailed in chapters 1 and 2. About 60 percent of these murders—1,609 to be exact—have been documented in Latin America, with Brazil, Colombia, Honduras, and Mexico consistently leading the pack for the highest number of murders each year. Nicaragua and Peru are also extremely dangerous places to be fighting for environmental human rights.[22] These numbers, which Global Witness bases on investigations that clearly link the murders to the work of environmental activism, is a significant

[21] See Tanya Wadhwa, "Guapinol Environmental Defenders Released from Prison after Long Battle for Freedom," People's Dispatch Website, February 28, 2022, https://peoplesdispatch.org/2022/02/28/guapinol-environmental-defenders-released-from-prison-after-long-battle-for-freedom/#:~:text=The%20environmental%20activists%20from%20the,them%20and%20ordered%20their%20release.

[22] See the annual reports of Global Witness at https://www.globalwitness.org/en/campaigns/environmental-activists/land-and-environmental-defenders-annual-report-archive/.

underestimate of the actual number of environmental defender murders that are actually taking place. Many cases go unreported and even in cases that do garner international attention, it is difficult to prove that the motive behind the killings is related to the victim's defense of environmental human rights.

In chapter 4, we will contemplate the stories of six environmental defenders from Brazil, Colombia, El Salvador, and Honduras. These stories represent the thousands of other stories that are less well known or remain altogether untold. A more complete list of murdered defenders can be found in the annual reports compiled by Global Witness, but again, even their list is incomplete. Furthermore, while each of these stories focuses on an individual defender, we would do well to remember that none of them acted alone, nor would they wish to be lifted up as "single savior" figures. As the women of Cherán are wont to say of their uprising to defend their forests, "*No fue una. Fuimos todas.*" It wasn't one of them, it was all of them.

So too, in each of these stories, every one of the featured individuals was surrounded by other individuals and whole communities and organizations that were and continue to be active agents of popular movements for environmental justice and ecological well-being. In fact, in many cases, the one individual whose story we will contemplate is not the only environmental defender who has been murdered in that particular context. Let us remember that, in the case of the Bajo Aguán region of Honduras, over 100 community leaders and water protectors were killed in about a five-year period. Therefore, as we contemplate these ecomartyrs, let us not forget that they concretely and symbolically represent the thousands of others who have been targeted for assassination, the millions more whose lives and livelihoods have been destroyed by racist and rapacious economic degradation of the earth, and even the suffering and destruction of the earth itself.

4

Narrating the Witness

In Memory of Murdered Land and Environmental Defenders

"You have the bullet, but I have the word. The bullet dies when it is detonated, but the word lives on when it is replicated." This proverb, now scattered across environmental justice spaces on the internet, is attributed to murdered environmental defender Berta Cáceres and often appears on the posters, banners, websites, and social media presence of environmental defenders who carry on her legacy. The "word" to which Berta refers here can take on many forms that land and environmental defenders embody every day: words of protest and denunciation of extractivism and the violence that it entails; words of hope and healing for Indigenous peoples and others whose communities have been fighting for liberation and environmental justice for generations; words expressing and inspiring the embodiment of an alternative world in which all of our worlds are free to coexist in reciprocal relationships of justice and peace with one another and with our common home. Another form of the "word" in which murdered environmental defenders live on is in the telling of their stories. Their lives were cut short violently and unjustly in an instant, but their stories live on when we refuse to let their murderers have the last word, when we remember them and refuse to let their witness be silenced. Telling their stories is essential to this task, which is why we now turn to the narratives of several murdered environmental defenders whose stories are treasured and told in their local communities, across Latin America, and even around the world.

In the Catholic tradition, saints and martyrs are commemorated by telling their stories. To be sure, they are remembered in feast day celebrations and processions; in veneration of their relics, statues, and other material culture; and in pilgrimages to sites of sacred significance. But they are also remembered in the telling of their stories. Telling the stories of saints and martyrs is often called hagiography—literally, writing about that which is holy. In the history of the tradition, these narratives often take the form of legend, based more in oral tradition than historically verifiable fact. Furthermore, hagiography rarely takes note of the human failings of a given figure, unless those failings took place prior to a conversion or transformation of some kind. In modern hagiography, whether religious or secular, we rely more on historical records and written reports than on oral traditions, but the holiness of a figure remains the focus of the narrative, stressing the ways in which their life and/or death bears witness to a given sacred quality of faith, beauty, justice, mercy, or love. Hagiography can thus reveal as much about the community of memory as it does about the remembered individual. As political scientist María José Méndez puts it, "Who are the figures that guide the way we live, relate, think and write? From where do we draw our strength? And what do these sources of inspiration say about the worlds we want to dismantle and those we seek to build? The figures we cite and honor matter as they reveal much about these worlds."[1] Telling the sacred stories of our sources of inspiration can run the risk of idealizing or romanticizing real human beings who had real human failings and who

---

[1]   María José Méndez, "'The River Told Me': Rethinking Intersectionality from the World of Berta Cáceres," *Capitalism, Nature, Socialism* 29, no. 1 (2018): 7–24.

struggled with very difficult choices in the midst of conflictual and ambiguous historical circumstances. At the same time, there is a clarity of vision presented in hagiography that can empower communities of memory in their identity formation, in their resistance to injustice and evil, in their articulation and embodiment of an alternative moral imagination, and in their communal power to act with love and justice in the face of violence and oppression.

When communities in Latin America remember the heroes and martyrs of decolonization, liberation, and environmental justice, they acknowledge and honor the humanity of these individuals, but they also tend to emphasize the ways in which they positively embodied these values and virtues. In chapter 6, we will delve deeper into the potential dangers of this hagiographic tendency with regard to theologies of martyrdom. But for now, it suffices to point out that the narratives of murdered land and environmental defenders included in this chapter are drawn from sources that hold up the memory of these individuals as exemplary witnesses to solidarity with Creation and with the marginalized communities who suffer the most immediate and severe consequences of the extractivist pillage of our common home.

The six witnesses whose narratives we will contemplate in these pages are individuals who have garnered international attention for their leadership in the church and/or in popular movements for social and environmental justice. Many of them received national and/or international awards recognizing the immense value of their work. I have chosen these six witnesses, however, not because they are any more worthy of recognition than other murdered environmental defenders, but because my research has confirmed that they are explicitly remembered as martyrs by their local communities and often by the larger environmental justice movement in Latin America and beyond. We will turn to what it means that they are remembered specifically as martyrs in chapter 6. I have also chosen these individuals because the details of their stories have been published extensively enough to weave together coherent narratives of their lives and deaths. The fact that their stories have been relatively widely published unfortunately indicates a certain degree of privilege due to racial, gender, religious, ecclesial, and/or educational status. Only two of the six are women, one of whom is white. Only one of the six is Black, and only one identified explicitly as Indigenous, though others had Indigenous heritage. Two of the six were ordained Catholic priests, and one was a vowed religious woman. Although all of them experienced various forms of intersectional oppression, they all came to the attention of the world because of other intersecting experiences of relative power and privilege. At the end of the chapter, we will briefly consider the witness of several other individuals who represent a fuller diversity of murdered environmental defenders, focusing particularly on individuals who have been killed in the years between Berta Cáceres's murder and the preparation of this book. But even in their cases it is important to remember that these individuals all represent a much broader and deeper collective movement for environmental justice. None of them were messianic figures whose leadership existed within a vacuum. None of them acted alone. All of them were inextricably woven into the lives and struggles of their communities. To reiterate, as the Purépecha women of Cherán put it, "*No fue una, fuimos todas.*" It wasn't one of them, it was all of them.

Father Josimo Morais Tavares (†1986)

Father Josimo Morais Tavares[2] was born in 1953 to a humble family of African descent in the state of Pará, Brazil. Much to his mother's chagrin, he left home at the age of eleven to attend seminary and was ordained a priest on January 20, 1979. His only sister died of

---

[2]   The following narrative of Fr. Josimo's life and assassination is based on the account set forth in Binka Le Breton, *A Land to Die For* (Atlanta: Clarity Press, 1997) and on accounts provided at the websites cited below.

malnutrition. As a poor, Black son of peasants, he faced many prejudices in his short lifetime, but rather than take advantage of his education and ecclesial status to flee from his roots, Josimo decided to dedicate his ministry to pastoral and social solidarity with landless rural workers. Most of his ministry took place during the time of Brazil's lengthy dictatorship, under which imprisonment, torture, and assassination

of human rights defenders were not uncommon occurrences. The rural oligarchy, made up of large landowners, enjoyed the protection of the dictatorship, while landless peasants had little recourse to political representation or legal protection in their struggles to defend their right to work the land for sustenance. Conflicts between landless peasants and the oligarchy over land tenure were common, but these conflicts intensified when the end of the dictatorial regime was announced. Fearful of land reform, the old rural oligarchy and new agents of agribusiness sought to reinforce their hold on power. At the same time, rural workers and landless peasants—in partnership with the church, the Pastoral Land Commission (CPT), workers' unions, and new social movements—were empowered in their struggles by "a hope to really see the Earth shared by all."[3]

---

[3] Gilvander Moreira, "Padre Josimo Tavares: 27 anos de martírio," Instituto Humanitas Unisinos Website, May 7, 2013, https://www.ihu.unisinos.br/noticias/519890-padre-josimo-tavares-27-anos-de-martirio.

In the midst of these movements, Father Josimo was tireless in his defense of small farmers, agricultural workers, and the landless rural poor. As coordinator of the CPT in Bico do Papagaio, a region known for intense land disputes, he "denounced land grabbers and the oppression of the landowners against the workers and he defended the rights of the people, making them aware of their strength."[4] Because of his clear commitment to vulnerable communities and to removing the fences that scar the earth and facilitate exploitation of the land and people alike, he was hated by the landowners, whom he called "sons of darkness" who love the "god of capital." He thus began to receive death threats. In an assassination attempt on April 15, 1986, five shots were fired at his vehicle.

Fr. Josimo was also subject to suspicion and misunderstanding by his fellow priests and pastoral workers. Due to his multiple death threats and the April 15 assassination attempt, he was required to submit a report on his pastoral work and to clarify the reasons for the many death threats that had been made against him. In what commentators call a "spiritual testament" delivered to the Diocesan Assembly of Tocantinópolis on April 27, just a few days before his murder, Josimo indicated that he knew that his death had already been decided. He clarified to the gathered assembly that his pastoral ministry was motivated by the Gospel and by his vocation as a priest:

> I want you to understand that what has been happening is not the result of any ideology or theological faction, not even myself or my personality. I believe that all of this can be attributed to the following three principal reasons:
>
> - Because God called me with the gift of the priestly vocation and I responded;

---

[4] Comunidade Intercongregacional Padre Josimo, "Fraternidade Padre Josimo," Instituto Cultural Padre Josimo Website, https://padrejosimo.com.br/site/fraternidade-padre-josimo/.

- Because the bishop, Dom Cornélio has ordained me as a priest;
- Because of the support of the people and the former vicar of Xambioá, Fr. João Caprioli, who helped me to complete my studies;

"The disciple is not greater than the Master. If they persecute me, they will persecute you too." I have to accept this. I am now committed to the struggle for the cause of poor and defenseless farmers, an oppressed people caught in the clutches of the large estates. If I am silent, who will defend them? Who will struggle on their behalf? At least I have nothing to lose. I have no wife, children, not even wealth; no one will grieve for me. Other than one person: my mother, who other than me has no one else. Poor. Widow. But you are there to care for her. Not even fear will stop me. It is time to accept this. I die for a just cause. Now I want you to understand this: everything that is happening is a logical consequence that results from my work in the struggle and the defense of the poor, for the sake of the Gospel that has led me to accept even the ultimate consequences. My life is worth nothing in light of the deaths of so many farmers who are parents—assassinated, violated, and forced off of their lands. Leaving women and children abandoned, without care, without food and without a home. It is time to stand up and make a difference! I die for a just cause.[5]

On May 10, 1986, Fr. Josimo was shot twice as he was entering the Pastoral Land Commission offices in Imperatriz. He was strong enough to walk to the hospital, but died of his wounds two hours later. Those who knew him remember him as a poet who played the guitar, loved to dance and play soccer and listen to people tell their

---

[5] Moreira, "Father Josimo Tavares: 27 anos."

stories. He had a gentle demeanor. He wore tattered Hawaiian flip-flops. Josimo was just thirty-three years old when he died.

In Brazil, Fr. Josimo is remembered as one of many *mártires da caminhada*, martyrs of the way, who lived and died under the inspiration of the Gospel to follow Jesus of Nazareth by making a preferential option for the poor and oppressed, whose lives are often so intimately tied to the accessibility and well-being of the land. Like the other martyrs of late twentieth-century Latin America, his people proclaim that he lives on in their struggles, "in the memory of the people, in the experience of popular educators, in the writings of liberation theology, and in the commitment of the few pastoral agents who continue to reaffirm the same commitment to the reign [of God] with the construction of a world with social, environmental, and urban justice and ecological sustainability." Communities, organizations, and programs that bear his name carry on his legacy in their pastoral work and socio-environmental projects, such as agroforestry, medicinal herb gardens, bioconstruction, creole seed houses, and diversification of food and energy production.[6] He lives on in the struggles of the people whom he empowered to become subjects of a history in which the fences of exclusion and hatred would be dismantled so that the earth and its inhabitants might be free to thrive and have access to life abundant. The words of the poet Pedro Tierra encapsulate Josimo's legacy well:

> *Who is this Black boy*
> *who defies limits?*
> *Just one man.*
> *Shabby sandals.*
> *Patience and indignation.*
> *A pure laugh.*

---

[6] See Instituto Cultural Padre Josimo Website at https://padrejosimo.com.br/.

Night honey.
Irrefutable dream.
He fought against fences.
All the fences.
The fences of fear.
The fences of hate.
The fences of the earth.
The fences of hunger.
The fences of the body.
The fences of the landowners....

[His] blood will rise up
like a rushing river
and it will break through the fences of the world.
A river of blood will be summoned
and will burst forth from your shirt
and that will be the flag
that flies over the rebellion.[7]

Father Josimo Tavares ... *presente!*

Francisco (Chico) Alves Mendes Filho (†1988)

Francisco (Chico) Alves Mendes Filho[8] was born on a rubber estate in the northwestern Amazonian state of Acre, Brazil, on December 15, 1944. Decades before his birth, the rubber boom in Brazil had ended due to the British cultivation of rubber plantations in

---

[7] Pedro Tierra, "A Morte Anunciada de Josimo Tavares," May 1986, https://www.escritas.org/pt/t/9619/a-morte-anunciada-de-josimo-tavares.

[8] This narrative of Chico Mendes's life and assassination is based on the accounts set forth in Chico Mendes and Tony Gross, *Fight for the Forest: Chico Mendes in His Own Words* (London: Latin America Bureau Research and Action, 1989), and Andrew Revkin, *The Burning Season: The Murder of Chico Mendes and the Fight for the Amazon Rain Forest* (New York: Houghton Mifflin, 1990).

Malaysia, but a resurgence in the demand for Brazilian rubber took place during World War II, when Allied forces lost access to Malaysian rubber. It was then that Chico's father migrated to the region as one of the tens of thousands of "rubber soldiers" drafted to meet U.S. and Brazilian demand for this valuable raw material. Both waves of migration to the Amazonian rubber estates that took place between the late-nineteenth century and the mid-twentieth century were mostly made up of mixed-race rural peasants fleeing drought and poverty in northeastern Brazil. Indigenous people of the region were forced either to flee or to labor on the estates, which operated on a system of debt bondage. While a traditional rubber estate did not even allow for rubber tappers to cultivate their own food, by the time Chico was born, many rubber tappers had learned to not only cultivate food but also live from the abundance of fruits, nuts, medicinal plants, and wild game that a healthy forest could provide. Much of this ecological learning came from cultural exchange and intermarriage with local Indigenous peoples. Rubber tappers were largely illiterate and innumerate, though, and Chico learned to read and write only when he was a young adult, under the tutelage of a rubber tapper from outside the region who had participated in revolutionary movements in Brazil and Bolivia. During this same process of gaining literacy, Chico began to gain critical consciousness of the vast inequalities and oppressive relations between the estate owners and rubber tappers.

In the region where Chico was born, the rubber estates gave way to ranchers in the 1960s and '70s, and the 1970s and '80s saw "growing conflict between ranchers clearing the forest for pasture, and rubber tappers, in many cases free of the oppressive relations with the *seringalista* [rubber estate], but facing eviction and loss of livelihood at the hands of the rancher."[9] Meanwhile, a 1964 military coup overthrew the progressive Labor Party government of João Goulart and installed a dictatorial regime designed to restore order to the country and prevent further subversion of the traditional economic system. "The military promoted a new economic and social model, attracting foreign capital for a programme of rapid industrialization by offering political stability and cheap, docile labour. They achieved this through wage control and the concentration of wealth, leading to the coexistence of high growth rates and increasing poverty. Opposition was suppressed by force."[10] It was in this context of conflict over land tenure and dictatorship that Chico came of age and began to organize rubber tappers to defend themselves and the forest from the violent incursions of land-grabbing ranchers. When rural workers' unions were formed in Acre, Chico was quick to join and stood out as a leader, though he noted that the unions were more in favor of preserving the status quo than defending the rubber tappers. At this same time, he was unexpectedly elected to municipal office as a representative of the opposition party and found that even fellow party members were also resistant to stopping the expulsion of rubber tappers from their lands. When the Workers' Party was formed,

---

[9] Mendes and Gross, 10.
[10] Mendes and Gross, 18.

Chico joined but ended up dedicating most of his energies to the Xapuri Rural Workers' Union from the early 1980s on.

In 1979, union leader Wilson Pinheiro led a group of 300 rubber tappers to drive out gunmen who were evicting land squatters in Boca do Acre. Armed with only knives and sickles, the tappers managed to oust the gunmen and confiscate their rifles, which the workers handed over to the local army unit. The army commander was enraged by the situation and accused the workers of wanting to turn the place into another Cuba. Local landowners were similarly disturbed by the uprising and had their gunmen shoot Wilson dead in the union office on the evening of July 21, 1980. Workers, enraged at the murder and refusal of law enforcement to investigate, seized one of the landowners known to have organized the murder and had him killed. The police responded with wholesale repression of the workers, arresting and torturing hundreds of rubber tappers.

Henceforth, Chico's hometown of Xapuri would become the organizational base of the rubber tappers' resistance to forced evictions and deforestation. For Chico, it was important for this new phase of the movement to be less centralized and truly participatory at the grassroots level. The first step in this process was to engage local communities in popular education projects aimed at literacy, conscientization, and encouraging rubber tappers "to identify more closely with the forest, to understand it, to learn more about it, and to defend it."[11] These efforts led to the organization and construction of eighteen schools. Meanwhile, the union also organized a rubber tappers' cooperative and engaged in multiple *empates*, or standoffs with landgrabbers who were evicting local communities and clear-cutting the forests. Throughout these projects and struggles, it became clear that

---

[11] Mendes and Gross, 32.

the movement was dedicated to more than worker and peasant rights to occupy the land; it was also dedicated to preventing deforestation, preserving the forest, and seeking alternative means of sustaining both the forest and the human communities that depended on it for their livelihood.

In collaboration with local unions and other allies, Chico played an instrumental role in bringing together representatives of rubber tappers from the whole Amazon region of Brazil at a National Rubber Tappers' Congress in October 1985. From this gathering emerged the idea of creating "extractive reserves," which are lands under public or otherwise communal ownership that allow rubber tappers and other forest dwellers the right to live and work there to earn a sustainable living from the flora and fauna of the forest. The National Council of Rubber Tappers (CNS) was formed to promote this vision and to gain recognition of "the rubber tappers as a particular group of workers fighting for a very important objective—the defence of the Amazon forest."[12] Whereas Indigenous peoples of the region and rubber tappers had been fighting each other for generations, the CNS sought to promote solidarity between the two groups. As Chico put it, "Our proposals are now not just ours alone, they are put forward together by Indians and rubber tappers. Our fight is the fight of all the peoples of the forest."[13]

Although the movement first grew in Acre, the CNS was keen to spread the resistance to the rest of the Amazon region. Internal support from other sectors in Brazil only came in response to the external support from environmental activists abroad and the international press. Support from the church was variable depending on how conservative the local clergy was, and

---

[12] Mendes and Gross, 46.
[13] Mendes and Gross, 46.

support from the government was nearly nonexistent. In Chico's own words,

> There was a time when the state government seemed to be paying a lot of attention to environmental problems and to the rubber tappers. But we soon realised it was just putting on a show of defending the environment so the international banks and other international organizations would approve its development projects. We can't see how the authorities can say they defend the ecological system while at the same time deploying police to protect those who are destroying the forest.[14]

The large landowners and the landgrabbers had all the economic and political power at their disposal—bribing authorities, appealing to law enforcement and the court system, and hiring gunmen to intimidate the rubber tappers. In cases of intimidation and violence, the police were unresponsive since, as Chico puts it, "the law has always been on the side of the rich," whom he characterizes as "very happy" to use violence.[15]

In the face of such violence and impunity, the rubber tappers' movement remained committed to nonviolent strategies, although Chico remarked that "if someday we need to use violence, it will be because we have been forced to do so by the circumstances, by the system and the policies of the landowners."[16] Nevertheless, he also expressed his fear of the bloodbath that would occur if the movement did end up resorting to violence:

> I don't want anybody getting killed. There is no point in me or any of my colleagues dying. I don't think that

---

[14] Mendes and Gross, 60.
[15] Mendes and Gross, 67.
[16] Mendes and Gross, 70.

dead bodies solve anything, and I know that if that's the way things go, this place will become an inferno. We are going to do our best to see it doesn't happen. But if it did become necessary, I'm sure there would be 100, 150, 200 workers who would be ready to fight and decide this thing once and for all. But that would mean a bloodbath here in Xapuri, repression, and a lot more besides.[17]

Ultimately, Chico and the CNS maintained their strategic commitment to nonviolence, and were able to achieve some significant successes, including the formation of an agro-extractive cooperative that brought together rubber tappers to escape their economic dependency on predatory middlemen and make a fair living from selling rubber and Brazil nuts at local markets. The great ecological success of the movement consisted in saving over 1.2 million hectares of forest during the course of fifteen years through *empates* that prevented clear-cutting by land-grabbers and through the formation of legally recognized extractive reserves.[18]

These successes came at great cost, though, with hundreds of arrests, dozens of cases of torture, and dozens of murders of public leaders and ordinary people involved in the movement to defend their communities and the forest from the violent destruction wrought by landowners and others intent on clearing the forest and its inhabitants for the sake of profit. Chico was not the first, nor was he the last person to be assassinated in this struggle. Given the penchant for violence and the impunity enjoyed by local landowners, he knew

---

[17] Mendes and Gross, 70–71.

[18] An "extractive reserve" is very different from an extractivist project or extractivist industry. In an extractive reserve, land is managed communally and local people "extract" products from the forest in an ecologically sustainable way to meet local needs for sustenance and supplemental income. Extractivism, on the other hand, sees the entire forest as extractable and places no value on ecological sustainability.

that death was a possibility, even before the death threats began to arrive in earnest. He did not want to die. He had a wife and two small children at home, and a lifetime of leadership in the struggle for environmental justice ahead of him. While he seemed to make some peace with the likelihood of imminent death, he did not want to die. In fact, Chico remarked in a letter shortly before his murder, "If a messenger from heaven came down and guaranteed that my death would help to strengthen the struggle, it could even be worth it. But experience teaches us the opposite. It is not with big funerals and demonstrations of support that we are going to save the Amazon. I want to live."[19] On the evening of December 22, 1988, just a week after his forty-fourth birthday and two days before Christmas Eve, Chico Mendes was shot to death by the son of a local rancher while relaxing with his family at his home in the town of Xapuri.

Chico lives on in the work of the rubber tappers of Acre, in the Chico Mendes Extractive Reserve, and in all of the extractive reserves of the Amazon that maintain ecological integrity while providing for the needs of forest dwellers. He lives on in the international environmental movement and the struggle for climate justice. He lives on in the species of bird that bears his name, Chico's tyrannulet (*Zimmerius chicomendesi*), and in the forest itself, which continues to be threatened and destroyed by powerful interests to this very day. As the popular Mexican rock group Maná puts it, he lives on in the rain that falls on the forest, in the tears of the angels who cry for all those who have been killed.

> *They killed Chico Mendes*
> *He was a defender and an angel*
> *of the whole Amazon*

---

[19] Mendes and Gross, 6.

He died in cold blood
Collor de Mello knew
and so did the police

When angels cry
rain falls on the village
rain over the bell tower
because someone died

An angel fell
an angel died
an angel left
and he won't return

When the assassin fled
Chico Mendes was dying
the forest was drowning in sobs

He left two beautiful children
a brave wife
and a forest in agony

When the angels cry
it's for every tree that dies
every star that goes out
oh no no

An angel fell
an angel died
an angel left
left flying into the sunrise.[20]

Chico Mendes ... *presente!*

---

[20] Maná, "Cuando los Ángeles Lloran," *Cuando los Ángeles Lloran* studio album (Record Plant, 1997).

Father Alcides Jiménez Chicangana (†1998)

Father Alcides Jiménez Chicangana[21] was born on January 30, 1949, to a humble peasant family in a predominantly Indigenous region of the Department of Cauca, Colombia. Indigenous influences in his heritage and upbringing contributed to a spiritual connection with and love for the natural world. Alcides attended primary school in his hometown of Santa Rosa, pre-seminary in Putumayo, high school at the major seminary in Nariño, and seminary with the Redemptorist Community in the Intermissional Seminary in Bogotá. He returned to his hometown to be ordained a priest and celebrate his first mass in 1978, after which he chose to carry out his ministry in the Puerto Caicedo municipality of the Department of Putumayo. Alcides's formation as a priest took place under the influence of the pastoral theology of Vatican II and the Latin American Bishops' meeting at Medellín in 1968. His decision to serve the church in the Department of Putumayo signified his commitment to a pastoral vision of prophetic peacemaking on behalf of human and ecological well-being. From the beginning, his mission was faced with a difficult task: "For decades, neglect by the state, exploitation of natural resources, illicit cultivation, and the presence of armed groups have sown seeds of death and hopelessness in the Putumayo region in the Colombian Amazon. Father Alcides Jiménez Chicangana confronted these things and was a victim of their violence."[22]

The region of Putumayo in which Father Alcides undertook his twenty years of ministry had, of course, been inhabited by

---

[21] In addition to other sources cited below, the following narrative of Father Alcides's life and assassination is based on the account set forth in Red Eclesial Panamazónica and SIGNIS ALC, "La Vida por La Amazonía-Capítulo 5-Padre Alcides Jiménez-Semillas del Putumayo," SIGNIS ALC YouTube Channel, September 14, 2018, https://youtu.be/kzDhvC9vZfo. Henceforth cited as REPAM/SIGNIS, "Semillas del Putumayo."

[22] REPAM/SIGNIS, "Semillas del Putumayo."

Indigenous peoples for
millennia. Migrants settled
in Putumayo in the early
twentieth century, when
the Colombian govern-
ment decided to establish
a penal colony there due
to the remoteness of the
region, which is located
between the mountains
of the Colombian Massif
and the rivers and plains of
the Amazon. As peniten-
tiaries were constructed,
migrants came to the
region to settle in villages

that would later become small towns and urban outposts. The same
rubber boom that affected the Brazilian Amazon contributed to an
early-twentieth-century wave of migration to the region, but by the
time Alicides arrived in the 1970s, that experience of cruelty and
exploitation had long passed. As the rubber boom faded, though,
petroleum extraction was already on the rise and the Transandino
pipeline was constructed in 1970 to transport oil from the Putumayo region to the port of Tumaco. The explosion in intensive
coca cultivation and production of cocaine began in the late 1970s
and proceeded at breakneck speed over the course of the next two
decades, coinciding with Father Alcides's ministry in the region.
Economic pressure and intimidation by drug cartels and narcotraffickers led to widespread cultivation of this illicit monoculture and
precipitated unprecedented violence in the region. The violence
was fueled even more by the armed conflict between left-wing
guerrilla fighters in the Revolutionary Armed Forces of Colombia

(FARC) and right-wing paramilitary groups, with both sides fighting for territorial control, especially of coca production, in this resource-rich region. Both oil extraction and illicit monoculture cultivation of coca thus mark the reality of the communities and the land to which Father Alcides dedicated his life and ministry.

In the midst of these twin terrors, Father Alcides was committed to cultivating peace among human beings and between human beings and the natural world. A central concern in his ministry was promoting food sovereignty, which was especially threatened by the intensive monoculture cultivation of coca. Álvaro Portilla is a small farmer who remembers Father Alcides's enthusiasm for the land and for food sovereignty:

> He was the first priest to come out to our farm. When he would come, he would be jumping, shouting, clapping, stomping around, and all, out in the fields of crops, going around to see whatever there was. There were tomatoes, there was cilantro, parsley, there were peanuts, and all the many plants that were cultivated in those times. And he would say "together we can do something better to defend out nutrition," because he knew that food sovereignty is the best. And most of all, everything he taught about having clean products, healthy, without having to attack the environment, which is the principal thing, that we should protect it.[23]

Álvaro also remembers how Father Alcides conveyed this message about food sovereignty in a symbolic, yet concrete way:

> He always wanted to leave you with an important message through the use of seeds. He said, "Come here." He said, "I want to give you some bean seeds," and then he got a pound of beans from the table and we talked so much about seeds and finally he took his hand and gave

---

[23] REPAM/SIGNIS, "Semillas del Putumayo."

me three of the beans. And so I was thinking and said, "Why, if you have a whole pound of beans, why do you give me three seeds?" And I took them to my house, and I planted them with much care, and I multiplied them. From each harvest, I multiplied them until I had almost half of a quarter of an hectare. And one day he came by and said to me, "I gave you some bean seeds," and I say, "Yes, father, you gave me some bean seeds." "There were three of them," he said. He remembered. I say, "Yes, there were three of them." And so he said, "And what did you do with them?" I say, "I multiplied them." He said, "That's what we want. If all the people did the same, then we'd have a good quantity of food."[24]

Father Alcides believed in the power of seeds to transform the reality of ordinary people's lives, and he believed in the power of ordinary people, particularly *campesinos* and *campesinas*, to work creatively with the power of seeds to transform their own reality. Intensive cultivation of coca was problematic for him not only because it was illegal, but because it was a fundamental threat to the land and to the creativity and identity of the people and their ability to provide healthy nutrition for their families and communities. In the words of local leader Luis Erazo, "The idea was to not lose our identity as *campesinos*, to not switch over to monocultures, not just coca, but other monocultures that would also threaten food sovereignty."[25]

Over the course of his twenty years in ministry with the people of Puerto Caicedo, Father Alcides also promoted recovery of popular knowledge about seed preservation and production of food and medicines that come from crops and plants native to the region. He was especially dedicated to empowering women to have a voice and vote in both the domestic realm and in the public

[24] REPAM/SIGNIS, "Semillas del Putumayo."
[25] REPAM/SIGNIS, "Semillas del Putumayo."

sphere. He encouraged women to become involved in the organization of the community and offered resources to facilitate training in food production for the sake of improving family nutrition and building up women's economic independence through local enterprise. He promoted the full participation of children and young people in the life of the community and laid the foundations for what would become a community radio station. Empowerment through conscientization and popular education was at the heart of his ministry, all for the sake of defending life: "My work is a project dedicated to life; it's an alternative ethic of life together; it's the defense of life-giving collaboration. It is a humble proposal in which highways, airports, and agribusiness count for nothing in the face of daily life, *campesino* agency, or the importance of breathing, of living, and of sharing."[26]

These commitments to food sovereignty, women's empowerment, and popular participation were all integrally connected to Father Alcides's spirituality of Creation. In Erazo's words again, Father Alcides "helped us to become an Amazonian Gospel, more integral, more inclusive, more participatory, more in tune with finding God all around in everything, in microorganisms, in water, in trees, in all of the seeds."[27] Father Alcides was known to celebrate Mass in the forest, surrounded by trees, which he encouraged congregants to meet as friends and offer the greeting, "Peace be with you!" A rare recording of Father Alcides celebrating Mass in the forest illuminates this spirituality further. In the recording, he proclaims, "This earth is like our mother, who gave birth to us one day. This earth covers us with the fraternity of her leaves. The trees, the rocks, and this little trickle of water." Even his eucharistic spirituality was

---

[26] Hugo Hernán Aparicio Reyes, "Alcides Jiménez: Chicangana in memoriam (Segunda y última parte)," *La Crónica del Quindío*, March 15, 2015, https://www.cronicadelquindio.com/noticias/general-1/alcides-jimnez-chicangana-in-memoriam-segunda-y-ltima-parte.

[27] REPAM/SIGNIS, "Semillas del Putumayo."

deeply integrated with his appreciation for the presence of God in the everyday elements of life drawn from the abundance of Creation:

> Today Jesus Christ comes to this mountain, as he liked to do. And he mingles with us and walks here. And he brings us together so we can share today *las yotas, la chicha, el guarapo*, friendship, some sweets, *un sancochi*. Father, send your spirit over this Mass, which is this Mass of nature and of ourselves.... This chalice represents the *chicha* of the Indigenous, of the *campesinos*, it's the *chicha* of friendship, and of love.[28]

For Father Alcides, the altar could be found anywhere that you could celebrate the presence of Christ. He was a priest who recognized and celebrated Christ's presence not only in the four walls of a church building, but in the forests and the fields, amid the reality of the natural world and the people.

In the face of violence against the earth and violent conflict among human beings over who would have the power to profit from the earth, Father Alcides advocated promotion of peace. He encouraged neutrality in the people's approach to the conflict between FARC and the paramilitaries, but he never encouraged passive resignation or silence. Rather, he encouraged and embodied active peacebuilding through denunciation of violence and exploitation and through construction of alternative forms of social and ecological organization. His leadership, preaching, and work in the community therefore represented a threat to the social and economic order that the multinational corporations and both sides of the armed conflict wanted to

---

[28] Nicolás Sánchez Arévalo, "Alcides Jiménez, el sacerdote al que asesinaron en plena misa," *MiPutumayo* Website, Podcast, September 16, 2019, https://miputumayo.com.co/2019/09/16/alcides-jimenez-el-sacerdote-al-que-asesinaron-en-plena-misa/. *La yota* is an edible fruit in the gourd family, also known as the poor man's potato. *La chicha* is a traditional drink made of fermented corn, *el guarapo* is a traditional drink made from fermented sugar cane, and *un sancochi* is a traditional stew.

construct.[29] Padre Eduardo Ordóñez remarks that "he confronted the narco-traffickers and the multinationals that threatened the land from the perspective of the people who were in need of food. And that led him into a process of sacrificing even his life."[30]

At six o'clock on Friday, September 11, 1998, the church bells at Our Lady of Carmen Parish rang out to announce the start of evening Mass. Fifteen or twenty minutes later, the church bells rang out again to alert the town to the travesty of Father Alcides's murder. During the Liturgy of the Eucharist, two gunmen entered the building and began to shoot at Father Alcides, who fled to the church patio in an attempt to escape. The sacristan Evangelina Andrade was hit by a stray bullet and died later in the hospital. The gunmen followed Alcides to the patio and killed him with eighteen bullets. He was forty-nine years old.

Father Alcides Jiménez lives on in the people of Puerto Caicedo, in the seeds that he planted among the people and in the earth. He lives on in the New Millennium Corporation and in the work of the women and young people he inspired. He lives on in the community radio station that was his dream and that flourishes today under his inspiration. He lives on in the young people of Putumayo who continue to learn from his words and his actions. As one of Father Alcides's protégés remarks:

> I look at Don Alvaro, at Liverman, at Lidia, at the young people and women who walked with him and I think the seeds that he planted and his spirit continue to bear fruit in this territory. The spirit of Padre Alcides exists in each one of us and while it is so, there is hope for the Amazon, for Putumayo.[31]

---

[29] Centro Nacional de Memoria Histórica, *"La Palabra del Señor,"* Centro Nacional de Memoria Histórica Website, September 14, 2016, https://centrodememoriahistorica.gov.co/tag/senor/.

[30] REPAM/SIGNIS, "Semillas del Putumayo."

[31] REPAM/SIGNIS, "Semillas del Putumayo."

The poem "Alcides," by Libardo Valdés expresses the pain and the hope of Father Alcides' legacy well:

> *Alcides*
> *Today more than ever*
> *I understand your struggles*
> *Alcides*
> *How you offered your life*
> *In favor of the people*
> *Today I feel your pain and your sadness*
> *Dreaming of new dawns in the springtime*
> *Your slow steps in solitude*
> *Your passions and your utopias*
> *You who were capable of defeating death*
> *Because you continue to sing on the street corners in*
> *favor of life*
> *Because you continue in each nook and cranny*
> *preventing forgetfulness*
> *There is sadness, Alcides, in your people*
> *The dark clouds with their mantle*
> *clothe the tender journey of life*
> *Forgetfulness abounds like a plague in every street*
> *Your journey continues, Alcides*
> *And you accompany ours*
> *The journey of tears, of steady steps*
> *Of embraces and affections*
> *Until new loves bloom again*[32]

Father Alcides Jiménez . . . ¡presente!

---

[32] This poem is featured at the end of REPAM/SIGNIS, "Semillas del Putumayo."

Sister Dorothy Mae Stang (†2005)

Dorothy Mae Stang[33] was born on June 7, 1931, just outside of the city of Dayton in the rural community of Shiloh, Ohio. She was the fourth of nine children in a white Catholic family of German and Irish descent. From a young age, Dorothy's Catholic faith and family upbringing instilled in her a sense of responsibility to care for others. She was responsible for getting her younger sister Barb ready for school every day; she volunteered with the Dominican Sisters of the Sick Poor to make bed pads for the indigent; she was a leader in a local Catholic youth association; and she worked part-time after school at a local pharmacy. At the age of seventeen, Dorothy joined the Sisters of Notre Dame de Namur alongside her dear friend Joan Krimm, with a sense of calling to missionary work in China. Her first post, however, was in Phoenix, Arizona, where she served as a school-teacher during the week and accompanied migrant farmworkers on the weekends. Dorothy's pastoral accompaniment of migrant farmworkers opened her eyes to the social and environmental injustices suffered by those subjected to harsh working conditions, inhumane living conditions, and exposure to harmful pesticides in the fields. The experience educated Dorothy on the unjust causes of poverty and fueled her desire to work with impoverished communities. She was thrilled, therefore, to be sent to work with poor farmers in northeastern Brazil in 1966, alongside four other Sisters of Notre Dame.

---

[33] The following narrative of Sister Dorothy's life and assassination is based on the accounts laid out in the following sources: Roseanne Murphy, *Martyr of the Amazon: The Life of Sister Dorothy Stang* (Maryknoll, NY: Orbis Books, 2007); Binka Le Breton, *The Greatest Gift: The Courageous Life and Martyrdom of Sister Dorothy Stang* (New York: Doubleday, 2008); Michele Murdock, *A Journey of Courage: The Amazing Story of Sister Dorothy Stang* (Cincinnati: Sisters of Notre Dame de Namur, 2009); *They Killed Sister Dorothy*, documentary film directed by Daniel Junge (First Run Features, 2008); and "Witness to Justice—Sister Dorothy Stang," Sisters of Notre Dame de Namur YouTube Channel, November 18, 2014, https://youtu.be/lHpQ8lONGtY.

Prior to beginning work in their mission site at Coroatá in the state of Maranhão, the newly arrived Sisters studied for several months at the Center for Intercultural Formation (CENFI) near Rio de Janeiro. At CENFI, they studied Portuguese, along with Brazilian history, politics, and culture, all from a perspective that promoted cultural competency and critical consciousness of Brazil's

colonization "by the cross and the sword." They learned under the tutelage of two of the founders of Latin American liberation theology, Fathers Gustavo Gutiérrez and Jon Sobrino, about "how the Gospel should be lived out in countries dominated by a few extremely wealthy families while the majority lived in appalling poverty."[34] In Sister Barbara English's words, the sisters left this training "with a commitment to respect the Brazilian culture, to question the world around us and understand it through the eyes of the poor."[35]

Dorothy's first charge with the Sisters in Coroatá was the traditional task of offering instruction in basic catechism and sacramental preparation. But the first thing that she and her fellow sisters came to understand was the economic oppression experienced by the people living in poverty, which was justified by the traditional, fatalistic theology that had been taught to them,

[34] Murphy, 27.
[35] Murphy, 28.

insisting that they were poor because God willed it to be so. In the region around Coroatá where Dorothy served, the people in the countryside were trapped in an oppressive system of debt bondage, wherein large landowners permitted the peasantry to farm the land, but the landowners also obligated them both to purchase seeds and other items from the landowners' store and to sell their crops back to the landowners at a very low price. The pastoral team of Italian priests and religious women at Our Lady of Mercy Parish in Coroatá began to work with first the men and then the women of the rural communities to empower lay leadership in the formation of biblical circles and, eventually, ecclesial base communities. They put an end to the favoritism and indulgence that the church had previously shown to the wealthy landowners and began to make what would come to be known in liberation theology and Catholic social teaching as a "preferential option for the poor."

In 1972, the Brazilian government offered the impoverished farmers plots of land in the Amazon rainforest and a wave of westward migration began. Dorothy and Sr. Rebecca Spires decided to start a new mission in the Diocese of Marabá, where they would accompany migrant communities in the state of Pará. While the Brazilian government's objective was to populate the region with settlers in order to facilitate a larger program of development dependent on destruction of the rainforest, the settlers were inspired by dreams of freedom and the opportunity to farm their own land without being beholden to the wealthy landowners. Sister Dorothy accompanied the communities not only on their journey westward, deeper into the Amazon, but in their process of learning to work the land in sustainable ways, in their reclamation of their dignity as human beings, and in their struggles for justice and human rights.

Dorothy first lived with a family and then built a house for herself. She worked with the community to build a school and a church. In 1982, the people created a farmers' union and led a strike to demand that the government fix the roads. The union established a community farm to supplement what each family could produce on their own; they bought rice and corn processing machines to facilitate cleaning and bagging their agricultural products; they built a communal well to access potable water; they organized to advocate for the donation of a truck to transport their produce to market; and the women collaborated to open a store. Working together, the communities were able to transform their realities with far more success than they would have had alone. Dorothy became one with the people in these struggles and is remembered as someone who "had a light all of her own which drew the attention of anyone of any age—children, young people, adults, and older people. She had a special way of approaching each person."[36] She also came to know, love, and experience communion with the Amazon rainforest, developing a spirituality of solidarity with both the poor and the earth.

During this same time, however, the people of the communities with whom Dorothy lived and worked began to experience constant invasion by ranchers, corporate soy farmers, and loggers who would invade the people's land and drive them away by force. The forest was being destroyed, and the crops and homes of the small farmers were burned, forcing them deeper into the forest where they would have to start their lives over again. This destructive cycle continued, as the rich and powerful landgrabbers moved deeper and deeper into the forest as well. Government and law enforcement were complicit with the violence, accepting bribes from the invaders, washing their hands of the reality, and looking away when the invaders resorted to violence, which they did often.

---

[36] "Amazonia, Dorothy Stang's Struggle," documentary film produced by the Chemin Neuf Community, distributed via the YouTube channel of the international prayer network "Net for God," April 8, 2016, https://youtu.be/hJhM4qC7lEg.

Indeed, between 1985 and 2005, more than 500 people were murdered over land disputes, with fewer than 10 murderers jailed. Once again, the people of the communities came together to take courage and resist the injustice of the landgrabbers' violence and oppression. For example, the union would send a group of people out to guard the land where crops were planted to prevent ranchers from destroying the crops and planting cattle grass.

Dorothy moved six times with the communities, finally landing in Anapu, where local communities were already being invaded. In the meantime, she became a member of the Pastoral Land Commission (CPT) and worked with the communities to apportion land that the Brazilian government was parceling out for sustainable farming and rainforest preservation under the Sustainable Development Program (PDS). She advocated for small farmers with local courts and law enforcement, petitioning for titles to lands that people had settled, and carrying with her, wherever she would go, documentation of landgrabbing, arson, and murder. She thus became a public figure who gave witness locally, regionally, and nationally to the situation of injustice, violence, and ecological degradation in the Amazon. Though quiet, unassuming, and always willing to dialogue, Dorothy made many enemies because of her witness. By the time of her murder, there was a $17,500 price on her head.

In early February 2005, an employee of a local rancher in Boa Esperança was illegally "sold" a plot of land that was already occupied by settlers under the PDS. One family on that land was repeatedly threatened and ordered to leave, culminating in a threat to kill every member of the family. Dorothy repeatedly warned the police that this was happening, but they did nothing to intervene. The family therefore fled to the forest and watched as the rancher and his men burned down the family's home and destroyed their crops. On February 11, Dorothy went into Boa Esperança to meet with community members and to bring food and clothing to the displaced family. While she was there, she was warned that there were two men in the area saying that they were going to kill her. She found these men and sat down with them to show them the maps that were proof that the land in question was part of the PDS. They responded that they were going to kill her and build the new landowner's house over her dead body. On the morning of February 12, Dorothy set out to go to the community meeting from the house where she had spent the night. On her way, she called out to one of the farmers named Cicero to ask if he was coming to the meeting, and he responded that he would be coming right behind her. After she made her way up a hill and around a bend, the two gunmen stepped into the road in front of her, beginning to argue with her again. As Dorothy began to walk away, one of the gunmen called her name, and she turned around to see that he was aiming a revolver at her. She reached in her bag, pulled out her Bible, and opened it to read the Beatitudes to them. When she read, "Blessed are the peacemakers," one of the gunmen opened fire at Dorothy three times, then approached her as she lay on the ground and shot her again three times, in the back of the head. Sr. Dorothy was seventy-three years old when she was killed.

Sr. Dorothy lives on in the Sisters of Notre Dame de Namur and in the ecclesial base communities of Anapu, where her loss is mourned deeply but her presence is felt daily. Her presence especially abounds in the local women's group that calls themselves "Dorothy's Seeds" to "honor her struggle and her work among us. We are the seeds that she left and she grows a little bit more every day."[37] She lives on in the achievements of this group and all of the communities of Anapu: in the trees planted to restore areas of the forest that have been destroyed; in the people's commitment

---

[37] "Amazonia, Dorothy Stang's Struggle."

to sustainable agriculture; and in the schools, health centers, and roads built to improve communal well-being. Dorothy lives on in Father Amaro, a Catholic parish priest in Anapu, whom she inspired to go to seminary and whom she accompanied in his pastoral internship. He remarks that "being here today in Anapu, where this friend shed her blood to give life, is everything for me."[38] Dorothy lives on in millions of acres of the forest that were declared national reserves by the Brazilian president within weeks of her murder, and in the newly documented Amazonian screech owl that bears her name, *Megascops stangiae*.[39] Greater than the many recognitions she was given during her lifetime and after her death is her continued presence in the people and the forest of the Brazilian Amazon. In the words of JP Miranda, a singer-songwriter from Xingu, "Dorothy Stang, you will never die!"

> *They killed the missionary*
> *whose age was almost a century.*
> *Courageous, strong warrior woman:*
> *to save the green and quench our thirst*
> *she faced even death.*
>
> *American and also Brazilian*
> *she gave her life for others.*
> *She wanted to defend the green and*
> *quench the thirst of the poor also.*
>
> *With the blood that bathed the earth*
> *hope never dies*

---

[38] "Amazonia, Dorothy Stang's Struggle."

[39] See "Brazilian Forest Reserves to Honor U.S. Nun," NBC News Website, February 17, 2005, https://www.nbcnews.com/id/wbna6989583, and "*Megascops Stangiae*: New Species of Owl Named in Honor of Sister of Notre Dame de Namur Dorothy Stang," Sisters of Notre Dame de Namur Website, July 2, 2021, https://www.sndohio.org/sisters-notre-dame/news/1714776/megascops-stangiae.

that here there will always be someone
to open paths and plant loving care
like Dorothy Stang did.

It was she herself who alerted us
that nature needs love.
It was she herself who told us one day
that the death of the forest is the end of our life.[40]

Dorothy Stang… *presente!*

Gustavo Marcelo Rivera Moreno (†2009)

Marcelo Rivera[41] was born in Cabañas, El Salvador, the eighth of nine children. Like other Salvadorans of his generation, Marcelo came of age during El Salvador's twelve-year civil war, which erupted in 1980 due to vast economic inequalities and political repression, including disappearances of social activists, throughout the 1970s. A coalition of armed guerrilla groups came together in 1980 to form the Farabundo Martí National Liberation Front (FMLN) and wage a coordinated revolution against the right-wing military regime that existed to serve the political and economic interests of a deeply entrenched Salvadoran oligarchy. Backed by the United States, the counterinsurgency tactics of the Salvadoran state intensified during

---

[40] JP Miranda, "Dorothy Stang, Tu Jamais Morrerás," jpmirandaomxingu YouTube channel, April 3, 2009, https://youtu.be/Hhxda7xvlew. Many thanks to Sister Kimberly Dalgarn for sharing the original Portuguese lyrics, with English translation, from the Sisters of Notre Dame de Namur archives.

[41] The following narrative of Marcelo Rivera's life and assassination, along with the larger story of the fight against gold mining in El Salvador, is drawn from the following sources: Robin Broad and John Cavanaugh, *The Water Defenders: How Ordinary People Saved a Country from Corporate Greed* (Boston: Beacon Press, 2021), and "Radio Victoria," Radio Ambulante Podcast, Season 11, Episode 28, April 12, 2022, https://radioambulante.org/en/audio-en/radio-victoria.

the war, in the form of massacres, disappearances, torture, and targeted assassinations. The armed conflict ultimately cost about 75,000 civilian lives, and the United Nations Truth Commission for El Salvador reported that the vast majority of human rights violations during the war were committed by agents of the Salvadoran state.[42] Among the departments hit hardest by the war was the department of Cabañas, which was divided between military strongholds and territory controlled by the FMLN. The area around San Isidro and neighboring Sensuntepeque was largely controlled by the military during the war, and commentators observe that this has not typically been a region characterized by popular resistance to the status quo.

After the Peace Accords of 1992, Marcelo and his brother Miguel Ángel started a library in their childhood home and then moved the library to an old building that had been a holding place for cadavers during the war. This would be the birthplace of the San Isidro Cultural Center. Soon to follow was Marcelo's forma-

---

[42] The United Nations Truth Commission for El Salvador received complaints of over 22,000 serious acts of violence, 60 percent of which included extrajudicial executions, over 25 percent of which concerned enforced disappearances, and over 20 percent of which involved torture. Responsibility for 85 percent of cases was attributed to agents of the State, including paramilitary groups and death squads. See "From Madness to Hope: The 12-Year War in El Salvador," Report of the UN Commission on the Truth for El Salvador, 1993, https://www.usip.org/sites/default/files/file/ElSalvador-Report.pdf.

Prime targets for acts of violence against opponents by agents of the state were individuals who were involved in activities aimed at the defense of the poor and the promotion of human rights and social justice. These folks were viewed by the government as "subversives" and were in constant danger of being arrested, tortured, disappeared, and/or executed. In her book-length study of martyrdom and progressive Catholicism during El Salvador's civil war, Anna L. Peterson indicates that by March 1980 government-sponsored forces were committing five hundred to eight hundred political murders per month. See Anna L. Peterson, *Martyrdom and the Politics of Religion: Progressive Catholicism in El Salvador's Civil War* (Albany: SUNY Press, 1997), 35.

tion of the Friends of San Isidro Cabañas Association (ASIC), an organization dedicated to human rights, gender equality, community development, and defense of the environment. ASIC developed close relations of solidarity and collaboration with other communal organizations in the region, especially the Association for Social and Economic Development (ADES) and Radio Victoria. Prior to

any awareness of the threat of gold mining in Cabañas, these groups worked together to resist the construction of a solid waste landfill near the banks of the Titihuapa River and the installation of a giant hog farm that would also contaminate the water supply. But it wasn't long before Marcelo, Miguel Ángel, and their friends at ADES and Radio Victoria realized that an even bigger issue was threatening their community's environmental well-being.

In the early 2000s, communities in the area began to notice wells drying up and an unusual number of livestock dying of mysterious causes. At the same time, men in white suits were arriving in town and large machines were removing long cylinders of rock from the earth. Trucks were coming and going to transport these strange rocks out of the communities. What the communities in and around San Isidro were experiencing were the effects of the multinational mining company, Pacific Rim, conducting exploration for gold in and around the abandoned El Dorado mine. Gold and silver deposits had been mined in El Salvador during the colonial period and for a brief time during the mid-twentieth century, and the El Dorado mine was opened and operated by a U.S. company for five years between 1947 and 1952. After the war, the Salvadoran government—still controlled by ARENA, the right-wing party founded by a military officer—adopted neoliberal economic policies that encouraged foreign investment, including investment in mining, as a motor of economic recovery and development. In 2002, the government "dangled a new mining law jam-packed with enticements for foreign firms."[43] The price of gold was on the rise, and the El Dorado mine in Cabañas, spanning 72 square kilometers, held an estimated 1.4 million ounces of gold, with a potential value of $1.3 billion. A new gold rush had begun. The dried-up wells and poisoned cows were the direct result. Pacific Rim's exploration for gold involved hundreds of perforations in the earth, which caused water sources to shift and thus dried up the wells. The use of cyanide in the gold extraction process was contaminating the water supply and thus killing the livestock.

While the communities originally had been optimistic when they heard news of a mining company that would bring jobs and economic development to their community, Marcelo questioned how beneficial the mine would actually be for the people and how destructive it might be for the land and water on which they depend to survive. Marcelo was among the first to raise the alarm, and Pacific Rim responded immediately to community concerns with an aggressive public relations campaign designed to convince people that modern mining is environmentally responsible and that their company would bring jobs and other great benefits to the community. They began to distribute gifts to the people, including farm animals, trees, and food supplies, and offered large sums of money to key individuals and organizations that they considered potential adversaries and/or allies.

---

[43] Broad and Cavanagh, 19.

Marcelo and his friends became very suspicious and therefore
began to educate themselves about metallic mining and its environmental consequences. Marcelo, Miguel, and colleagues from ADES
made the trek across the border to visit communities affected by
mining projects in Honduras. There they witnessed firsthand
the environmental impact of mining, returning to Cabañas with
"horror stories: of rivers poisoned by cyanide, of dying fish and
skin diseases, of displaced communities, denuded forests, and
corruption and conflict catalyzed by mining company payoffs."[44]
Furthermore, the group learned that mining operations utilize an
exorbitant amount of water, which would further accelerate the
water scarcity crisis that communities in Cabañas and throughout
the entire country were already facing. They also came to understand that local people would only be qualified for the lowest-paid
and most dangerous jobs, and that the company would take 98
percent of its profits back home to Canada, leaving just 2 percent
for appropriation by local and national governments. Their minds
were made up, and the struggle against mining began in earnest.

Marcelo and friends from ASIC, ADES, and Radio Victoria
also visited other mining operations in El Salvador and began to
network at the national level, eventually forming the National
Working Group Against Metallic Mining in El Salvador. The coalition led popular education campaigns and protest marches against
mining in Cabañas, and the pressure seemed to have an effect. In
2008, likely out of concern for the upcoming presidential elections in which the FMLN opponent was anti-mining, the formerly
pro-mining ARENA government assured that it would not issue
permission for mining extraction without environmental impact
studies and without norms to regulate the industry. An unlikely
partnership between the right and the left was thus forged in
the face of the overwhelming dangers of metallic mining for the

---

[44] Broad and Cavanagh, 38.

Salvadoran people. When presidential elections in 2009 resulted in the first-ever victory for an FMLN candidate, it became clear that Pacific Rim's plan to proceed with extraction would be delayed indefinitely.

In response, Pacific Rim took El Salvador to court at the World Bank's International Centre for Settlement of Investment Disputes (ICSID), suing the country for $250 million in lost investments and future profits. Meanwhile, the company had already ramped up an intimidation campaign aimed at the water defenders, who had been getting in the way of their progress for years. Marcelo, Miguel Ángel, their colleagues at ADES and Radio Victoria, and community members involved in the struggle received repeated threats via emails, telephone calls, and text messages. They were followed and watched, and mysterious callers made it known that their daily activities were being tracked. Not long before his assassination, Marcelo and his brother were the targets of a vehicle attack by an employee of the pro-mining mayor of San Isidro while they were walking down a narrow street in their hometown. And then, on June 18, 2009, Marcelo disappeared from a bus stop outside San Isidro.

The Rivera family frantically searched for Marcelo for twelve long days before they received an anonymous call telling them where his body could be found—at the bottom of a 30-meter-deep abandoned well in a cornfield not far from the bus stop where he had last been seen. Marcelo's body was horrifically disfigured, with signs of torture reminiscent of the counterinsurgency tactics employed by the Salvadoran military and paramilitary forces in the 1970s and '80s. His family was told that DNA tests would need to be done to officially identify the body and, when they traveled to San Salvador to get permission to retrieve Marcelo's remains, they were told that he had already been buried in a common grave. It wasn't until eleven days later that they would finally recover his body and take him home to San Isidro for a proper funeral and burial. Authorities insisted that the crime could be attributed to common delinquency—that Marcelo had been drinking with some gang members and had been killed in a drunken brawl. But his family and fellow water defenders knew better. Marcelo didn't drink. He was a teacher who was "an avid reader, a person who loved theater and the arts and a good practical joke."[45] He was thirty-seven years old when he died.

Over the next two years, four other anti-mining activists were killed in Cabañas. Just weeks after Marcelo's murder, Ramiro Rivera Gómez, vice-president of the Cabañas Environmental Committee (CAC), miraculously survived an attack in which he was shot eight times. Despite police protection, he was gunned down and killed later that year on December 20, 2009. His wife, Felícita Echeverría, was also killed and his thirteen-year-old daughter was wounded. Six days later, a gunman shot and killed Dora Alicia Recinos Sorto, a thirty-two-year-old mother of seven, pregnant with her eighth child. Alicia, as she was known, was involved in the anti-mining struggle, and her husband, one of the primary spokespersons for the CAC, had survived an assassination attempt in 2008 and was still being threatened with violence for his activism. The gunman also shot at and killed Alicia's unborn baby and shot her two-year-old son in the foot. Finally, thirty-year-old student activist Juan Francisco Durán Ayala disappeared on June 3, 2011, after being warned to stop posting flyers and distributing pamphlets for the CAC anti-mining campaign the day before.[46]

Marcelo Rivera lives on in the work of the San Isidro Cultural Center, which bears his name and his image, and in the work of ASIC, ADES, and Radio Victoria. He lives on in young people's activism as part of the Marcelo Rivera Cell of the Bloque Popular

---

[45] Broad and Cavanagh, 3.

[46] For documentation of these cases, see the "Conflictos Mineros en América Latina" mapping database at https://mapa.conflictosmineros.net/ocmal_db-v2/.

Juvenil. He and the other murdered water defenders live on in the victories of the anti-mining movement in El Salvador and beyond. Pacific Rim—now Oceana Gold—lost its case against El Salvador at the World Bank in 2016, and El Salvador became the first country in the world to ban all forms of metallic mining in 2017. In the case of metallic mining, at least, the Salvadoran water defenders' declaration that "water is life" prevailed. Marcelo, Ramiro, Felícita, Alicia, and Juan Francisco are also present in the continued vigilance of the anti-mining movement against threats to the mining ban and in the movement to pass a law in El Salvador that would both codify water as a basic human right and prohibit the privatization of water. This movement is spurred on by the witness of their martyrs, whose story is told by Óscar Domínguez in song:

> *In San Isidro, Cabañas, resistance is born*
> *The death of the San Francisco River put them on alert*
>
> *First the garbage, then came the water,*
> *   then the mining*
> *Cabañas is in danger*
>
> *Francisco, take charge, and prepare for battle*
> *the people accompany you*
> *They have now raised consciousness*
> *and formed the Committee of Environmentalists*
>
> *Cabañas is prepared to confront the battle*
> *the first objective is to take down the machines*
> *The struggle becomes tense, and the threats begin*
>
> *They assassinate Marcelo, Ramiro, and Dora,*
> *eight months pregnant*
> *and finally young Paco*
>
> *They try to silence Radio Victoria*
> *with death threats to their employees*

Assassinating these four, they tried to put out the fire
But instead of putting it out, it became stronger

. . .

We are Salvadorans
in defense of life
We are Salvadorans
they are Canadians
We are Salvadorans
And the struggle won't be held back![47]

Marcelo Rivera . . . *¡presente!*

Berta Isabel Cáceres Flores (†2016)

Berta Cáceres[48] was born in La Esperanza, Honduras, on March 4, 1971, to a Catholic family that for generations had been distanced from the Indigenous identity and spirituality of their ancestors, the Lenca people. Berta's mother was a social activist, midwife, and humanitarian, though, and, in her youth, Berta traveled to neighboring El Salvador to offer support and solidarity for the Salvadoran revolution. Returning to Honduras as a firsthand witness to the bloodshed of war, Berta sought paths of nonviolent transformation

---

[47] Óscar Domínguez, "Ambientalistas de Cabañas," mp.3. Many thanks to Isabelo Cortez of Radio Victoria and the Cabañas FMLN, for sharing this song with me.

[48] The following narrative of Berta Cácares's life and assassination is drawn from Nina Lakhani, *Who Killed Berta Cáceres? Dams, Death Squads, and an Indigenous Defender's Battle for the Planet* (New York: Verso, 2020); "Las Semillas de Berta Cáceres," documentary film produced by the Entre Pueblos journalism project, EntrePueblos YouTube Channel, March 3, 2021, https://youtu.be/gBC5I16oKO4; and "Guardiana de los Ríos," documentary film produced by Campaña Madre Tierra and distributed by Radio Progreso (www.radioprogresohn.net), Radio Progreso YouTube Channel, September 13, 2016, https://youtu.be/Lwwe4MOGfmo.

that would resist socioeconomic injustice, defend the territories of Indigenous and other rural Hondurans from extractivism and militarism, and construct alternatives grounded in grassroots democratic participation and recuperation of Indigenous identity, culture, and cosmovision. In 1993, Berta co-founded the Civic Council of Popular and Indigenous Organizations of Honduras (COPINH), which would go on to successfully resist multiple extractivist projects in the mountainous region of western Honduras.

Berta's reclamation of her family's Indigenous identity went hand in hand with her insistence on the rights of the Lenca people to defend their sacred lands and rivers. Berta herself explains that the Lenca people are deeply connected to the land and that their "cosmovision is centered in the land and in corn, in the equilibrium that should be maintained between all beings." Under Berta's leadership, COPINH also incorporated anti-patriarchal analysis and feminist praxis, promoting the full incorporation and leadership of women and LGBTQ+ folks in the work of the organization. In her estimation, it is vital to confront "projects of death" with a critical perspective on how these projects are based in a paradigm of multiple dominations: not just capitalism, but patriarchy and racism as well. The anti-capitalist struggle must therefore also be anti-patriarchal and anti-racist in its analysis, vision, strategies, and everyday life.

Over the course of more than two decades in this struggle for the defense of the land and waters of western Honduras, Berta and other members of COPINH were the targets of smear campaigns and received many death threats, along with threats to their families. These threats increased in the years following the 2009 coup d'état, which ousted the center-left President Manuel Zelaya and installed a U.S.-backed regime that declared Honduras to be "open for business," meaning deregulated and eager to attract foreign investment for extractivist development projects carried out by national and multinational corporations. The new administration quickly approved the construction of forty-seven new hydroelectric dams in order to provide power for other industries, especially hundreds of mining projects. In the words of Afro-Honduran Gurifuna human rights defender and dear friend of Berta, Miriam Miranda, to understand the context of Honduras after the 2009 coup, one must understand "what it means for Honduras to be a country that became a political laboratory for destroying the institutions" of civil society. This situation has exacerbated the historical control that the oligarchy and political elites have over natural resources. In Miranda's words again, "In the majority of cases, those who control the resources—and here I mean the water, the forests, all of the resources of the soil and the subsoil—are the investors. They have a map of all the resources, a map of the resources, but not of the people who have co-existed here for centuries."[49]

That investors' map of resources includes the Gualcarque River, which is sacred to the Lenca people, and is essential to the life of the Río Blanco community. In 2006, the Chinese engineering company Sinohydro partnered with the Honduran energy company DESA to plan four hydroelectric dam projects in the Gualcarque with financing from the World Bank. Construction on the Agua Zarca dam near the Río Blanco community began in 2012, but the companies had violated the rights of Indigenous peoples to prior, free, and

---

[49] "Las Semillas de Berta Cáceres."

informed consultation on the project. COPINH had organized the population to discuss the project, and in two open town halls and more than 150 Indigenous assemblies, the people expressed their resistance to the Agua Zarca dam project and to any damage to or privatization of their sacred waters. The project proceeded anyway, with falsified signatures based on names and identification numbers taken from election rolls. COPINH took the people's resistance to the capital, but no one would listen. The Lenca people therefore blocked the road to the construction site for two whole years, even in the face of harassment and violent attacks. During a peaceful protest on July 15, 2013, the Honduran military opened fire, killing Tomás García, one of the leaders of the Lenca community in Río Blanco. The community was indignant, and their persistent pressure led to Sinohydro's withdrawal from the project. Funding from the World Bank was also withdrawn due to concerns over human rights violations. Berta's mother remarks that Berta was untiring in her commitment to this struggle, arriving home exhausted at 11 p.m., with her boots all muddy, and she would be back up and out working at 6 a.m. the next morning. But she had faith and hope that the work would not be in vain. When the struggle against the Agua Zarca dam began, Berta went down to the Gualcarque River and waded into the waters. She was able to speak with the river, to feel what it had to say to her: "And I knew how hard it was going to be. But I knew we were going to triumph. The river told me so."[50]

Berta was awarded the prestigious Goldman Environmental Prize in 2015 for her role in the struggle against the Agua Zarca dam project. Her acceptance speech deserves to be read in full:

> In our cosmovisions, we are beings who have emerged from the earth, from water, and from corn. The Lenca people are

---

[50] "Berta Cáceres, galardonada del Premio Goldman 2015, Honduras," Goldman Environmental Prize YouTube Channel, April 20, 2015, https://youtu.be/S-2Muwo1jls.

ancestral custodians of rivers, which are further protected by the spirits of young girls who teach us that to give our lives in multiple ways for the defense of the rivers, is to give our lives for the good of humanity and this planet. COPINH, walking alongside people struggling for emancipation, ratifies this commitment to continue protecting the water, the rivers, and the common goods of nature, along with our rights as peoples.

Wake up! Wake up, humanity! We are out of time. Our consciences will be shaken by the fact that we have only been contemplating the self-destruction caused by the predations of capitalism, racism, and patriarchy. The Gualcarque River has called upon us, as have all the rivers that are seriously threatened in our world. We must answer the call. Our Mother Earth—militarized, fenced in, poisoned, where basic rights are systematically violated—demands that we take action. Let us build, then, societies that are capable of co-existing in a way that is just, dignified, life-giving. Let us come together and move forward with hope as we defend and care for the blood of the Earth and its spirits. I dedicate this award to all the rebels out there: to my mother, to the Lenca people, to Río Blanco, to COPINH, and to the martyrs who have died defending the goods of the natural world.[51]

The struggle against the Agua Zarca dam continued after Berta returned home from being awarded the Goldman Prize. She was scheduled to visit Europe to put pressure on banks and corporations to divest from the project and other extractivist investments like it, but that trip never came to pass. Late in the night of

---

[51] "Berta Cáceres Acceptance Speech, 2015 Goldman Prize Ceremony," Goldman Environmental Prize YouTube Channel, April 22, 2015, https://www.youtube.com/watch?v=AR1kwx8b0ms. Translation adapted from the English subtitles included in the video.

March 2, 2016, Berta Cáceres was shot to death while burning the midnight oil, working tirelessly in her home in La Esperanza. She was forty-four years old, just two days before her forty-fifth birthday, when she died.

Berta's murder was part of a coordinated response—by "shareholders, executives, managers, and employees of Desarrollos Energéticos, S.A. (DESA); private security companies working for DESA; and public officials and State security agencies"[52]—to COPINH's protection of the Gualcarque River and surrounding communities from social and ecological devastation by the Agua Zarca hydroelectric dam project. The Honduran state did nothing to protect her and, in fact, laid the foundations of militarism and corruption that led to her murder and that continued to enable attacks on environmental defenders after her death. In the words of Miriam Miranda:

> How is it that we live in a country that is so screwed, in which it was possible and it's possible to kill a person like Berta? I don't think anyone measures up to the woman who they gave a prize to, who had international recognition, so you have to realize how vulnerable we have been made by the state and that we are disposable. That's what hurts.

And yet, like so many who knew Berta, Miriam insists that her opponents did not succeed in ultimately killing her: "I think they made a mistake thinking they could kill Berta and kill the struggle, the resistance. I said it in the moment when we went to plant [bury] Berta, when I said that Berta had multiplied. Even in the midst of the pain, I felt Berta there." Just as Berta was there for Miriam in the most difficult moments of her own

---

[52] Grupo Asesor Internacional de Personas Expertas, "Dam Violence: The Plan That Killed Berta Cáceres," November 2017, https://www.gaipe.net/wp-content/uploads/2017/10/Exec-Summ-Dam-Violencia-EN-FINAL.pdf.

struggle—moments when she was attacked, kidnapped, and arrested—Miriam feels Berta's presence with her even today. But she still laments, "It's not so easy to lose someone as important in your life as Berta. It's not easy."[53]

Berta lives on in Miriam Miranda, in the work of COPINH, in her four children, in her daughters who continue her struggle, and in the work of international solidarity groups pressuring banks and corporations to divest from not only the Agua Zarca dam projects but also other extractivist projects that generate violent conflict and ecological ruin. She lives on in her own prophetic words shared across the world on YouTube videos, posters, murals, t-shirts, and more. As Miriam and so many of those devoted to her legacy declare: "Berta did not die, she multiplied!" In the words of Rosalina Domínguez, another water protector from Río Blanco, "Berta's death was not the end, it was a seed that she planted that has multiplied. Every time I go to the river, I feel her presence walking there.... Berta is there. It's that you feel the energy and the strength that she gives us to speak, to not be afraid."[54] One year after Berta's assassination, three young Indigenous women took to the stage at the Goldman Environmental Prize ceremony and offered this tribute to Berta's legacy:

> *Berta, as Indigenous women, we know that death is just the earth's way of reminding us of who we belong to. The land.*

> *Tonight, we summon you as courage. As mother, as teacher, as patience, as joy, as activist with a contagious smile who cut her teeth on revolution for the love of the people in the land of Honduras.*

> *Last year on this very stage you said, "We come from the land, water, and corn. Somos seres surgidos de la tierra,*

---

[53] Miriam Miranda's comments here are taken from "Las Semillas de Berta Cáceres."

[54] "Las Semillas de Berta Cáceres."

el agua, y el maíz." *You were carrying the power of clenched fists and sacred rivers in your speech. Río Blanco and the Río Gualcarque. Sources of life and medicine for the Lenca people. It's why you were so fearless against the threats. The river had already warned you that your victory would be difficult but you stood brave and tonight the river runs throughout this room, a living vein connecting all of us to this planet, a call to protect Mother Earth, just as lovingly and fiercely as you did, Berta.*

Tonight we celebrate your spirit, your passion, and what you gave your life to, the Council of Popular and Indigenous Organizations of Honduras. The rivers of the earth and the goddesses that protect them. Your passion for human rights and the oxygen of resistance. Your voice echoes like the heartbeat of every Indigena's *fight for dignity.*

Tonight, we celebrate you, Berta.

You taught me that as an Indigenous woman, the true path towards justice is to accept the fact that the land never belonged to us. That we have always belonged to the land. You taught me how to press my ear to the soil, how to plant my feet in the river and listen, as my ancestors whisper me responsible for protecting the sacredness of where all of us come from.

You taught me how to love this land both unconditionally and fearlessly, how to hold hands with the river and protect her vulnerability. How to bathe in the eternal gaze of her wisdom. And listen to the songs of liberation flowing through her current. Thank you for showing me the ghosts connecting land to life, and the holiness of their stories that lie beneath the water.

You taught me the meaning of courage and solidarity. You've reminded us just how far chants of justice can travel. Since you've joined the spirit world, thousands have converged in Tegucigalpa demanding truth. Ten buses of Indigenous and Black Hondurans were stopped en route to the capital. Many walked by foot when forced to leave the buses. From San Francisco to D.C. a call to action was summoned in your honor. In New York City, hundreds of women gathered chanting, "Berta didn't die, she multiplied!"

Berta, it was you who said, "Let us come together and move forward in hope to defend and care for the earth and its spirits." We will look for you in the villages of stars every night. We will listen for your voice like a whispering wind and hear your laughter in every crashing wave. We will stand for justice and feel our feet planted in every ounce of soil that we have always belonged to, knowing that we are safe, knowing that when you return to us, we will become millions. Berta, we will always carry you with us, your resistance, your vision will continue to be passed on in every sacred drop of water that surrounds us.[55]

Berta Cáceres ... *¡presente!*

Invisibility, Impunity, and an Incomprehensible Cloud of Witnesses

Each of the murdered environmental defenders whose stories we have just contemplated have been featured in books, videos, documentaries, music, and artwork at an international level. Many of them received awards from local authorities, and/or from national and international environmental justice organizations. Some of

---

[55] Leslie Valencia, Terisa Siagatonu, and Erika Vivianna Céspedes, "Tribute to Berta Cáceres at the 2016 Goldman Environmental Prize Ceremony," produced by Corwin Creative, Goldman Environmental Prize YouTube Channel, April 21, 2016, https://youtu.be/yMybBm6RT5g.

their stories are even featured on the website associated with the 2019 Vatican Synod for the Pan-Amazonian Region. Despite widespread impunity in cases of human rights violations in each of their particular contexts, local activism and international pressure led to the arrest and trial of a significant number of individuals involved in their murders, though arrest and conviction of the intellectual authors of their murders has been achieved in very rare cases and only after years of struggle against impunity and for justice. Most environmental defenders whose human rights are violated and/or who are ultimately killed never receive the widespread recognition or modicum of justice that these six individuals have received. In almost all of their cases, impunity reigns and their witness remains invisible to the world beyond their own local communities.

In recent years and with the proliferation of online news sources, the murder of environmental defenders has gained significantly greater attention. As I conducted research for this book, I paid close attention to Global Witness yearly reports, Spanish and Portuguese news sources, and the online presence of environmental justice organizations in Latin America. It seemed like each month, I would encounter more and more stories of environmental defenders threatened and killed. Since the murder of Berta Cáceres in 2016, hundreds of other defenders have been murdered in Latin America alone. What follows are six cases—a selection of just one per year since Berta's death.[56]

- Carlos Maaz Coc was a Maya Q'eqchi' leader in an artisanal fishermen's guild that collaborates with other organizations in Guatemala to defend the Maya Q'eqchi' from contamination of their lands and waters due to nickel mining. Carlos was killed on May 27, 2017, during a peaceful protest demanding government action on the contamination of Lake Izabal.

---

[56] Each of these cases is documented on the Frontline Defenders Website at https://www.frontlinedefenders.org/.

- Juana Raymundo was a twenty-five-year-old Maya Ixil nurse and local coordinator of the Farmers' Development Committee (CODECA), which promotes social participation, protests electricity privatization, and defends the human rights of Indigenous farmers in the Nebaj Quiché region of Guatemala. Juana's body was found on the side of a road showing signs of torture on July 28, 2018.

- Dilma Ferreira Silva was a forty-seven-year-old prominent leader in the Movement of People Affected by Dams in Brazil. For over three decades, Dilma had fought for the rights of people affected by the Tucuruí hydroelectric dam on the Toncantins River. She was killed in her home, along with her husband, Claudionor Costa da Silva, and friend of the family Hilton Lopes on March 22, 2019.

- Homero Gómez González was the manager of El Rosario monarch butterfly sanctuary in the state of Michoacán, Mexico. Raúl Hernández Romero was a tour guide. Both were dedicated to the conservation of the land and protection of the monarch from illegal loggers. Homero disappeared on January 13, 2020, and his body was found more than two weeks later. Meanwhile, Raúl disappeared on January 27 and his body was found six days later, two days after Homero's funeral.

- Alberth Snider Centeno Tomás, Suami Aparicio Mejía García, Gerardo Mizael Rochez Cálix, and Milton Joel Martínez Álvarez were all Afro-Indigenous members of the Garifuna people along the Caribbean coast of Honduras. They formed part of the Black Fraternal Organization of Honduras (OFRANEH), an organization that defends the rights of Garifuna communities against threats to their ancestral land and territory. Alberth was the twenty-seven-year-old elected leader of his community, an advocate of compensation for stolen lands, and a defender of the Punto

Izopo wetlands against drug traffickers and African palm oil plantations. On July 18, 2020, all four men, along with one other man from Belize, were taken from their homes by men wearing Honduran Investigative Police vests and Honduran Military Police uniforms. To date, they are still missing.[57]

- Fernando dos Santos Araújo was a 39-year-old landless worker, gay man, and advocate for LGBTQ+ rights, land rights, and agrarian reform in the state of Pará, Brazil. On May 24, 2017, police arrived at his camp of landless workers and massacred ten people, including Fernando's partner Bruno, under whose body he hid. Fernando fled to the woods and eventually entered the Victim and Witness Protection Program as an eyewitness to the massacre. Nevertheless, he made the decision to return to the region to rejoin the struggle of his community for land rights and agrarian reform. After receiving multiple threats, he was shot and killed on January 26, 2021.[58]

- Luz Marina Arteaga was a rural leader, doctor, and defender of the land rights of peasant and Indigenous communities in the Meta department of Colombia. She worked with the Norman Pérez Bello Claretian Corporation, an ecumenical faith-based organization that accompanies the land reclamation efforts of Indigenous people in the Orinoquía watershed bioregion. As a leader who was prominent in the land claims process, Luz Marina received multiple death threats. She disappeared on January 13, 2022, and her body was found on the banks of the Meta River five days later.

[57] See also School of the Americas Watch, "Take Action: Garifuna Land Defenders Forcibly Disappeared," July 31, 2020, https://soaw.org/take-action-garifuna-land-defenders-forcibly-disappeared.

[58] See also Nation Nyoka, "Agrarian Reform and Queer Rights Go Hand in Hand," New Frame Website, June 11, 2021, https://www.newframe.com/agrarian-reform-and-queer-rights-go-hand-in-hand/.

These stories of violent death are horrifically astounding. Perhaps even more astounding is the fact that most land and environmental defenders know that their continued activism puts them at heightened risk of harm. Indeed, most who are assassinated receive prior notice of the danger that they are in via death threats and other forms of intimidation. What are the theological commitments, spiritualities, and cosmovisions that underlie such unwavering commitment to social justice and ecological well-being? What are the spiritual and theological wellsprings of faith, hope, and love that empower such courage? How is it even possible to love so fully even in the face of death? What is the greater reality to which these individuals and their communities bear witness? In the chapters that follow, we will turn to theological reflection on these very questions.

5

WELLSPRINGS OF THE WITNESS

The Ecological Imaginations of Land and Environmental Defenders

In the first half of this book, we explored the social and historical contexts in which land and environmental defenders are being threatened and killed for their commitment to human and ecological well-being. We examined the root causes of these murders in the racist, patriarchal, and extractivist structures of colonialism, capitalism, and neoliberalism, and we identified these structures in theological language as sinful, rooted in an anti-social and anti-ecological imaginary. We pinpointed specific industries, along with local, national, and transnational networks of violent power wielded against land and environmental defenders by organized crime, politicians, law enforcement, banks, and corporations. And we contemplated the stories of several environmental defenders who have been assassinated, with consideration for the local specificities of power and violence that led to their murders.

In this present chapter, we turn to a different kind of analysis, moving from the social, political, and economic question of why environmental defenders are being killed to the theological question of why they persevere in their commitments to social and environmental justice, even in the face of death. Rather than flee from the danger that they knew they were in, the defenders whose stories we have just contemplated were willing to risk their lives for love of their people, their territories, their land, their waters, and the natural world as a whole. To be sure, countless communities of Indigenous people, Afro-descendent people, and rural poor have experienced brutal massacres by powerful forces intent on gaining access to their land and its natural resources. Many such communities are not even afforded the option of fleeing or seeking refuge to protect themselves. In the case of the murdered environmental defenders under consideration in this book, however, we are talking about people who were *decidedly willing* to live and struggle, suffer and die for the sake of love, liberation, and justice for their lands, ecosystems, and people. Their willingness to suffer such violence does not justify the violence, nor does it give the violence redemptive value. Nor does it invalidate the immense moral courage of those who do flee from violence to preserve their lives and the lives of their families. The mystery here, though, is that suffering and death were sacrifices that ecomartyrs did not run away from. Like most martyrs, they knew the potential cost of their commitment, and while the prospect of death was by no means a welcome one, they placed greater value on their desire for justice, peace, and ecological well-being than on their own physical survival.

What kind of love is this that looks death in the eye and, like Jesus, says, "No one takes my life from me, I give it freely" (Jn 10:18)?[1] What are the wellsprings of such love? What are its foundations? What motivates it? And what can we learn from the wellsprings, foundations, and aspirations of such love? As

---

[1]   Gustavo Gutiérrez reflects on the meaning of this statement in light of the martyrdom of Ignacio Ellacuría, S.J., in El Salvador, in "No One Takes My Life from Me; I Give It Freely," in *Love That Produces Hope: The Thought of Ignacio Ellacuría*, ed. Robert Lassalle-Klein and Kevin Burke (Collegeville, MN: Liturgical Press, 2006), 68–72.

Honduran singer-songwriter Karla Lara wonders: "Where does so much strength come from?… Where do so many Bertas come from?… Let the river run, let it run."[2]

In this chapter, we will discover that the wellsprings of "so many Bertas" are as diverse and complex as a watershed in which many springs, creeks, and streams feed into a sacred, life-giving river, which in turn feeds into other rivers. Ecomartyrs in the Americas embody and therefore bear witness to the ecological imaginations of Indigenous cosmovisions; African-heritage religions; Catholic or other Christian social ethics; liberation theologies; ecospiritualities; ecosocialism; decolonial struggle; and/or ecofeminism (and more). These streams of inspiration and motivation are not always reducible to a single spiritual source or worldview and they are diverse even within themselves. Therefore, we will not attempt to make exclusive correlations between specific ecomartyrs and specific wellsprings, although we will take into account examples from specific martyrs to illustrate the various ecological imaginations that inspire and motivate committed action for human and ecological well-being. In some communities and individuals, a specific ecological imagination is very distinctively embodied with little outside influence, while in other communities and individuals, some or all of these ecological imaginations overlap and mutually critique and/or inform one another.

We will proceed in two parts. First, we will consider four frameworks for considering the common ground, or watersheds, in which the wellsprings of ecological imaginations flow. Many of these ecological imaginations are diverse manifestations of what Pope Francis calls "integral ecology," though we would do better to refer to them in the plural as "integral ecologies," since many of them are so distinctive as to be irreducible to any of the others. Another term that might encompass the commonalities of these

---

2   Karla Lara, "Que corra el río," Karla Lara YouTube Channel, April 7, 2017, https://youtu.be/KmLdzihTGfo.

ecological imaginations while preserving their diversity is the Latin American concept of "*buen vivir*," or good living, which again might be better articulated as "*buenos vivires*," or plural visions and practices of good living. A third term that encompasses the commonalities between them is the concept of "the commons," or the practice of human communities managing the life-giving resources of Creation communally, for the sake of communal and ecological well-being, rather than for private gain. Finally, many of the ecological imaginations are linked together by "decolonial feminism," which is a critical lens that can help to refine and decolonize the other frameworks. Attempting to bring such disparate ecological imaginations together under any one of these umbrella terms is a venture that risks reductionism and cognitive colonization of worldviews that are distinctively non-Western and potentially incompatible with predominant forms of Western reasoning. We will do our best, therefore, to honor each of these ecological imaginations in its distinctiveness, while placing them in fruitful conversation with one another.

Next, we will reflect on three ecological imaginations that I have identified as most prevalent within the wellsprings of contemporary ecomartyrdom in the Americas, keeping in mind that each of these categories is itself diverse, fluid, and impossible to pin down as one thing or another. We will begin with Indigenous cosmovisions, because they have the deepest roots in Abya Yala and Turtle Island. We will proceed to consider African-heritage religious traditions brought to the Americas by enslaved Africans and passed on to their descendants; then we will conclude with post–Vatican II Catholic social thought, theologies of liberation, and ecospiritualities, under the umbrella of the "sacramental imagination." Again, these categories are all diverse in and of themselves, and they can synthesize or resist synthesis with the others, making for beautifully "pluriversal" wellsprings and watersheds of commitment to a world in which many worlds, human and more-than-human, are able to coexist in relationships of solidarity, peace, and justice with one another, their local landscapes, and the earth as a whole.[3]

Common Ground: Watersheds of Resistance

The chorus and final line of a song by the Puerto Rican hip-hop band Calle 13 beautifully encapsulate the common ground, or the common watersheds of resistance, that are fed by the wellsprings of prophetic ecological imaginations in the Americas:

> *You can't buy the wind*
> *You can't buy the sun*
> *You can't buy the rain*
> *You can't buy the heat*
> *You can't buy the clouds*
> *You can't buy the colors*
> *You can't buy my joy*
> *You can't buy my pain*
>
> . . .
>
> *You can't buy my life*[4]

This song is like a prayer lamenting that which has been stolen from the land and people of Latin America. The lyrics exude pride in the beauty and love of the land and the peoples who share what

---

[3] See chapter 1, note 29, for the origins of this vision in the Zapatista movement. Decolonial scholars use the term "pluriversality" to contrast such a vision with the "universality" of totalizing, colonizing worldviews in which one vision and praxis of reality is imposed on all others. See, e.g., Bernd Reiter, ed., *Constructing the Pluriverse: The Geopolitics of Knowledge* (Durham, NC: Duke University Press, 2018), and Arturo Escobar, *Pluriversal Politics: The Real and the Possible* (Durham, NC: Duke University Press, 2020).

[4] Calle 13, "Latinoamérica," from the studio album *Entren Los Que Quieran* (Sony Music Latin, 2010).

they have and who keep on walking even "without legs." And this chorus especially points to a common, foundational commitment that is characteristic of the ecological imaginations that we will be contemplating in this chapter: the life-giving goods of Creation are not for sale! You can't buy or sell the sources and sustenance of life itself! In prophetic contrast with the anti-ecological imaginary of extractivism, in which the goods of Creation (including human labors) are inert commodities appropriated by anyone who has enough wealth or weapons to do so, the ecological imaginations of ecomartyrs are characterized by a deep sense of Creation—both human and the more-than-human Creation—as sacred. The goods of Creation are sacred in and of themselves and are also sacred in relation to their capacity to reproduce and sustain life for human beings as an integral part of Creation. This sacred sense of shared well-being among human beings and the rest of Creation is expressed in four different conceptual and practical frameworks that help to encapsulate some commonalities between the wellsprings of ecomartyrs' witness: integral ecology, *buen vivir*, commoning, and decolonial feminism.

Integral Ecologies

In 2015, Pope Francis issued a landmark encyclical titled *Laudato Si': On Care for Our Common Home*, in which he uses the term "integral ecology" to describe the interconnection of all reality, with an emphasis on the interconnections between human and ecological well-being. While it seems that Pope Francis is introducing a new paradigm here, he is simply using new language to describe (a) the sacred nature of reality as interdependent; (b) worldviews that recognize the sacred, interdependent nature of reality; and (c) ways of coexisting in the world that honor and embody the sacred interdependence of all Creation. In other words, the paradigm of integral ecology can be read as an acknowledgment of and tribute to the many and varied human communities that have already been embodying the sacred reality of human and ecological interdependence since time immemorial. Land and environmental defenders have been witnessing to this reality for decades, even centuries or millennia, prior to the invention of this term. It is not that the *concept* of "integral ecology" itself, as described by Pope Francis, is the wellspring or inspiration for land and environmental defenders. Rather, the term attempts to articulate that which lies deep within the ecological imaginations of those who dedicate their lives to the interconnected well-being of human and more-than-human communities. This paradigm offers an open and flexible enough framework that seems to get at some of the key characteristics of how land and environmental defenders are conceptualizing and embodying alternative ways of being human in relation to the vulnerability and beauty of life in this world.

Pope Francis roots his own integral ecology in the biblical tradition and the Christian doctrine of Creation, but integral ecology as a whole and each of the dimensions of it can be elaborated, extended, corrected, and embodied in conversation with other religious, spiritual, philosophical, and even scientific communities. For this reason, I suggest that we speak of not just one integral ecology, but many. Broadly speaking, integral ecologies are pluriversal ways of being human that recognize and live into the interdependence of all reality and the interconnections between social, political, economic, spiritual, cultural, and ecological well-being. Let's take a closer look at three dimensions of integral ecologies that are particularly salient in the ecological imaginations of ecomartyrs.

First, integral ecology is a paradigm for being human that sees the world in terms of sacred abundance rather than scarcity and seeks to share and care for the earth's abundance for the sake of meeting both human needs and the needs of Creation. This affirmation of gracious abundance does not deny ecological limits, human vulnerability, or the vulnerability of Creation, but rather recognizes that the gracious gift of Creation must be tilled and kept carefully, gratefully, and communally in order to distribute the goods of this gift justly and maintain it for generations to come. Recall Father Alcides's insistence that the abundance of Creation can be found in the smallness and simplicity of seeds—when we plant seeds and tend to them with care, they multiply. Moreover, when we share what we have, there is always enough. Land and environmental defenders both resist the ways in which extractivism violates the earth's abundance and create alternative communities of solidarity with one another and Creation, seeking ways of honoring and caring for the interdependence of human and ecological needs.

Second, as already discussed, integral ecology is a paradigm for being human that sees all things as interconnected and therefore refuses to fearfully extract or divide one element or dimension of existence from the others. True to its name, the anti-ecological imaginary of the extractivist paradigm extracts humanity from the rest of Creation, insists on a dichotomy between economic growth and ecological well-being, and depends on the persistence of hierarchical dualisms between not only humanity and the nonhuman natural world, but between rich and poor, men and women, white people and people of color, and so on. Integral ecologies are generally oriented toward the deconstruction of these binaries that characterize both capitalist extractivism and Western Christian patriarchy. Pope Francis's own integral ecology participates in this deconstruction insofar as he critiques the dualisms that pertain specifically to politics, economics, and ecology. However, in the realms of gender and sexuality, Francis's adherence to traditional Catholic teaching about the nature of "man" and "woman" overlooks the way in which the binaries of sex and gender in Western Christian patriarchy were and continue to be formative in the perpetuation of racist, colonial, and extractivist paradigms.[5] While not all land and environmental

---

[5] For an excellent critique of Francis's integral ecology on this point, see Melissa Pagán, "Cultivating a Decolonial Feminist Integral Ecology: Extrac-

defenders surpass Francis's entrenched gender dualism, many do seek paths of interdependence and interconnection that explicitly and/or implicitly overcome these binaries and embody a holistic vision of human existence, even in the face of vulnerability, conflict, and even violence. Interestingly, the two Catholic priests and one Catholic religious woman whose ecomartyrdom we have contemplated in this book all saw the leadership of women as central to the struggle for land and ecological well-being. As we will discuss under the framework of decolonial feminism, Berta Cáceres was even more visionary and prophetic in her insistence that patriarchy must be dismantled along with capitalism and racism in order to liberate people and the planet from the rapacious violence of extractivist ecologies.

Third, integral ecology is a paradigm for being human that eschews violence and seeks creative and nonviolent paths of resistance and alternative living. While armed self-defense is sometimes necessary and entirely justified, a worldview that sees all life as sacred and interconnected is fundamentally invested in the preservation of life and the promotion of peaceful coexistence. Most environmental defenders have seen enough violence in their contexts to know, both strategically and spiritually, that violent conflict always ends up harming the earth and marginalized communities more than anyone else. Furthermore, land and environmental defenders know firsthand the power of creative forms of resistance that re-imagine and re-embody the world in both everyday life and larger struggles for social and environmental justice. As we have already seen Berta Cáceres profess in chapter 4, "You have the bullet. I have the word. The bullet dies when it is detonated. The word lives on when it is replicated." The bullet and the bulldozer alike seek invulnerability for some human beings at the expense of exacerbated vulnerability

---

tive Zones and the Nexus of the Coloniality of Being/Coloniality of Gender," *Journal of Hispanic/Latino Theology* 22, no. 1 (Spring 2020).

for others. And yet eventually the violence of bullets and bulldozers ensures self-destruction for us all. Environmental defenders know this and seek another way.

Buenos Vivires

Buen vivir, or good living, is a term that emerged in the 1990s and early 2000s from the Andean countries of South America—primarily Bolivia and Ecuador—to describe "a way of living in harmony with oneself (identity), with society (equity), and with nature (sustainability)."[6] Broadly speaking, the concept describes political, economic, cultural, and ecological postures that issue radical critiques of neoliberal development and embody alternative proposals for well-being and coexistence between human beings and the rest of the natural world. More specifically, discourses around *buen vivir* derived originally from the Quechua concept of *sumak kawsay*, which refers more to an ideal vision of "life in plentitude" or "harmonious life" than to the practical and ethical aspirations of living everyday life in relationships of interdependent harmony with other creatures at the level of personal, familial, communal, and intercommunal existence. This latter concept, which seems to correspond more directly to *buen vivir* or good living, is more accurately identified with the Quechua phrase *alli kawsay*. Concepts similar to both *sumak kawsay* and *alli kawsay* exist in other Indigenous cultures, and the language of *buen vivir* has been adopted by other Indigenous communities to describe their own ancestral practices of communitarian values, collective landholdings, and reciprocity with the natural world. We will discuss these Indigenous wellsprings of ecomartyrdom at greater length below.

---

[6] Antonio Luis Hidalgo-Capitán and Ana Patricia Cubillo-Guevara, "Deconstruction and Genealogy of Latin American Good Living (*Buen Vivir*): The (Triune) Good Living and Its Diverse Intellectual Wellsprings," *International Development Policy* 9 (2019): 23–50.

While the origins of *buen vivir* lie in Indigenous traditions, the concept also draws on sources of inspiration in other critiques of Western modernity. As Uruguayan intellectual Eduardo Gudynas puts it, *buen vivir* is a mixed formulation that

> results from connections between contributions from certain indigenous ways of knowing and from other critical currents within Western modernity. The contribution of indigenous ways of knowing is determinative; without them the original postures of *Buen Vivir* cannot be understood. But *Buen Vivir* is not a synonym for a specific indigenous culture, nor does it defend a return to a pre-colonial Andean past. Neither can it be reduced to Western concepts such as quality of life or well-being, or Greek philosophy.[7]

Given the multiple interpretations and expressions of *buen vivir*, Gudynas suggests that it is a phenomenon best understood in the plural; hence, *buenos vivires*. Indeed, other scholars offer a detailed deconstruction and genealogy of *buen vivir* as flowing from three different wellsprings: (1) "indigenist good living," which stems from the concepts of *sumak kawsay* and *alli kawsay* discussed above; (2) "socialist and statist good living," which stems from governmental processes in early twenty-first century Bolivia and Ecuador in which extractivist industries would be harnessed by the state to produce greater social equity; and (3) "ecologist and post-developmentalist good living," which stems from the anti-development and biocentric proposals of Latin American intellectuals and social-environmental movements.[8]

While contradictions and inequities exist among these three conceptions of Good Living, there are also ways in which they

---

[7] Eduardo Gudynas, "Alternativas al Desarrollo y Buen Vivir," in *El Buen Vivir como paradigma societal alternativo*, Economistas sin Fronteras, Dossieres EsF no. 23 (Otoño, 2016), 7.

[8] Hidalgo-Capitán and Cubillo-Guevara, "Deconstruction and Genealogy of Latin American Good Living."

overlap and mutually critique and inform one another. Many land environmental defenders operate out of a prophetic ecological imagination imbued with one or more of these conceptions of good living, whether they use this specific language or not.

Traditions of Commoning

In most integral ecologies and conceptions of *buen vivir*, the interdependence of all reality is experienced and embodied in communal practices of mutual care among humanity, the more-than-human world, and the divine. For almost all of our two or three hundred thousand years of existence as a species, human beings organized our habitation on the earth and our consumption of its goods communally, with almost all human land and water usage conducted on what "commoners" and political ecologists often call the "commons." Put very simply, commons are the diverse and often quite complex systems that human beings have created and implemented throughout human history to organize and manage our use of various goods of Creation communally. There are many different kinds of commons, but the commons to which many ecomartyrs have dedicated their lives are usually organized around goods necessary for the reproduction and sustained maintenance of human life—for example, common fields for farming or grazing livestock; common forests for foraging, hunting, and/or gathering firewood; and common rivers for fishing, drinking, irrigating crops, bathing, and washing clothes. Commons are not these natural resources themselves, but rather, in the words of commons scholar and activist David Bollier, the social, political, cultural and ecological "paradigms that combine a distinct community with a set of social practices, values and norms that are used to manage a resource. Put another way, a commons is *a resource + a community + a set of social protocols*."[9] Any given practice

---

[9] David Bollier, *Thinking Like a Commoner: A Short Introduction to the*

of commoning, therefore, requires shared or overlapping ecological imaginations that provide the cultural and/or religious framework within which commons are supported and maintained not only socially and ecologically but ceremonially and spiritually.

Commons are *not* the open-ended, free-for-all resource grabs that ecologist Garrett Hardin erroneously assumed them to be in his 1968 essay called "The Tragedy of the Commons."[10] Rather, commons are carefully organized means of managing collective property rights and usage that often take into careful account the needs of not only the human community of commoners but also the needs of the local landscape, waterways, flora, fauna, and other natural resources as well. Commons are therefore highly contextual, and the localized forms that they take vary immensely across time and place, according to the distinctiveness of any given local culture and ecosystem, even from one village to the next. They run the spectrum from egalitarian to hierarchical, and can be more or less ecologically sustainable. The most successful, long-standing commons, though—commons that best meet basic human needs over generations, or even millennia—are typically supported by decentralized, widespread, and active participation of commoners and by cultural, spiritual, and ecological practices that encourage and embody relationships of harmony and reciprocity with the more-than-human world.

Extractivism requires enclosure of the commons, so it is important to remember the history of commons enclosure in Europe, which is where the story of colonization and enclosure of the commons begins and then gets imposed on the rest of the world. Like most of the rest of Europe, British land tenure was managed collectively in the pre-Roman Iron Age, and commoners

---

Life of the Commons (Gabriola Island, BC: New Society Publishers, 2014), 15. Emphasis in the original.

[10] Garrett Hardin, "The Tragedy of the Commons," *Science* 162, no. 3859 (December 13, 1968): 1243–48.

continued to enjoy usufruct rights to land usage under Roman rule. This all begins to change in the early Middle Ages, when communal property was "brought under the control of local land-owners within a manorial system."[11] But even under feudalism, which was quite cruel and inhumane in many other ways, laws allowed commoners regulated access to the fields and forests that ensured provision of their daily bread. Slowly but surely, though, the lords of the manor brought more and more land under their direct control by force, for their own benefit and use, and the erosion of English commons accelerated from the sixteenth century to the nineteenth century. This process is known as the "enclosure of the commons." Bollier sums up the English enclosure movement quite plainly:

> The king, aristocracy and/or landed gentry stole the pastures, forests, wild game and water used by commoners, and declared them private property. Sometimes the enclosers seized lands with the formal sanction of Parliament, and sometimes they just took them by force. To keep commoners out, it was customary to evict them from the land and erect fences or hedges. Sheriffs and gangs of thugs made sure that no commoner would poach game from the king's land.[12]

Commoners suffered greatly under this process, and though they resisted in myriad ways, they were by and large forced to migrate to the towns and cities to work for a pittance in the growing proletariat of the industrial revolution, or to languish as beggars and paupers, who were criminalized, incarcerated, and/or shipped off to the newly established British colonies in the Americas and Australia.

---

[11] Derek Wall, *The Commons in History: Culture, Conflict, and Ecology* (Cambridge, MA: MIT Press, 2014), 25.

[12] Bollier, 42.

Silvia Federici reminds us that the enclosure of the commons affected women and gender roles in particularly harmful ways. Women were especially dependent on the commons for their "subsistence, autonomy, and sociality," and they were denied the private property rights that some men managed to acquire after enclosure. Furthermore, enclosure of the commons facilitated the rise of modern capitalist patriarchy, in which men generally left home to work in the industrial revolution, while women came to be more and more confined to the domestic realm, expected to reproduce laborers for the growing workforce. Women who resisted enclosures, who attempted to maintain the old ways of commoning (e.g., gathering medicinal plants from the woods), or who were not dependent on a male authority were too often accused of being witches and were subsequently drowned or burned at the stake.[13]

The rest of Europe followed a similar pattern of enclosure and displacement, as did the conquest and colonization of the Americas by European powers starting in the late fifteenth century, with the racist and genocidal addition of widespread slaughter of Indigenous people, along with the enslavement of Indigenous and then African persons. The landed aristocracy who sought to expand their empires in the "new world" were ironically, tragically, aided and abetted by displaced European commoners (and their descendants), many of whom benefited from the access to land grants under settler colonialism. Under Latin American colonialism, significant access to common lands persisted, albeit under the control of European rulers and *encomenderos*. These lands, however, were also enclosed over the course of the nineteenth and twentieth centuries, further displacing Indigenous and *campesino* communities and further concentrating access to land in the hands of national oligarchies and transnational corporations.

---

[13] Silvia Federici, *Caliban and the Witch: Women, the Body, and Primitive Accumulation* (New York: Autonomedia, 2004).

Nevertheless, a robust movement of resistance to commons enclosure persisted throughout this period, and the resistance of Indigenous peoples to European conquest and colonization of the Americas can also be understood as resistance to violent enclosures of Indigenous commons. Land and environmental defenders carry on a long tradition, therefore, of resistance to enclosure of the many and varied commons of Creation. Recall the poem dedicated to Father Josimo, remembering this particular ecomartyr for his struggle against fences: the fences of fear and of hatred, of the land and of hunger, of the body and of the landowner. To a certain extent, Josimo, like many other defenders, also persisted in tearing down the fences of gender hierarchies to recover the sacred power of women in managing and maintaining the commons. Land and environmental defenders' practices of commoning therefore represent alternatives to the extractivist imaginary, and the roots of such practices are watered and nourished by the wellsprings to which we will shortly turn.

Decolonial Feminisms

One final framework that draws together various commonalities among some land and environmental defenders in the Americas is "decolonial feminism." By no means are all land and environmental defenders feminists, let alone decolonial feminists. Nevertheless, a common thread that runs through many defenders' work is a commitment to intersectional analysis of the overlapping oppressions imposed by the persistent coloniality of knowledge, being, and power in the world. The term "coloniality" refers to the matrix of power relations put into place under European colonialism that continues to define who can produce knowledge, who counts as a full human being, and who controls the military, political, and economic reins of power in the current world system. Eurocentrism and white supremacy, patriarchy and heteronormativity, capitalism and extractivism—these oppressive forces are all legacies of colonialism that continue to destroy human lives and are progressively destroying the planet to this very day. It is white, wealthy, cisgender, straight men who have the right to produce knowledge; to count as full human beings with dignity and autonomy; and to maintain a stranglehold on military, political, and economic power over other human beings and the earth itself. It is usually these same men, and those adjacent to them, who are disproportionately agents and beneficiaries of the extractivist projects that land and environmental defenders resist.

Eurocentric feminism neglects the intersections of oppression that coalesce to form the colonial matrix of power, focusing only on gender and often seeking equal footing in the white male power structure. Even ecofeminism, which links the domination of women to the domination of the earth, tends to neglect the roles of race, class, and sexuality, let alone colonialism, in the systems of domination that it seeks to critique. Decolonial feminism, in contrast, is nourished by the critiques and liberatory praxes of Black feminism, womanism, feminisms of color, and "two-thirds world" feminisms, along with the embodied struggles of marginalized women in the face of class, race, gender, and sexual oppressions. In the United States, the term "intersectionality" has come to stand for the way in which identity, oppression, and/or power and privilege result from these multiple, intersecting systems of domination.[14] Decolonial feminism places this framework in global perspective, with a critical analysis of colonialism and coloniality as the origin of various structures of hierarchy and oppression. Berta Cáceres's analysis is clear on this point, although she uses the term "*coloniaje*" to describe the problem, rather than "coloniality":

> It is the same thing. The names change, but it's the same. It is colonialism, the same colonialism from five hundred years ago,

---

[14]   See the forthcoming collection of writings by the legal scholar who coined the term intersectionality: Kimberlé Crenshaw, *On Intersectionality: Essential Writings* (New York: The New Press, 2023).

and now we see an even more aggressive capitalist onslaught on Indigenous peoples. We got to a point where we have to fight for the survival of Indigenous peoples. We got to a point where, if we do not fight, we will disappear in a short time.[15]

The incursion of extractivist projects, military bases, cultural hegemony, and media propaganda all contribute to the *coloniaje* that Berta and many other land and environmental defenders resist. In Ochy Curiel's words:

We could say that Berta Cáceres's *coloniaje* is another way of calling a pattern of power that has implied extractivism, the economic dependence of countries of the South on those of the North, based on the exploitation of some groups and the unequal distribution of wealth at a global level, but also within the countries of the South, all of which has caused the material, social, and spiritual dehumanization of certain groups that have been historically placed in the lowest social hierarchies, such as Indigenous peoples, Black people, and farmworkers.[16]

Based on her analysis of *coloniaje*, Berta insisted that the struggle against oppression and ecological degradation must resist fragmentation and seek integration of the struggles against all forms of oppression and domination, especially capitalism, racism, and patriarchy.

On the flip side of resistance, decolonial feminisms are rooted in a socially and ecologically wholistic vision and praxis of "a world in which many worlds are free to co-exist."[17] This vision is

---

[15] Berta Cáceres quoted in Ochy Curiel, "Berta Cáceres and Decolonial Feminism," trans. Bruna Barros and Jess Oliveira, *WSQ: Women's Studies Quarterly* 49 (Fall/Winter 2021): 72.

[16] Curiel, 72.

[17] Comité Clandestino Revolucionario Indígena-Comandancia General

nourished by a diversity of social and ecological imaginations—these are the more specific wellsprings of the witness to which we now turn.

Prophetic Ecological Imaginations: Wellsprings of the Witness

It is possible to articulate (literally, draw together) the ecological imaginations of land and environmental defenders in broad terms of integral ecologies, *buenos vivires*, traditions of commoning, and decolonial feminisms. But these are simply umbrella frameworks that help us think about linkages between the worldviews that fuel the commitments of the various ecomartyrs whose witness we are contemplating in this book. However, each of these individuals and their communities embody distinctive ecological imaginations that sometimes stand in stark contrast to one another and/or sometimes overlap and synthesize well together. Therefore, it is important to seek the deeper sources of the cultural, spiritual, and theological worldviews that motivate their witness. These deeper wellsprings transcend and extend beyond the following three families of ecological imagination, but considering these three particular wellsprings can be helpful for deepening our understanding of the sources from which ecomartyrs draw their inspiration, courage, compassion, and hope.

Indigenous Cosmovisions

The Indigenous cosmovisions of Abya Yala and Turtle Island are as diverse as the landscapes that Indigenous peoples inhabit, the languages they speak, the ritual ceremonies they practice, and the colonial histories that they have navigated over the course of the

---

del Ejército Zapatista de Liberación Nacional, "Cuarta Declaración de la Selva Lacandona," January 1, 1996, enlacezapatista.ezln.org.mx.

past 500+ years. It is impossible to reduce such diversity to any one essential characteristic or definition of indigeneity, let alone any one characteristically Indigenous cosmovision. To attempt such reduction runs the risk of romanticization, objectification, and even re-colonization of a vast array of living, breathing, dynamic human cultures. Nevertheless, Native peoples and scholars of Indigenous cosmovisions do identify some family resemblances that are particularly conducive to shared identity and collaboration among Indigenous communities, and that are often influential in Latin American communities that may not explicitly identify as Indigenous but are of at least partial Indigenous descent. In what follows, we will seek a basic understanding of some salient Indigenous family resemblances that show up in the ecological imaginations of many land and environmental defenders. The witness of Lenca river guardian Berta Cáceres is particularly illuminating for these family resemblances,[18] but we will also consider selected examples from other Indigenous contexts as well.

First, Indigenous cosmovisions are often deeply rooted in particular places, in particular lands and landscapes, and in relation to the more-than-human elements and inhabitants of these places, lands, and landscapes. Place-based spiritualities are fostered in and through sacred relationships with highly localized but cosmically significant places and elements of the more-than-human world. Native scholars of religion have articulated this foundation in space and place as a salient point of contrast with the traditional Western Christian emphasis on linear time and salvation history. Vine Deloria Jr. made this critique plain in his 1971 book *God Is Red*, and George Tinker has rearticulated this distinction for

---

[18] For a more robust analysis of the Indigenous spirituality that animated Berta Cáceres's leadership, see Mónica A. Maher, "A Rebellion of Spirituality: On the Power of Indigenous Civil Resistance in Honduras," in *Civil Resistance and Violent Conflict in Latin America: Mobilizing for Rights*, ed. Cécile Mouly and Esperanza Hernández Delgado (Cham: Springer International, 2019), 41–63.

the twenty-first century with a clear emphasis on the primacy of Creation, of the earth, and of the land in American Indian spirituality.[19] Human beings are always situated locally, within our particular niches on the earth, within Creation, as relatives to one another and to all that exists. Robin Wall Kimmerer has facilitated communication of this emphasis on place-based spirituality to a more popular audience in her best-selling book *Braiding Sweetgrass*, where she posits that human beings are the "newest arrivals on earth." Having emerged from the more-than-human world—and in some cosmovisions like that of the Maya, having been fashioned from corn—we are the younger siblings of the rest of Creation. Human beings would therefore do well to pay attention to and learn from our elders in the web of life.[20] Cultivating a sacred sense of human origination from and place within the more-than-human world is essential to not only knowing but also embodying the truth of our embeddedness in the sacred whole.

Berta Cáceres also articulated the primary relationship between human beings and the more-than-human world in the Lenca cosmovision as one of origination: "In our cosmovisions, we are beings who have emerged from the earth, from water, and from corn."[21] In other words, the foundation of human existence lies in the land, the waterways, and the more-than-human elements that give us life. Therefore, in the Lenca cosmovision, particular places from whence the people draw existence and continued sustenance are considered sacred. The Gualcarque River that Berta and COPINH were fighting to protect when she was killed is a sacred river, a place that is a source of life and

---

[19] See Vine Deloria Jr., *God Is Red: A Native View of Religion*, 30th Anniversary Edition (Golden, CO: Fulcrum, 2003), and George E. "Tink" Tinker, *American Indian Liberation: A Theology of Sovereignty* (Maryknoll, NY: Orbis Books, 2008).

[20] Robin Wall Kimmerer, *Braiding Sweetgrass: Indigenous Wisdom, Scientific Knowledge, and the Teachings of Plants* (Minneapolis: Milkweed Editions, 2011).

[21] "Berta Cáceres Acceptance Speech."

fertility for the people and the land, a place that is inhabited by girl spirits that protect the river and the Lenca people.[22]

Other Indigenous struggles for land and environmental justice are similarly founded in a commitment to the sacredness of the earth in general and local lands and waterways in particular. For example, the movement of Indigenous water protectors against the Dakota Access Pipeline at Standing Rock has been fueled by a commitment to the sacred nature of the lands and rivers that would be harmed and desecrated by the pipeline. The conjunction of the Cannonball and Missouri Rivers is a place of sacred significance in the cosmovision and spirituality of the Standing Rock Sioux, and it had already been irreparably disturbed in previous interventions by the U.S. Army Corps of Engineers.[23] What appears to be a straightforward struggle for environmental justice is deeply rooted in a sacred, place-based spirituality. The motto "Water is Life" is by no means simply a pragmatic or transactional understanding of the value of water to human existence. Rather, it conveys the sacredness of water as a site of creation and re-creation in a broader cosmovision, within which human life is a sacred part of a larger sacred whole. For this reason, another motto of the movement is "Defend the Sacred."

Similarly, the women of Cherán in Michoacán, Mexico, were motivated at least in part by the sacredness of the forests and waterways of their territory when they rose up against the violence of illegal logging and monocrop agriculture in 2011. Even prior to this uprising, the Purépecha community in Cherán had been engaged in a long struggle to recover their Indigenous territory, culture, and identity. Much of this struggle has been centered on recovery of the Purépecha language and customs, but

---

[22] Claudia Korol, *Las Revoluciones de Berta: Conversaciones con Claudia Korol* (Buenos Aires: Ediciones América Libre, 2018), 159.

[23] Jon Eagle Sr., "When Man Changes the Land, It Is Changed Forever," *Indian Country Today,* September 12, 2018, https://indiancountrytoday.com/archive/when-man-changes-the-land-it-is-changed-forever.

above all, the force behind the recovery of Purépecha territory, culture, and identity is concentrated in the forest and its sacred significance to the community. Consider the following litany of Purépecha women's reflections on the sacredness of the forests that surround Cherán:

- The forest has always given us all that we need to exist as a community, and so we've inherited from generation to generation a sense of being Purépecha in Cherán that has to do with respect for and connection with the forest that's instilled in us from a young age.
- The forest is our home. It's our home, and the forest is also the people. The forest is the trees, the hills, the animals, the plants, the air. The forest is everything.
- The forest for me is very important. Many call it the lungs of the earth, but for me it's more like the heart.
- For me it's like unity, territory, something that's important to all of Cherán, like our *mamá*, like our mother. At the end of the day, it's mysterious, a little scary, and really fantastical, or in this case, a little mystical.
- There's a wise word [in the Purépecha language] ... that means "where the sources of water abound," where everything you need to live as a human being is there.... There's work, there are plants, there are mushrooms, there are fruits. For us the forest has a meaning that is enormous. There are animals, rabbits, deer, squirrels, which we also draw sustenance from. For us, really, that's where we find what we need to exist on this earth. What greater meaning could there be? It's everything.
- We can't explain who we are without the forest. It's more than just a place. It has much spirituality; it has much that is symbolic; it has much that we believe in.

- The forest also provides water for everything needed to live, and the sources of water in the forest are sacred wellsprings of existence and flourishing for the forest as a whole and the people that depend on the forest for life.[24]

Flowing from this rootedness of spirituality in Creation and in the particularities of place, a second family resemblance among Indigenous cosmovisions emerges in what Kimmerer calls "the grammar of animacy." Western anthropologists' use of the category of "animism" to describe Indigenous worldviews often presupposes and thus superimposes a hierarchical dualism between spirit and matter. But the grammar of animacy refuses any such bifurcation of created existence. Lands, landscapes, and waterways, along with the plant, animal, and mineral elements of local ecosystems, are not only sacred in Indigenous cosmovisions; they are often understood to be sentient subjects of interrelational coexistence, communication, and co-creation with one another and their human relatives. Kimmerer notes that recognition of and respect for this animacy is woven into the Ojibwe language, in which all elements and inhabitants of Creation are imbued with an aliveness that is expressed in the form of verbs that express their particular ways of being in the world. When she first encountered this phenomenon while studying Ojibwe, she was resistant to the idea that a "Saturday" or a "bay" could be expressed as a verb, but refusing to surrender to the logic of Western Christian missionaries and boarding schools, she says she "heard the zap of synapses firing":

> An electric current sizzled down my arm and through my finger, and practically scorched the page where that one word [*wiikwegamaa*] lay. In that moment I could smell the water of the bay, watch it rock against the shore and

---

[24] *Mujeres del Fuego* [Women of Fire] podcast, November 4, 2021, Audible.com.

hear it sift onto the sand. A bay is a noun only if water is dead. When bay is a noun, it is defined by humans, trapped between its shores and contained by the word. But the verb *wiikwegamaa*—to be a bay—releases the water from bondage and lets it live. "To be a bay" holds the wonder that, for this moment, the living water has decided to shelter itself between these shores, conversing with cedar roots and a flock of baby mergansers. Because it could do otherwise— become a stream or an ocean or a waterfall, and there are verbs for that, too. To be a hill, to be a sandy beach, to be a Saturday, all are possible verbs in a world where everything is alive. Water, land, and even a day, the language a mirror for seeing the animacy of the world, the life that pulses through all things, through pines and nuthatches and mushrooms. This is the language I hear in the woods; this is the language that lets us speak of what wells up all around us. And the vestiges of boarding schools, the soap-wielding missionary wraiths, hang their heads in defeat.[25]

Berta Cáceres attested to this "language that lets us speak of what wells up all around us" in and through her immersion in the Lenca cosmovision. Lenca recognition of more-than-human animacy is passed down by women in the community through ceremonies and everyday practices that challenge the primacy of human agency with an affirmation of both the agency of guardian spirits within the more-than-human world, on the one hand, and the subjectivity of the more-than-human world itself, on the other. And yet the agency and subjectivity at work here contrasts sharply with Western conceptions of the autonomous individual. The alive- ness and agency of human beings and the more-than-human world are constituted precisely in and through relationality and intercon- nection. Berta's own accounts of her defense of the Gualcarque

---

[25] Kimmerer, *Braiding Sweetgrass*, 55.

River from the Agua Zarca hydroelectric dam project indicate that the Gualcarque River is *protected* by the spirits of young girls, and it *beckons* to the Lenca people to swim in its calming waters. The river *told* Berta that the movement to protect the Gualcarque would prevail. And the Gualcarque and all the threatened rivers of the world *call* on humanity to take action on behalf of the rights of rivers and of Mother Earth.

Indigenous resistance to the anthropocentrism of modern liberal agency and respect for the living sentience, relationality, and agency of the more-than-human world tends to cultivate relationships of deep respect, humble listening, and mutual protection between human beings, the divine, the earth, and all of its inhabitants: Between human beings and the divine creator of all that exists. Between human beings and the land, with all of its living spirits, its soil, animals, plants, and trees. And between human beings and rivers, their living spirits, their water, fish, shrimp, and swimming holes. A cosmovision grounded and expressed in a grammar and experience of animacy affirms all of this beautiful abundance, along with all of the limitations and constraints that must accompany building a commons that exists within the bounds of such relationships. What is more, the animacy and sentience of the more-than-human world requires local, contextual relationships of mutuality with the land, water, and creatures in the places where human beings reside and make our homes, not just a hierarchical stewardship of inanimate resources.

This leads to a third family resemblance among Indigenous cosmovisions: interdependency and reciprocity between human beings and the more-than-human world. Recognizing the sacredness and animacy of place and of more-than-human creatures situates human beings in relationships with the sacred subjects of Creation that must be carefully tended in order to maintain balance and harmony in the world. Tinker explains the concept and practice of reciprocity well:

> Reciprocity involves first of all a spiritual understanding of
> the cosmos and the place of humans in the process of the
> cosmic whole. It begins with an understanding that every-
> thing that humans do has an effect on the rest of the world
> around us. Even when we cannot clearly know what that
> effect is in any particular act, we know that there is an effect.
> Thus, Indian peoples, in different cultural configurations,
> have always struggled to know how to act appropriately in
> the world. Knowing that every action has its unique effect
> has always meant that there had to be some sort of built-in
> compensation for human actions, some act of reciprocity.[26]

The need for acts of reciprocity is especially important when
human beings commit acts of violence that are necessary for human
survival and sustenance. Taking more-than-human life in order for
humans to live—taking the lives of plants and certainly the lives
of animals—must be accompanied by acts of "spiritual reciproca-
tion" that restore the balance of existence. Tinker thus explains
that in many Indigenous cultures, "a ceremony of reciprocity must
accompany the harvesting of vegetable foods such as corn or the
harvesting of medicinals, such as cedar, even when only part of a
plant is taken."[27] These ceremonies cultivate respect for the land and
our more-than-human relatives such that gratuitous and unthinking
acts of violence should be avoided and only that which is required
for the fullness of human life should be taken from the earth.
Extractivism and neoliberal development projects are antithetical
to this cosmovision, for as Tinker notes, "there is no ceremony for
clear-cutting an entire forest."[28]

Berta learned the ins and outs of reciprocity with the earth
from the Lenca people, and she studied ceremonial practices of

---

[26] Tinker, 68.
[27] Tinker, 68.
[28] Tinker, 70.

reciprocity under the tutelage of María Pascuala Vásquez—a
Lenca elder known as "Pascualita," who serves as the spiritual teacher and *primera dama*, or first lady, of COPINH.[29]
Pascualita regularly presides over traditional ceremonies called
"*composturas*," in which the community assembles an altar full
of offerings to Mother Earth in "payment" and thanksgiving for
the abundance that the land provides.[30] The altar includes plants,
flowers, candles, incense, *chicha* (alcohol), *chilate* (a fermented
corn drink), food products, fireworks, chocolate, and/or a cross.
Even where this latter Christian symbol is incorporated into
the offering, the ceremony retains an Indigenous sense of reciprocity with the earth that fosters respect for the sacred power
of Creation to provide for the flourishing of life. COPINH
often begins their activities with a *compostura* smoke ceremony
indicating this sense of mutual relationality and reciprocity with
the elements of the more-than-human world. The *compostura* is a
reminder that, as Pascualita remarks, "From the beginning, it was
a political *and* a spiritual fight."[31]

Each of these elements of Indigenous cosmovisions—place-
based spiritualities, the animacy of all Creation, and human
reciprocity with the more-than-human world—all flow together
with myriad other Indigenous traditions. Taken together, these
elements form wellsprings of collective spiritual power that offer
Indigenous land and environmental defenders not only a life-giving
ecological imagination but also the strength, protection, creativity,
and joy that are necessary for a struggle that involves many risks.
As Berta put it, "Here it is easy to be killed. The cost we pay is very

---

[29] See Nina Lakhani, *Who Killed Berta Cáceres? Dams, Death Squads, and
an Indigenous Defender's Battle for the Planet* (New York: Verso, 2020), 45.

[30] Nora Sagastume, "Compostura a la Madre Tierra," Interview with
María Pascuala Vásquez, https://soundcloud.com/discover/sets/track-
stations:3016031.

[31] See Lakhani, 45.

high. But most important is that we have a force that comes from our ancestors, a heritage of thousands of years, of which we are proud. That is our nourishment and our conviction at the hour of struggle."[32]

Religions of the African Diaspora

Another web of ancestral traditions that animate many land and environmental defenders in the Americas lies in the cosmovisions and spiritual practices of African diasporic religions. When enslaved Africans were kidnapped and forcibly transported as chattel to the Americas, they brought with them the Indigenous cosmovisions of African religions and the agricultural practices of their people. Leah Penniman, founder of Soul Fire Farm in upstate New York, tells the stories of African ancestors who braided seeds into one another's hair in order to preserve the possibility of life in their unknown destination; of enslaved ancestors who, "with those seeds, carried Indigenous ways of knowing the land"; and of Black farmers who practiced Afro-Indigenous forms of agrarianism in the American South before being driven off their lands by racial terrorism in the century after emancipation.[33] Ecowomanism and Black agrarianism are overlapping frameworks for healing and recovering these ancestral legacies in the United States and Canada. Ecowomanist theologian and ethicist Melanie Harris warns, however, that such recovery must be undertaken with care, given the colonial legacies of mainstream environmentalism: "In the frantic urgency of climate change, environmentalists of every discourse are often left scrambling, ready to pounce and exploit the very blackness and African cosmological connection embedded in African indig-

---

[32] Cited and translated in Maher, 50.

[33] "Black Agrarian Wisdom—Young Farmers Conference 2019," Stone Barns Center for Food and Agriculture YouTube channel, December 5, 2019, https://youtu.be/nEQOqCxKHXY. Soul Fire Farm is "an Afro-Indigenous centered community farm committed to uprooting racism and seeding sovereignty in the food system." See https://www.soulfirefarm.org/.

enous religions for the sake of saving their own (colonial) ecological home (or their ecological souls)."[34]

Nevertheless, Harris argues that rooting ecowomanism in African cosmologies is not doomed to participate in this colonial legacy of exploitation:

> Ecowomanism honors its African cosmological roots as a valid and authentic epistemology of how to be an ethical earthling, living on the planet today. As many African peoples' values are shaped by their religion and religious practice, so, too, are ecowomanism's values shaped by their identity as descendants of Africa, carrying embodied and actual indigenous roots. To honor African cosmologies— and the theories and practices of environmental justice that are informed by them—is an act and method of resistance in that it joins the postcolonial move to expose the remnants of colonial ecology and dismantle this by infusing the field with true ecowomanist epistemology. Womanist earth stories, African American agricultural knowledge, and African ethical worldviews model inter-connectedness and help us honor the earth and live faithfully on the planet with others.[35]

The preservation and recovery of Afro-Indigenous cosmovisions and spiritual practices, therefore, often serves as a wellspring of resistance, creativity, and courage for ecological healing, environmental justice, food sovereignty, and land reclamation in Black communities of North America.

In Latin America and the Caribbean, meanwhile, Afro-Indigenous ways of knowing and belonging to the land have been

---

[34] Melanie L. Harris, *Ecowomanism: African American Women and Earth-Honoring Faiths* (Maryknoll, NY: Orbis Books, 2017), 75.

[35] Harris, 76.

preserved and animated by the centuries-old practice of African-derived religions such as Candomblé and Umbanda in Brazil, Santería in Cuba, Vodon in Haiti, and Dugu among the Garifuna people of Central America's Caribbean coast. In many of these locations, African-derived religions were historically outlawed and persecuted by church and state, but managed to survive and thrive in remote and isolated contexts such as *quilombos* in Brazil, under the cover of a Catholic façade, and/or in syncretic relationship with Catholicism.

As a country where the majority of the African diaspora in the Americas resides and nearly half of the population can claim African ancestry, Brazil is a particularly illuminating context for understanding the staying power of Afro-Indigenous religions as wellsprings of the struggle for environmental justice and ecological well-being. While religious persecution is no longer legal in Brazil, violence against African-based religions such as Candomblé has been on the rise, due in large part to the rise in fervent Evangelicalism and Pentecostalism among gang members. Nevertheless, these traditions persist and give life not only to social and cultural struggles for identity, Black pride, and racial justice, but also to movements for environmental justice and ecological well-being.

Valdina Oliveira Pinto, respectfully known as Makota Valdina, is an environmental ethicist, human rights advocate, and ritual elder of a Candomblé temple, in Bahia, Brazil.[36] She explains the nature of Candomblé from her perspective as devotee and spiritual leader of the tradition:

> Candomblé is the traditions, the rites, the practices that we Afro-Brazilians recreated in Brazil, from what

---

[36] See Valdina Oliveira Pinto and Rachel E. Harding, "Afro-Brazilian Religion, Resistance and Environmental Ethics," in *Ecowomanism, Religion, and Ecology*, ed. Melanie L. Harris (Leiden: Brill, 2017), 70–80.

the Africans who were enslaved brought with them. We recreated and gave new meanings to those African rites, rituals, traditions and worldviews and made Candomblé. For us, Black people in Brazil, Candomblé is much more than just a form of spirituality or a religion. Candomblé is an expression of resistance. It is a way of affirming an identity that was taken through the process of enslavement. Candomblé is a way of reconstructing a family that was dispersed through the slave trade. Candomblé is a way of life that differs from Western visions of the world.[37]

Combining cultural, linguistic, and religious elements from the various West African peoples that were enslaved and brought to Brazil, Candomblé was born in the *quilombo* communities of fugitive slaves. While the first forms of the tradition did not have physical temples, Makota Valdina remarks, "We had nature. We had earth, water, plants, stones, the animals. We had the essence.... Our temple was the natural world."[38] Today, *quilombolas* are on the front lines of defending land and environmental human rights, and Candomblé remains an animating force for many of them.

Since the emergence of Candomblé in *quilombos*, its traditions evolved and diversified over time, resulting in various "nations," in which distinct groups preserve the distinct spiritual practices, sacred songs, movements, and prayers in the ritual language particular to the given "nation." Each nation cultivates the spiritual realm of *nkisis*, *orixá*, or *vodun*—all of which refer in different ritual languages to the divine life-forces or energies that manifest in the sacred powers of the natural world. These life-forces are often associated with particular West African deities and/or Roman Catholic

---

[37] Pinto and Harding, 72.
[38] Pinto and Harding, 73.

saints who once served as cover for West African cosmologies or became syncretized with them. Regardless of the ritual language used to refer to these life-forces, though, Makota Valdina notes that all of these terms refer to the same thing: "Because earth is earth,.... And for as many languages as there are in the world, there are that many names for the earth. But the essence of the earth is one." The *nkisis, orixá,* and *vodun* have their essence in the natural world—in the land, water, stones, plants, and animals, all of which are ancestors to human beings. "Plants, water, the mineral and vegetal life, even the animals that we say are 'irrational'—they are all our ancestors. We arrived here after them. All of those life-forms had to exist first in order for us humans to exist."

Makota Valdina remarks that the Creator God or Goddess knew that we would need these elements for human life, but Candomblé is far from an anthropocentric worldview. As with the Indigenous cosmovisions discussed above, Candomblé understands human beings to be late arrivals to the earth. This understanding cultivates ecological humility among human beings, who "[s]ometimes think we are so special, so remarkable, but we're not. We need the natural world. We need nature."[39] Also like Indigenous spiritualities in the Americas, Candomblé fosters an ecological imagination in which human beings can and should practice relationships of reciprocity and communication with the spiritual vibrancy of the more-than-human creatures and natural elements in our world. For example, Makota Valdina advocates speaking with the stars and talking to the sun. And yet this cosmocentric worldview also honors the beauty and sacred power of human beings, who are also stars and suns in our own right—"Each one of us is a sun."[40] The ecological imagination of Candomblé can thus provide access to the animating forces of

---

[39] Pinto and Harding, 74.
[40] Pinto and Harding, 75.

the universe that reproduce and preserve the continuation of life on earth. Practitioners of Candomblé draw on this wellspring for daily sustenance and for the strength and empowerment required to face down the extractivist forces of destruction that seek to steal *quilombo* lands, clear-cut forests, build mega-dams, and pollute the land and water.

The Garifuna people (Garinagu) of the Caribbean coast of Central America (primarily in Belize, Guatamala, and Honduras) are similarly animated by ancestral traditions that harken back to African roots and processes of intercultural influence and syncretism that took place in the Caribbean over the course of centuries. Previously referred to by the British as "Black Caribs," the Garifuna people originated in the coming together of Carib and Arawak[41] Indigenous peoples with enslaved West Africans on the island of St. Vincent. Garifuna spirituality thus integrates core elements of West African and Indigenous religions, emphasizing the values of relationality and harmony in both. While the Garinagu place highest priority on reciprocity in relation to ancestors, their philosophy also requires cultivation of harmony with the environment. According to one Garifuna commentator in Belize,

> The basic idea is that there should be harmony, a balance in the relationship between the individual and everything around him including the social, spiritual and environment in which he is an integral part. We see our oneness with the world around us. Our existence and our future are inextricably linked with the world and the environ-

---

[41] Keri Vacanti Brondo notes that the Garifuna use these terms to describe their history, contrasting with the archaeological and scholarly use of the term "Taíno." I follow her lead in referring to the Garifuna as she reports that they refer to themselves. See Keri Vacanti Brondo, "Land Loss and Garifuna Women's Activism on Honduras' North Coast," *Journal of International Women's Studies* 9, no. 1 (November 2007).

ment [social, spiritual, and physical].[42]

All aspects of the environment—social, spiritual, and physical—are considered to be sacred, and Garifuna spirituality cultivates a sense of connection to and responsibility for the land and the earth, which symbolizes life.

For example, the daily process of making bread from the cassava root is imbued with both gratitude for the goods of the earth as gifts provided by God and responsibility for returning the gift (in the form of cassava peelings) to the earth so that the cycle of life and regeneration can continue. In the words of Jerris Valentine: "Our Garifuna people believed that God in Her goodness will provide and make the earth yield plenty. Therefore there is respect for the land. We leave the tender parts of the cassava in the ground for its nourishment so that we can come back—and if not us—others after us can return to the harvest and be fed."[43] Similarly, traditional healers embody reverence and respect for the earth when they gather herbal medicines with care, blessing the land with holy water, asking permission of the plants, gathering plants only at certain times of day, and only gathering what is necessary. Furthermore, Garifuna spirituality also embodies a cosmic connection beyond the land to include the sun, which is recognized as an essential element of life and is greeted and dismissed each day with songs at sunrise and sunset. Perhaps even more pertinent to the issue of murdered land and environmental defenders is the fact that Garifuna culture is matrifocal (maternally focused): women are at the center of the Garifuna relationship to the earth, and land

---

[42] Barbara Flores, "The Garifuna *Dugu* Ritual in Belize: A Celebration of Relationships," in *Gender, Ethnicity, and Religion: Views from the Other Sides,* ed. by Rosemary Radford Ruether (Minneapolis: Fortress Press, 2002), 149.

[43] Rev. Jerris Valentine, "Traditional Social Life, Garifuna Perspective and the Contribution of the Garifuna Woman" (unpublished paper, January 1996), 4. Cited in Flores, "The Garifuna *Dugu* Ritual," 151.

tenure passes down through women.[44] Garifuna women, like Berta
Cáceres's dear friend Miriam Miranda, therefore play a key role in
the work of defending the land and environment from incursion
by extractivist projects like palm oil plantations and the tourist
industry. Such women are therefore prime targets of violence by
the networks of power that seek to appropriate Garifuna territory
for profit.[45]

In sum, the values of relationality, reciprocity, balance, and
harmony with the earth, along with respect and care for the environment, are deeply embedded in African-based traditions as
disparate as ecowomanism, Black agrarianism, Candomblé, and
Garifuna spirituality. The wellsprings of land and environmental
defense in the religions and cultures of the African diaspora run
wide and deep indeed.

The Sacramental Imagination of Postconciliar Catholicism

Another significant wellspring that provides an animating soulforce
for many land and environmental defenders, especially in Latin
America, is the sacramental imagination, which Mary Catherine
Hilkert describes as a worldview that "emphasizes the presence of the
God who is self-communicating love" and "the creation of human
beings in the image of God." Hilkert roots the sacramental imagination in the mystery of the incarnation of God in Jesus of Nazareth,
whose crucifixion impels Christians to "proclaim the cross in a world
of radical suffering."[46] The sacramental imagination of the Catholic
tradition in the Americas became explicitly attuned to the crosses
of human history and the structural sins of injustice, oppression,
and violence in the wake of Vatican II, the development of libera-

---

[44] See Brondo, 104–106.

[45] See Brondo.

[46] Mary Catherine Hilkert, *Naming Grace: Preaching and the Sacramental
Imagination* (New York: Continuum, 1997), 193.

tion theology, and the emergence of ecclesial base communities in the late twentieth century. As these expressions of the sacramental imagination developed over the past fifty years, they also began to tap into deeper wellsprings of ecological consciousness and Creation spirituality present in the Christian tradition and beyond.

Before delving further into this wellspring, however, it is important to remember that Western Catholic theology and European Christianity in general have been complicit in the anti-ecological imaginaries of colonialism, capitalism, and the forms of extractivism that have resulted in the twin horrors of ecocide and genocide in the Americas. Much ink has been spilled on Christianity's responsibility for environmental degradation since Lynn White's famous 1968 essay, "The Historical Roots of Our Ecological Crisis." Most of this work neglects to consider the responsibility of Christian colonialism for the crisis, but colonial Christianity provided theological justification for the displacement of human beings from the land through a hierarchical racialization of humanity and a colonizing conception of gender and the natural world. "To be saved" by European Christianity was to be forcibly removed or extracted from the places that Indigenous and African communities had belonged to for generations and even millennia. This sin of theological extractivism contributed to the logic of economic extractivism that took hold in the Americas and has accelerated in its intensity to this day.

To some, the wellsprings of Western Christianity are therefore irredeemably colonial and toxic, and will only continue to contribute to the intersecting oppressions of capitalism, racism, and patriarchy. This position has its merits and is understandable, especially given the horrors of Western Christian history and the seemingly intractable nature of Christian forms of anthropocentrism, patriarchy, and white supremacy. However, the coloniality of the Catholic tradition began to crack in the twentieth century, allowing for the deeper, socially and ecologically liberating wellsprings of biblical faith and the sacramental imagination to flow through. While the reforms of the Second Vatican Council did not entirely undo the theological or ecclesial coloniality of Roman Catholicism, its spirit of *aggiornamento* did provide some new theological and pastoral openings that have great potential for decolonizing and reimagining the tradition.

When at the start of the council Pope John XXIII communicated that he desired for the church to become a "church of the poor," and the bishops who signed the Pact of the Catacombs committed themselves to this aim, they began to realign the church with the liberating gospel of Jesus Christ, as opposed to the idolatrous and colonizing gospel of Empire. When the council declared in *Gaudium et Spes* that "the joys and hopes, the grief and anguish of the people of our time, especially of those who are poor or afflicted, are the joys and hopes, the grief and anguish of the followers of Christ as well,"[47] it opened a colonial church up to learning from and entering into solidarity with movements of colonized and impoverished peoples struggling for liberation. When the council made the initial steps of recognizing the value and truth that is present in the religions of the world, it offered the possibility of dialogue and friendship with non-Christian peoples, rather than conquest and conversion. When the Latin American bishops met at Medellín in 1968 and Puebla in 1979 to implement the reforms of the council in their own context, they committed the Latin American church to both a prophetic critique of the social structures that cause injustice and violence and a ministry of solidarity and accompaniment grounded in God's own preferential option for the poor. When the Catholic social tradition then evolved to incorporate the preferential option for the poor, the church took one step further toward the life-giving and liberating gospel of Jesus. When liberation theo-

---

[47] Second Vatican Council, *Gaudium et Spes: Pastoral Constitution on the Church in the Modern World*, December 7, 1965, www.vatican.va, § 1.

logians in Latin America and around the world recognized and entered into solidarity with grassroots movements for social, cultural, economic, and political liberation, they were not only de-linking the church from centuries of alliance with Empire. They were also following the God of the Exodus and the Jesus of the Gospels by realigning the church with the *anawim*, the marginalized in our world, and honoring the power of the *anawim* in history.[48] Finally, when and where the Latin American church sought to empower the laity at the base of the church and society in the formation of ecclesial base communities, an ecclesiogenesis took place in which the church was born again as a truly incarnate church of the poor and oppressed.[49]

There are many biblical sources and theological reflections that attest to a faith in the God of Life that flowers forth in these expressions of ecclesial opening to and communion with communities that had been historically conquered and colonized by the forces of Western Christendom. One way to think theologically about such faith is in terms of the "sacramental imagination," which is a way of seeing the world in which the community of believers discerns the presence of the divine throughout Creation, but most especially in those who are vulnerable, suffering, and oppressed. The God of the Hebrew Bible and Christian Scriptures is a God who is not only

---

[48] See Gustavo Gutiérrez, *The Power of the Poor in History* (Maryknoll, NY: Orbis Books, 1983).

[49] See Leonardo Boff, *Ecclesiogenesis: The Base Communities Reinvent the Church* (Maryknoll, NY: Orbis Books, 1986) and *Church: Charism and Power* (New York: Crossroad, 1985). While scholarly attention to ecclesial base communities (or CEBs, by the Spanish acronym) has waned in the twenty-first century, these communities are alive and well in Latin America and garnering renewed pastoral attention thanks to the ministry of Pope Francis and the 2019 Synod for the Pan-Amazon Region. For recent reflection on the journey of the CEBs in the context of El Salvador, see Elizabeth O'Donnell Gandolfo and Laurel Marshall Potter, *Re-membering the Reign of God: The Decolonial Witness of El Salvador's Church of the Poor* (Lanham, MD: Lexington Books, 2022).

an advocate for suffering humanity but also present and active in our midst. A liberating Christian faith sees Jesus of Nazareth as definitive confirmation of God's incarnate presence in those who suffer—a God who suffers an early and unjust death as one of the oppressed, and who comes to proclaim good news to the poor and to set the oppressed free (cf. Isaiah 61:1 and Luke 4:18). Where and whenever human beings are oppressed in any way or suffering violence of any kind, the sacramental imagination of the Catholic tradition sees the image of God violated and Christ crucified once again. Liberation theology and the ecclesial base communities add to this imagination a recognition of Christ the liberator, risen and active in the midst of oppressed peoples struggling for freedom, justice, and peace.

In the late twentieth century, an entire generation of Latin American Christians was violently persecuted for following Jesus, liberator of the oppressed, in their communities' daily lives and in broader social movements seeking a new world characterized by human dignity and equal access to the goods of Creation. While these Christians were committed to justice and liberation in a variety of sectors of society, a significant number of them were land defenders and/or advocates for land reform. Centuries of land theft and enclosures under colonialism and neocolonialism had driven countless rural peoples off their ancestral lands to become landless rural workers for large landowners; impoverished subsistence farmers, barely eking out a living from small and barely arable plots of land; or displaced residents of crowded, unsanitary, and unsafe *favelas* or slums. When Indigenous, Afro-descendent, and *campesino* communities fought back against the incursion of land-grabbers in their territories, formed agricultural cooperatives, and/or collaborated in movements advocating land reform, the powerful forces of the state fought back (with support from the economic and military power of the United States). Tens of thousands of land defenders and advocates for land reform were imprisoned, tortured, disappeared, and assassinated in late twentieth-century Latin America, many of them inspired in their struggle by their faith in a God who sides with the oppressed and promises a future in which everyone "shall sit under their own vines and under their own fig trees, and no one shall make them afraid" (Micah 4:4). Some of the more well-known Latin American martyrs, like Saint Óscar Arnulfo Romero and Blessed Rutilio Grande, were advocates for the rights of rural workers and proponents of land reform. The vast majority of those who were persecuted, though, were impoverished *campesinos* and rural workers themselves.

In chapter 6, we will discuss the connections between these late-twentieth-century land defenders and contemporary ecomartyrdom. The witness of Father Josimo Tavares, whose story we contemplated in chapter 4, is like a bridge between these forms of martyrdom, and his story is particularly illuminating for understanding the sacramental imagination as a wellspring for land defenders. Father Josimo was deeply motivated by his faith in the gospel of Jesus Christ, his commitment to a preferential option for the poor, and his vocation to the priesthood. As one witness to Josimo's ministry put it,

> Josimo used to say that everyone should have a piece of land to plant what he needed to feed himself. Of course, the ranchers didn't like that. They want us to be dependent on them all our lives. Josimo said we are all children of God, and God is our father. No father wants some of his children to be very rich and have everything they want while the others are poor and have nothing. A father wants all his children to have a decent life. God didn't make the earth and say, "All right, the ranchers can have it all and the rest can have nothing." He made the earth for all of us. But Josimo made himself a lot of enemies talking that way.[50]

---

[50] Binka Le Breton, *A Land to Die For* (Atlanta: Clarity Press, 1997), 66.

While he preached that all Christians are called to participate in this gospel of liberation, Josimo experienced a particular calling to the work of defending the poor as an ordained priest in the Catholic Church. He saw his threefold ministry as pastor, prophet, and priest to be aligned with Jesus' own ministry: "He should live simply among the poor, sharing their struggles and bringing them the presence of God in the midst of violence and inhumanity. He should help them to unite, so that together they could work to transform their daily life. He should be courageous and unwavering, denouncing injustice and awakening hope in the midst of crisis."[51] As his ordination approached, he sent out invitations with the following poem, attesting to the wellspring of his ministry in a sacramental imagination:

> *To be a priest*
> *is to feel life*
> *springing forth;*
> *rendering service*
> *to God and to the poor*
> *above all.*
>
> *The justice of God*
> *is like the wind;*
> *either it blows gently*
> *like a breeze,*
> *or it explodes*
> *like a tempest!*
>
> *It is pleasing to God*
> *to serve the poor*
> *the sick,*
> *those on the edges of life.*
>
> *To be a priest*
> *is to seek to live*

---

[51] Le Breton, 22.

the life of Christ
through the strength
of communal love.

A padre is
a prophet in injustice,
a pastor on the journey
a humble priest
who seeks
to offer
righteous offerings
to God![52]

Father Josimo offered his own life to God in order to respond in love and justice to "the cry of the poor." By standing in solidarity with impoverished Brazilians seeking access to land and the goods of Creation, he bore witness to the solidarity of God with the struggles of the oppressed.

Father Josimo's commitment to solidarity with land defenders was rooted in a gospel-inspired vision of social justice and political liberation from the tyranny of the landowning and land-grabbing elites. It does not seem that an *ecologically* oriented faith was at the heart of his ministry, and sadly he did not live long enough for that dimension of his theology and spirituality to develop. His concern was primarily the "cry of the poor." Later land defenders and water protectors inspired by a sacramental imagination carried on the legacy of land reform proposals, advocacy for landless communities, and defense of small and communal landholdings with a more explicit integration of the "cry of the poor" with "the cry of the earth,"[53] sensing divine presence both in the poor and in the earth itself.

---

[52] Le Breton, 22–23.

[53] See Leonardo Boff, *Cry of the Earth, Cry of the Poor* (Maryknoll, NY: Orbis Books, 1997).

Father Alcides Jiménez and Sister Dorothy Stang are prime examples of defenders who fought for human communities and the earth in tandem because of how they knew the suffering, beauty, and liberating power of the divine to be present in both. They saw the struggle for social justice and environmental justice as one struggle because both human beings and the planet are part and parcel of God's good Creation and because human and planetary well-being are intricately interconnected. Recall that Father Alcides saw Christ in the trees and invited the congregants at Mass in the forest to offer the sign of peace to the trees as their friends and neighbors. And Sister Dorothy embodied what one of the younger Brazilian sisters remarked was a "cosmic" spirituality: "Everything revealed God's presence to her."[54] Like Alcides, Dorothy was especially attuned to the life-giving dynamics of human communities as sites of God's presence. She herself remarked:

> In the midst of all this violence, there are many small communities that have learned the secret of life . . . sharing, solidarity, confidence, equality, pardon, working together. It doesn't matter what the religious beliefs are as long as human values guide them. God is present . . . generator and sustainer of all life. Thus life is productive and transforming in the midst of all this.[55]

Dorothy was always painfully aware of the deforestation of the Amazon and often wore a t-shirt that read, "The death of the forest is the end of our lives." But her sacramental imagination deepened even further through her encounter with Creation spirituality while on sabbatical in 1991 with the Institute of Culture and Creation Spirituality at Holy Names College in California. In conversation with Matthew Fox, who was then a Dominican friar, Dorothy

---

[54] Roseanne Murphy, *Martyr of the Amazon: The Life of Sister Dorothy Stang* (Maryknoll, NY: Orbis Books, 2007), 92.

[55] Murphy, 93.

began to connect more deeply to God in Creation and was able to bring Creation spirituality together with liberation theology and Latin American struggles for justice. She saw intimate connections between and stood in resolute solidarity with the struggles of both the crucified people—beaten down by centuries of colonialism, slavery, debt bondage, and landlessness—and the crucified earth— degraded by centuries of logging, mining, intensive monocrop agriculture, and contamination, all for the sake of profit.

Creation spirituality and other ecospiritualities that perceive and honor God's presence throughout Creation often deepen the social, economic, and political concerns of the sacramental imagination through an appeal to Creation-centered themes in Scripture, contemplative strands of the Christian tradition, and what many call the "new cosmology."[56] Proponents of the new cosmology argue that humanity needs a new Creation story based on post-modern scientific understandings of the universe and its origins. This new Creation story posits a common origin and end, as well as an inherent interconnectedness to all reality, and it cultivates a sense of awe and wonder at the beauty, complexity, and immense worth of life in this 13.8-billion-year-old, incomprehensibly vast cosmos. Some land and environmental defenders have undoubtedly drawn on this wellspring alone as an animating force for seeking human and ecological well-being. In fact, it might even be possible to consider the new cosmology as a wellspring unto itself. However, for our purposes in this chapter, it suffices to say that, for some land and environmental defenders (like Sister Dorothy) the Catholic sacramental imagination has been expanded, deepened, and enhanced by contemplation of the new cosmology. As Brian Swimme puts it in the film *Journey of the Universe*, "What is the creativity that brought forth a trillion galaxies?" Within the

---

[56] See, e.g., Brian Thomas Swimme and Mary Evelyn Tucker, *Journey of the Universe* (New Haven, CT: Yale University Press, 2011), and the documentary film, podcast, and courses related to the book.

Catholic sacramental imagination, the creative force in question here is animated by a God who seeks interconnection, communion, beauty, playfulness, and solidarity. Dialogue between science, the new cosmology, and the Catholic sacramental imagination, therefore, draws together multiple wellsprings that inspire and empower love and defense of human communities and the more-than-human world on which human beings depend.

The sacramental imagination is fundamentally open and even committed to finding "God in all things," as Ignatian spirituality would put it. Therefore, interreligious dialogue is, or should be, part and parcel of the Catholic sacramental imagination. In addition to the dialogue with science and the new cosmology, some Catholic land and environmental defenders are also inspired by their dialogue with the Indigenous cosmovisions and religions of the African diaspora described above. This has been especially true of the church in the Amazon, where the synodal process leading up to the 2019 Synod for the Pan-Amazon Region was marked by concerted efforts at listening to the wisdom of Indigenous peoples and the ways in which Indigenous expressions of "good living" are an important ecological challenge to the church and world. Furthermore, many Catholic land and environmental defenders themselves identify as Indigenous and/ or Afro-descendent, or have been influenced in myriad ways by their Indigenous and/or African ancestry. For those who embody them in everyday life, these wellsprings are not contradictory or mutually exclusive, but rather potential partners in the work of cultivating human communities that honor the earth and seek to live in relationships of harmony with one another and the rest of Creation.

Drinking from Many Wells

A significant turning point for Latin American liberation theology took place in the early 1980s when Gustavo Gutiérrez published a book titled *We Drink from Our Own Wells: The Spiritual Journey of a*

People.[57] Whereas critics were accusing liberation theology of lacking a spirituality and manipulating the gospel for ideological purposes, Gutiérrez attested that the wellsprings of liberatory praxis lie deep within the spiritual journey of the Latin American people. Similarly, other forms of liberation theology in the Americas and around the world have demonstrated that their own respective commitments to liberation lie within their own cultural knowledge and spiritual experience of the divine. So too, land and environmental defenders live out their commitments to human and ecological well-being by drinking from their own wells of cultural and spiritual sustenance. In this chapter, we have sought to dip a toe into the waters of the wellsprings that have nurtured and lent strength to "so many Bertas." I have identified several frameworks for thinking about these well-springs and several traditions of spiritual sustenance that feed these wellsprings with prophetic ecological imaginations in which the dichotomizing and dominating impulses of extractivism's anti-ecological imaginary are undone. Ecomartyrs bear witness to these diverse wellsprings, but perhaps even more deeply, they bear witness to the deepest wellspring of all—the divine yearning of human beings, as creatures of the earth, for not only survival but also relationships of care and communion with one another and with the more-than-human Creation that gives us life and hope for a future on this imperiled planet. In the language of Christian theology, the fire of this yearning for life and communion is lit and fueled by the presence of God, incarnate in the midst of Creation. Whereas in chapter 1 we saw Atahualpa Yupanquí conclude that God dines at the table of the masters, ecomartyrs witness to and embody the presence of the divine at the table of Creation, in solidarity with the struggles of margin-alized and oppressed communities to love, honor, and protect their own well-being and that of the earth, our common home.

---

[57] Gustavo Gutiérrez, *We Drink from Our Own Wells* (Maryknoll, NY: Orbis Books, 1984).

6

Remembering the Witness

Ecomartyrdom in Christian Theological Perspective

> *Indigenous America*
> *Black, mixed race*
> *of white invasions*
> *your history, our story*
> *chapters of sorrow*
> *verses of light*
> *passion in cultivation*
> *greed in exploitation*
> *songs and graces*
> *cries and misfortunes,*
> *hallelujahs and struggles*
> *vigils and sorrows*
> *in defense of life*
> *of our common home*
> *women and men*
> *of yesterday and today*
> *points of light*
> *persistence and resistance*
> *living and resurrected*
> *walking in the reign*
> *of heaven and earth*[1]

---

[1] This poem is featured in the video "Mártires da Caminhada," Verbo Filmes

In many Latin American popular movements and in certain sectors of the Latin American church, the yearly calendar is marked not only by holidays, holy days, and traditional saints' feast days, but also by anniversaries of martyrdom. From small gatherings in homes and chapels, to Masses and marches tens of thousands strong in capital cities, communities and churches come together to remember the "women and men / of yesterday and today" who have been "points of light / persistence and resistance" in the intersecting struggles against oppression, violence, and ecological degradation across the continent. Those who have been killed for their commitment to these struggles are often named by surviving communities as "martyrs," and sometimes "martyrs of the way," in reference to the liberating, anti-imperialistic path traversed by those whose journey resembles that of Jesus of Nazareth. Beyond the martyrology of the yearly liturgical calendar, women and men like Josimo Tavares, Chico Mendes, Alcides Jiménez, Dorothy Stang, Marcelo Rivera, and Berta Cáceres are palpably present in local communities and cooperatives that bear their names; in poetry and song dedicated to their legacy; on posters, murals, and t-shirts emblazoned with their image and prophetic words. Their stories are passed on and dramatized in oral traditions, local theater productions, books, cartoons, popular education materials, and documentary films. But more importantly, the resurrection of these martyrs takes place in their people's continued journey toward a new heaven and a new earth—a world in which exploitation of human beings and our common home will be no more, and in which all people are free to live life in abundance and harmony with the rest of Creation. Like Saint Óscar Romero and so many others who suffered martyrdom before them, they are risen again

---

YouTube channel, November 21, 2021, https://youtu.be/sH3GuQHXk9g. Portuguese text written by Cireneu Kuhn, SVD, and English translation adapted from that of Pedro Andrés Sánchez.

in their people and in all those who join in solidarity with their struggles for liberation, justice, peace, and the integrity of Creation.

This chapter offers historical and theological reflection on the meaning of martyrdom in the Christian tradition and why it is that murdered land and environmental defenders are considered to be martyrs by many of the communities and movements that carry on their legacy, especially in Latin America today. We begin with ecotheological reflection on the dangerous memory of suffering in the Christian tradition and beyond. Then, after considering the dangers involved in remembering the murder of these individuals as instances of martyrdom, we turn to a brief overview of how the theological category of martyrdom has functioned and evolved in the Christian tradition, with particular attention to the way in which the concept underwent a dramatic transformation in twentieth-century Latin America. The chapter then reflects on how the category of ecomartyrdom extends and enriches, while deepening, and offering important critiques of the theological legacy of twentieth-century Latin American martyrdom. Finally, we conclude with the challenging call to action that ecomartyrdom places on the lives of Christians and all people of good will who hope to offer our children and grandchildren a more just and livable future.

Dangerous Memory in Ecotheological Perspective

In the field of memory studies, anthropologists and sociologists insist that the way in which human beings remember the past functions to uphold and/or challenge the status quo in the present, as well as our vision of the future. Collective memory has political consequences, and in light of this study of extractivism and ecomartyrdom, it also has ecological consequences. For Christians who remember ecomartyrdom, the way in which this memory functions to inspire eco-political praxis for liberation is not only a sociological or anthropological fact. Rather, it is also a theological mandate, albeit a risky one. The memory of suffering in general and the memory of Jesus of Nazareth's suffering in particular place on Christians the demand that we respond to suffering with compassion and struggle for liberation from unjust causes of suffering *no matter what the cost*. Ecomartyrs have heeded this demand and paid with their lives. Christian disciples are called to do likewise in our own contexts of suffering and hope. Some clarification on this point is in order.

German political theologian Johann Baptist Metz argues that the memory of suffering has, or should have, a practical effect in that it points to a future of freedom and moves those who remember to hopeful praxis on behalf of that future. Furthermore, Metz maintains that the Christian memory of the suffering, death, and resurrection of Jesus Christ is a "dangerous memory" that not only incites liberating praxis in the believer but promises a future of freedom for both the living and the dead, whom God wills to be subjects in God's presence. The hope inspired by this promise must find its defense in the form of liberatory praxis in solidarity with all those whose subjectivity has been threatened or denied. For many land and environmental defenders, and from the perspective of ecologically informed Christian theology, this praxis extends to solidarity with the threatened and destroyed subjectivity of the more-than-human Creation. Or rather, such solidarity entails the praxis of intersubjectivity, interdependency, and reciprocity with other human beings and the other creatures, lands, waters, and elements of our common home.

It is in reference to the praxis of solidarity that Metz denotes the memory of suffering as "dangerous memory," for such memory not only incites criticism of ideologies that perpetuate or legitimate unjust suffering but also points toward a positive future of freedom and liberation. Unjust suffering in and of itself is not a good thing, nor does it fulfill a divinely ordained purpose, but *remembering* such suffering should incite praxis on behalf of a more just future, the way things *ought* to be. As such, Metz argues that

> Christian *memoria* insists that humanity's history of suffering does not belong simply to the prehistory of freedom, but that it is and will continue to be an inner moment of the history of freedom. Imagining freedom in the future is nourished by the memory of suffering, and freedom goes sour when those who suffer are for the most part devalued or treated via cliches. This means, however, that Christian *memoria* becomes a memory that rouses us from becoming too quickly reconciled to the "facts" and "trends" of technological society. It becomes a dangerous-liberating memory over and against the mechanisms and forces of the ruling consciousness and its abstract ideal of emancipation.[2]

The freedom to which Metz aspires here is not the bourgeois or neoliberal freedom to conduct one's individual or corporate affairs unencumbered by the constraints of responsibility for justice, ecological well-being, or the common good. In fact, memory of suffering is dangerous precisely because it calls such libertarian ideals into question. In decolonial perspective, such memory can interrupt colonial histories and point to an alternative future of pluriversal freedom— a world in which many worlds are free to co-exist.[3] Consequently, dangerous memory of suffering threatens the status quo, calls into question the present order of things, and demands a fundamental change in our consciousness and praxis.

---

[2] Johann Baptist Metz, *Faith in History and Society: Toward a Practical Fundamental Theology*, trans. J. Matthew Ashley (New York: Crossroad, 2007), 108.

[3] See chapter 1, note 29, and chapter 5, note 3.

Metz's emphasis on memory in his practical fundamental theology is clearly not an appeal to the past as a safe and unthreatening influence on the present. Rather, memory of the past for him necessarily means the dangerous memory of suffering, which radically reorients our lives and praxis toward a future of freedom. Christian memory of Jesus Christ promises such freedom for all people and, thus, demands of believers a life praxis in accordance with the hope inspired by that promise. And for Metz, Christian hope finds both its fulfillment and its justification in a praxis that responds to the memory of suffering by struggling in solidarity for the subjectivity of all of suffering humanity. If we weave Metz's theology of remembering Jesus together with an ecotheological perspective on the cosmic Christ, present in all of Creation, it becomes clear that remembering the suffering of the more-than-human Creation also requires solidarity with the earth. Indeed, it is remembering the suffering of the earth community—grounded in a desire for the well-being of and the communion between humanity and Creation—that has led so many ecomartyrs to their deaths. Later in this chapter, we will see that remembering murdered land and environmental defenders as martyrs requires a commitment to carrying on their praxis of solidarity with both the human and more-than-human Creation whose subjectivity has been threatened and denied.

Reading Metz's theology of "dangerous memory" in ecological perspective thus provides fresh insights for the praxis of memory and solidarity aimed at care for and defense of our common home. Placing these insights in conversation with what Melanie Harris calls the ecowomanist praxis of "ecomemory" deepens and corrects Metzian "dangerous memory" even further in at least three ways.[4] First, Harris draws on the work of Emilie Townes to posit

---

[4] Each of these insights is drawn from Melanie L. Harris, *Ecowomanism: African American Women and Earth-Honoring Faiths* (Maryknoll, NY: Orbis Books, 2017), 27–38.

that ecomemory is a form of "counter-memory" that calls into question traditional environmental histories that center white environmentalism and thus erase the "voices, experiences, and histories of black peoples" and other people of color in the environmental justice movement. Ecomemory centers the ways in which colonized, marginalized, and oppressed communities of color have been primary agents of care for and defense of the earth. Second, for Harris, ecomemory also refuses to ignore or suppress the ecological wounds and trauma experienced by Black peoples that have been occasioned by histories of displacement from homelands during the transatlantic slave trade, forced agricultural labor during chattel slavery in the Americas, and displacement from the land once again under the reign of racial terrorism in the Jim Crow South. Harris maintains that ecomemory, which includes reparations, is necessary in order to heal these wounds and reclaim a healthy and life-giving relationship with the earth for Black people in particular, but also for other colonized peoples and for people of European descent who have perpetrated and/or benefited from the infliction of such wounds. Third, Harris moves ecotheology and environmental ethics away from approaches grounded in Christian supremacy, contending that ecowomanism and ecomemory are necessarily interfaith and interreligious endeavors. Whether in conversation with ancestral African cosmovisions or contemporary Buddhism, Harris's approach privileges dialogue and collaboration for the sake of deepening ecological wisdom and furthering the praxis of environmental justice.

The dangerous memory of murdered land and environmental defenders is refined by each of these insights. Environmental justice struggles of marginalized and oppressed communities of color are necessarily centered by a praxis of ecomemory that centers ecomartyrdom, since murders of land and environmental defenders are taking place almost entirely (though not exclusively) in communities of color in the Global South. One caveat here is that focusing on those who are actually murdered for their defense of land and the environment has the potential to elide the environmental justice struggles of Indigenous, Afro-descendent, and poor communities in the Global North, where racially motivated violence is widespread but no longer so directly related to defense of land rights or ecological issues. Therefore, it is important to recognize that racially and economically marginalized communities in the Global North are also plagued by the criminalization, defamation, and other human rights violations suffered by their counterparts fighting for environmental justice in the Global South. The problem of extractivist violence disproportionately affects communities of color around the world, and violent repression of environmental justice movements varies only by degree, not by kind, between North and South. Vigilance and solidarity in the face of such repression is just as necessary in the United States and Canada as it is in Mexico, Honduras, Colombia, and Brazil.

Harris's insistence on the need for ecomemory to heal the wounds of ecological trauma are also prescient for guiding our memory of murdered land and environmental defenders. Memory of such individuals within and beyond the communities where they lived and died is not only empowering for active participation in the environmental justice struggle. At a deeper level, it is essential to the process of healing that we must all undergo, in different ways, if we are to re-imagine and re-embody the relationship between human beings and the earth. And finally, Harris's commitment to interfaith dialogue points to the ways in which so many murdered land and environmental defenders were often inspired by not only one faith tradition or spirituality, but many. Though each tradition is beautiful and life-giving on its own, the wellsprings of the ecomartyrs' witness that we contemplated in chapter 5 often merge, flow together, and diverge in powerful ways both within individual ecomartyrs' lives and among various communities of struggle. There is no way forward for a future on this planet if the religious, spiritual, and humanist traditions of the world do not find a way to dialogue, collaborate, and practice dangerous memory together for the sake of a liberating, life-giving, and ecologically healthy future.

The Dangers of Memory: Caveats for a Theology of Ecomartyrdom

Before continuing to develop an argument for remembering murdered land and environmental defenders as ecomartyrs, it is important to consider the potential pitfalls that such an enterprise can entail. These dangers of theologizing martyrdom, when left unchecked, can prove counterproductive and even harmful for the communities and ecological landscapes to which ecomartyrs dedicated their lives. Any theology of martyrdom in general, or ecomartyrdom in particular, must take care not to fall into these potentially toxic patterns.

First, like so much religious rhetoric, the category of martyrdom is easily manipulated and can be applied to anyone who dies for the sake of any cause, however morally reprehensible that cause may be. In the Western Christian tradition alone, the rhetoric of martyrdom has been used to support the expansion of Christendom and the colonial hegemony of Eurocentric Christian supremacy. During the conquest and colonization of the Americas, for example, European missionaries killed by Indigenous peoples were extolled by the church as martyrs of the gospel who died for the sake of expanding the reign of Christendom and bringing salvation and civilization to the "heathen" populations of the "New World." More recently, evangelical Christianity in the United States has constructed a narrative of persecution and martyrdom in which secular culture and liberal values are weapons in the war against Christians (and, apparently, even Christmas!). Persecuted missionaries are also considered martyrs in this orbit, even in extreme cases such as that of John Allen Chau, who was killed when he attempted to contact and evangelize the isolated tribes of the North Sentinel Islands in 2018 (a feat that the tribes resisted for both cultural and medical reasons, given the dangers of exposure to illness for which they have no immunity).[5] Political manipulation of martyrdom rhetoric is also characteristic of the white Christian nationalist movement within the United States, as has become evident in the case of Ashli Babbitt, the woman who was killed by a police officer while she was participating in the assault on the U.S. Capitol on January 6, 2021. Babbitt has been extolled by supporters of Donald Trump as a martyr for truth and liberty, but the causes for which she stood included the demonstrably false and anti-democratic claim that Trump won the 2020 presidential election and the QAnon conspiracy theory, which "centers on the baseless belief that Trump has secretly battled deep-state enemies and a cabal of Satan-worshiping cannibals that includes prominent Democrats who operate a child sex trafficking ring."[6] As we will see below, martyrdom is at its core defined by witness to truth. Each of these cases involves extolling death for the sake of colonial expansion, racist ideology, Christian supremacy, and conspiracy theories. Clearly, the rhetoric of martyrdom can be distorted by falsehoods,

---

[5] See J. Oliver Conroy, "The Life and Death of John Allen Chau, the Man Who Tried to Convert His Killers," *Guardian*, February 3, 2019, https://www.theguardian.com/world/2019/feb/03/john-chau-christian-missionary-death-sentinelese.

[6] Michael Bisecker, "Ashli Babbitt a Martyr? Her Past Tells a More Complex Story," *San Diego Tribune*, January 3, 2022, https://www.sandiegouniontribune.com/news/california/story/2022-01-02/ashli-babbitt-a-martyr-her-past-tells-a-more-complex-story. See also Jeff Sharlet, "January 6 Was Only the Beginning," *Vanity Fair*, June 22, 2022, https://www.vanityfair.com/news/2022/06/trump-ashli-babbitt-christians.

fanatical political ideologies, and the desire to consolidate power over vulnerable communities. It is important, therefore, to be very clear about how ecomartyrdom witnesses to historical and moral truth, the politics of justice and compassion, and the desire to distribute power more justly and equitably among human beings and between human beings and Creation.

Second, theologies and spiritualities that center martyrdom run the risk of justifying injustice and perpetuating the suffering and sacrifice of marginalized and oppressed communities. Feminist and womanist theologians have been especially wary of theological systems that revolve around paradigms of self-sacrifice and redemptive suffering. In womanist Christology, for example, Jacquelyn Grant has drawn on Black women's experiences of servitude to call into question the redemptive suffering of servanthood that is central to both Jesus' own mission and the vocation of Christian disciples.[7] And Delores Williams has appealed to Black women's surrogacy experiences in her critique of theologies that center the redemptive suffering of Jesus' surrogacy for humanity on the cross.[8] Over the course of the half century or so that women have been admitted to the theological academy, dozens of other arguments have been made against such theologies of sacrifice and redemptive suffering, and in favor of theologies that center abundant life and liberation for women and all marginalized peoples. Latin American liberation theologies and spiritualities of martyrdom have not adequately responded to these critiques of sacrifice and redemptive suffering, but the case can be made that martyrdom in liberationist

---

[7]   See Jacquelyn Grant, *White Women's Christ and Black Women's Jesus: Feminist Christology and Womanist Response* (Atlanta: Scholars Press, 1989), and "The Sin of Servanthood and the Deliverance of Discipleship," in *A Troubling in My Soul: Womanist Perspectives on Evil and Suffering*, ed. Emilie M. Townes (Maryknoll, NY: Orbis Books, 1993).

[8]   See Delores S. Williams, *Sisters in the Wilderness: The Challenge of Womanist God-Talk* (Maryknoll, NY: Orbis Books, 1993).

perspective is an outcome of commitment to resisting ideologies and systems that justify the sacrifice and suffering of the world's poor majorities for the sake of satiating the consumptive desires of the wealthy and powerful minority. In other words, martyrdom in liberationist perspective is a protest against unjust sacrifice and suffering and is far from a justification of such violent realities.[9] We would do well to keep these distinctions in mind as we theologize and remember the sacrifices that ecomartyrs have been forced to make in their pursuit of human and ecological liberation and well-being.

A third caveat to keep in mind relates to the patriarchal, racist, and clericalist nature of remembering saints and moral exemplars, especially martyrs.[10] Lifting up individual martyrs as privileged exemplars of political and ecological holiness can tend to elide the communal web of struggle and commitment that not only formed the martyrs in their own personal commitments, but is also made up of dozens, hundreds, even thousands of other human beings running the same risks and potentially suffering the same fate as the individuals we know about. Privileging a handful of exemplary individuals rather than whole communities of struggle and commitment can feed into the patriarchal, white supremacist, and capitalist ideal of the self-sufficient, autonomous individual. Furthermore, the moral exemplars that we remember in the Christian tradition are too often ordained European and/or Euro-descendent men.

Latin American memory of martyrdom does subvert this tendency in many ways by shifting the church's focus to the

---

[9] For a more extensive analysis on this point, see Elizabeth O'Donnell Gandolfo, "Women and Martyrdom: Feminist Liberation Theology in Dialogue with a Latin American Paradigm," *Horizons* 34, no. 1 (2007): 26–53.

[10] I also raise this point in Gandolfo, "Women and Martyrdom," but without consciousness of how white supremacy culture contributes to not only privileging memory of lighter-skinned martyrs but also reinforcing the patriarchal and white racist ideal of the self-sufficient individual.

Global South, but the major figures recognized in Latin American martyrology are still predominantly ordained, lighter-skinned men who held significant positions of ecclesial power, like Saint Óscar Romero and Blessed Enrique Angelelli, both members of the church hierarchy. These men were remarkable, to be sure, and their commitment to the gospel of love and liberation cannot be overemphasized. But their visibility does tend to elide the everyday martyrdom of the thousands of ordinary people who have committed their lives to that same gospel and with the same violent outcome. Recognizing contemporary ecomartyrdom can help correct this tendency, but this category does privilege rural communities over urban sectors, and the individuals whose stories are best known, especially at an international level, still enjoy some privileged status. This is even true, to a certain extent, of all six of the stories we contemplated in chapter 4. It is important to constantly remember, then, that the ecomartyrs we know about are just a handful of many thousands who have been killed for defending land and environmental causes, let alone other human rights causes in other sectors of society, in the past several decades alone. We should not imagine them standing on their own as moral exemplars, but rather as a members of a great cloud of witnesses, living and dead, who beckon us to join our lives to their legacy of communal commitment to care for and defend one another and our common home.

Fourth and finally, martyrdom is not a uniquely Christian category, but Latin American theologies and spiritualities of martyrdom are predominantly Christian in origin, interpretation, and expression. Many ecomartyrs are Christian and can be considered martyrs because they died bearing witness to the liberating gospel truth of God's desire for all of Creation to flourish, which Christians believe to be definitively revealed in Jesus Christ. However, many ecomartyrs are not Christian, and may even have deep, well-founded suspicions about the nature of Christian faith, given its history of complicity with racism, patriarchy, and colonialism. Nevertheless, murdered land and environmental defenders who are not Christian most certainly also bear witness to the truths of their own wellsprings and to the sacred interdependence of humanity and the more-than-human world. But does calling non-Christians "martyrs" amount to yet another colonial imposition of a foreign theological category? Or would it be even more problematic to exclude non-Christians from this category?

An adequate resolution to this dilemma is not really possible or even necessary. Rather, the dilemma points to the care with which Christians must operate in contexts of interreligious encounter and collaboration. The category of martyrdom exceeds the narrow bounds of Christian doctrine and identity, as do the sacred realities of truth, justice, and ecological interdependency to which martyrs witness. Therefore, as we will discuss further below, it is entirely possible to interpret the murders of non-Christian land and environmental defenders in terms of martyrdom. However, in doing so, care must be taken on at least two fronts. First, it is important to keep in mind that the realities to which non-Christian martyrs bear witness are not reducible to Christian or more broadly Western or modern theological and philosophical concepts. The wellsprings of non-Christian, non-Western religious experience must be respected as truly other, and should not be whitewashed to fit into categories that are familiar to modern Western Christians. Humble respect for the real differences that exist and what can be learned from such differences is imperative. Second, a good rule of thumb is to honor the wishes of any given non-Christian community that may express an aversion to the rhetoric of martyrdom. It is possible to recognize and protest the murder of non-Christian land and environmental defenders without using this category, and it is imperative to do so if a non-

Christian community indicates that the category of martyrdom is undesirable or offensive to their own cultural and religious sensibilities. For this reason, the six ecomartyrs whom I lift up in chapter 4 of this book are all individuals around whom robust communities of memory already exist that interpret their lives and deaths in terms of martyrdom. In short, this is a tricky dilemma that must be navigated with great care.

Despite these dangers of remembering murdered land and environmental defenders as martyrs, the spiritual and theological fruits of interpreting their deaths in this way are plentiful. In what follows, we will briefly survey the history of martyrdom in the Christian tradition and how this concept evolved in twentieth-century Latin America. We will then turn to a consideration of how ecomartyrdom and its fruits can extend, deepen, and even correct theologies and spiritualities of martyrdom in liberation theologies and beyond.

Martyrdom in Twentieth-Century Latin America[11]

Traditionally, the church has typically defined martyrdom as witness to the Christian faith and passive acceptance of death because of the persecutors' hatred of the faith (*odium fidei*). This definition stresses both the passivity of the martyr and the intention of the persecutors, who are assumed to be non-Christian. As Karl Rahner points out, such a concept of martyrdom excludes death in an active struggle, for the whole or any given part of the Christian faith, in favor of a passive resistance to renunciation of the faith in the face of persecution.[12] It also presumes that the persecutors are not Christian and

---

[11] This section is a revised version of text that appears in Gandolfo, "Women and Martyrdom."

[12] Karl Rahner, "Dimensions of Martyrdom: A Plea for the Broadening of a Classical Concept," in *Martyrdom Today* (*Concilium* 163), ed. Johannes-Baptist Metz and Edward Schillebeeckx (Edinburgh: T & T Clark, 1983), 9.

have a hatred of the Christian faith as a whole. In light of this traditional emphasis on passivity and *odium fidei*, it becomes problematic to recognize as martyrs those who were killed, often by people who identify themselves as Christians, because of their active struggles for peace and justice. However, Jon Sobrino argues that the traditional concept of martyrdom is a *historical* notion, "which means that it can continue changing throughout history."[13] In the years since the Second Vatican Council, the concept has changed significantly, thanks in great part to the contributions of Latin American liberation theologians. These thinkers and the popular church that they serve have gifted the universal church with a new category of martyrdom: what Sobrino calls the "Jesus martyrs," or those persons who, like Jesus, live and consequently die for the sake of the liberation and justice of God's reign.

A second category of martyrdom introduced by liberation theologians is that of the "crucified people," which refers to those countless women, men, and children who suffer a silent and violent death—either slowly or abruptly—because they are made to carry the weight of the world's sins and injustice on their backs.[14] These are the nameless, countless billions who endure hunger, lack of

---

[13] Jon Sobrino, *Witnesses to the Kingdom: The Martyrs of El Salvador and the Crucified Peoples* (Maryknoll, NY: Orbis Books 2003), 120.

[14] For a detailed account of the identity of the oppressed masses as the "crucified people" and the "Suffering Servant of Yahweh," see the following: Pedro Casaldáliga, "The 'Crucified Indians': A Case of Anonymous Collective Martyrdom," in Metz and Schillebeeckx, *Martyrdom Today*, 9–11; Ignacio Ellacuría, "The Crucified People," in *Mysterium Liberationis: Fundamental Concepts of Liberation Theology*, ed. Ignacio Ellacuría and Jon Sobrino (Maryknoll, NY: Orbis Books 1993), 580–603; Jon Sobrino, *Jesus the Liberator* (Maryknoll, NY: Orbis Books 1993), 254–271; Jon Sobrino, "Our World: Cruelty and Compassion," in *Rethinking Martyrdom* (*Concilium* 1), ed. Teresa Okure et al. (London: SCM Press, 2003), 15–23; Sobrino, *Witnesses to the Kingdom*, 155–166; and Kevin Burke, "The Crucified People as 'Light for the Nations': A Reflection on Ignacio Ellacuría," in Okure et al., *Rethinking Martyrdom*, 120–130.

dignified housing and medical care, horrid working conditions, a life of fear and exploitation, the violence of war, torture, rape, assassinations, massacres, and outright genocide. They suffer and die defenselessly, without the possibility of escape.[15] To harken back to the song by Atahualpa Yupanquí cited in chapter 1, these are the poor majorities of the world who must "spit out blood" so that "others might live a more comfortable life." Latin American theologians often call these untold masses "martyrs," despite the fact that most of these victims do not lose their lives, like the Jesus martyrs, because of their active promotion of the reign of God. They are considered martyrs, as the name "crucified people" suggests, because in their suffering and death, they, like Jesus, also shoulder the weight of the sin and injustice wrought by the *anti-reino* (that which opposes God's reign of love and justice). They are martyrs because their deaths bear clear and direct witness, in the words of Elsa Tamez, to "the wickedness and sin of the world that vents its anger on Christian prophets and also on innocent people."[16] For this reason, Michael Lee calls the crucified people "martyrs of reality."[17] The crucified people must be remembered and rescued from anonymity in order to name that wickedness for what it is, in order to restore dignity and hope to the victims, and in order that the injustice they have endured (and continue to endure) might be redressed and occur *nunca más*, never again. While the category of "crucified people" carries with it its own dangers of valorizing redemptive suffering, the poor and oppressed majorities are a central reality for any theology that takes seriously the signs

---

[15] Cf. Jon Sobrino, "Los mártires jesuánicos en el tercer mundo," *Revista Latinoamericana de Teología* 16, no. 48 (San Salvador: Centro de Reflexión Teológica, 1999), 253.

[16] Elsa Tamez, "Martyrs of Latin America," in Okure et al., *Rethinking Martyrdom*, 35.

[17] Michael E. Lee, *Revolutionary Saint: The Theological Vision of Óscar Romero* (Maryknoll, NY: Orbis Books, 2018), 171.

of the times, for in them God is present, both hidden and revealed, throughout history. As we will see shortly, the same can be said for the "crucified earth."

It is important to note that, for theologians like Sobrino, the crucified peoples are always the point of reference when we talk about the Jesus martyrs because they are the ones "who shed light on the 'why' of the Jesuanic martyrs and on the martyr Jesus. The latter have been killed for defending these crucified peoples from the slow death of poverty and the violent death of repression."[18] The poor and oppressed are the ones who are "there first" and for whom Jesus and the Jesus martyrs have died in the struggle to take the crucified peoples down from their crosses, *and* to transform the systems that erect such crosses in the first place. Again, we will see that the same can be said for the crucified earth as a reference point for ecomartyrdom.

Roots of a Changing Concept of Martyrdom

In the years of heightened persecution that followed Medellín, the rise of liberation theology, and the formation of ecclesial base communities, certain sectors of the Latin American church began to recognize as martyrs those who gave their lives as part of a nonviolent struggle for a more just and peaceful society.[19] This grassroots

---

[18] Jon Sobrino, "The Kingdom of God and the Theologal Dimension of the Poor: The Jesuanic Principle," trans. J. Matthew Ashley, in *Who Do You Say That I Am? Confessing the Mystery of Christ*, ed. John Cavadini and Laura Holt (Notre Dame, IN: University of Notre Dame Press, 2004), 145. Like most translators of Sobrino, Ashley prefers the neologism "Jesuanic" as a more literal English translation of Sobrino's term "jesuánico," but I prefer to simply modify "martyrs" or "martyrdom" with the attributive noun "Jesus."

[19] Many people in the Latin American popular church also regard armed revolutionaries who fell in combat as martyrs. Others regard these individuals as "heroes," reserving the term "martyr" for those who died without recourse to violence. Thomas Aquinas affirms that soldiers can be considered martyrs in certain cases (Cf. *In IV Sent.* dis. XLIX, q.V, a.3, quaest. 2, art. 11, cited

reaction to the unjust deaths of fellow Christians and other activists was both a result of and a motivation for Latin American liberation theologians' attempts to make religious sense of the countless political executions and "disappearances" taking place on a daily basis throughout the continent. These theologians did not have to look far to find support in the Catholic tradition for recognizing these individuals as martyrs. In the *Summa Theologica*, Thomas Aquinas argued that "martyrdom consists essentially in standing firmly to truth and justice against the assaults of persecution."[20] For him, dying for the pursuit of justice, which is the proper effect of truth, was as much a cause for martyrdom as dying for the truth of the faith itself. Indeed, the truth of faith is made manifest in works (James 2:18), including works of justice, and this is why Aquinas maintained that virtuous deeds are themselves professions of faith when they are referred to God and can thus be the cause of martyrdom.[21] It is in this same sense that "[a] human good can become divine good if it is referred to God; therefore any human good can be a cause of martyrdom, insofar as it is referred to God."[22] Ultimately, however, Aquinas posited that it is *love* that directs and perfects the life and death of a martyr and conforms her to Christ.[23] The Christian witness, then, is not only one who has faith *in* Christ but also one who becomes *like* Christ insofar as she "performs virtuous actions in the spirit of Christ."[24]

---

in Sobrino, "Los mártires jesuánicos en el tercer mundo," 253), and Rahner argues for broadening the concept of martyrdom to include those who engage in justified battle ("Dimensions of Martyrdom," 11). However, other theologians, especially strict pacifists, would argue that nonviolence is a requirement of Christian martyrdom. The full implications of this controversy exceed the scope of this book. For the sake of clarity, I will remain within the bounds of a concept of martyrdom that precludes the use of violence.

[20] St. Thomas Aquinas, *Summa Theologica*, II-II, q. 124, art. 1.

[21] Aquinas, art. 5.

[22] Aquinas, art. 5.

[23] Aquinas, art. 3.

[24] Aquinas, art. 5.

In an attempt to broaden the concept of martyrdom to include both Christians and non-Christians who die in the struggle for the common good, Leonardo Boff appropriates Aquinas's assertion that any human good which is referred to God can be the cause of martyrdom. According to his interpretation of Aquinas, dying for the common good can be considered martyrdom because the cause of such a death is ultimately a divine good. The common good is a human good, and, as such, it can be referred to God and can thus become a divine good. But Boff argues that all virtuous acts are ultimately referred to God because "[t]his reference to God should be understood in its fullest sense; it is not only to be found in the simple act of consciously referring to something of God; a virtuous act in itself, by its ontic structure, contains reference to the principle of all virtue which is God."[25] All virtuous deeds on behalf of justice and the common good are therefore, by their very nature, inspired by the spirit of Christ and referred to the divine good. Therefore, anyone who dies in the authentic pursuit of the common good can be considered a martyr.

Given the above considerations, dialogue with Aquinas's theology of martyrdom has expanded the concept of martyrdom on two fronts. First, martyrdom for the Christian faith can include death due to an active struggle on behalf of the moral truths and virtues of the faith, including love, justice, and the common good. Second, non-Christians and even nonreligious people who are killed for performing these same virtuous actions can also be considered martyrs. The concept of martyrdom can be understood, then, as witness not only to the Christian faith but also to moral truth and justice.

While the documents of the Second Vatican Council do not address the topic of martyrdom in detail, *Lumen Gentium* does

---

[25] Leonardo Boff, "Martyrdom: An Attempt at Systematic Reflection," in Metz and Schillebeeckx, eds., *Martyrdom Today*, 15.

take up the first aspect of the above expansion of the concept of
martyrdom by designating martyrdom as a witness to Christ-like
love: "By martyrdom, a disciple is transformed into an image of his
Master, who freely accepted death on behalf of the world's salvation; he perfects that image even to the shedding of blood.... The
Church, therefore, considers martyrdom as an exceptional gift and
as the highest proof of love."[26] The Catholic tradition here moves
to recognize as martyrs those who conform their lives to the life
of love led by Jesus and, as a result, die like Jesus. Therefore, the
Roman Catholic Church has officially recognized as martyrs
individuals such as Maximilian Kolbe, who volunteered to die in
another man's place in the German death camp at Auschwitz, and
Óscar Romero, who prophetically denounced economic and military violence waged by the Salvadoran state against the people of
El Salvador.

Conforming one's life to that of Jesus and, thus, to the way of
love and justice necessarily involves active witness to moral truth
through denunciation of sin and injustice as well as annunciation
and actualization of the reign of God here and now. According to
Boff, that reign is nothing other than "God entering into history
and carrying out his word. And the true name of God is justice,
love, peace without qualification; true faithfulness to God... is
faithfulness to truth, justice and the requirements of peace."[27] As
such, Boff calls those who die, like Jesus, for these values "martyrs
for the reign of God." Michael Lee calls them "martyrs of solidarity." Martyrs for the reign of truth, justice, love, charity, and
peace—these are human beings who lived like Jesus, making a preferential option for solidarity with the poor and oppressed. And like
Jesus, they were killed out of an *odium fidei* that encompasses far

---

[26] Second Vatican Council, *Lumen Gentium: Dogmatic Constitution on
the Church*, November 21, 1964, www.vatican.va, § 42.

[27] Boff, "Martyrdom," 15.

more than hatred of the dogmatic truths of the Christian faith. In the case of these martyrs, who lived and died like Jesus, *odium fidei* means hatred of truth, justice, love, charity, and peace; ultimately, it means hatred of solidarity, hatred of the oppressed, and, thus, hatred of humanity. Because they lived and died like Jesus, Sobrino calls these persons the "Jesus martyrs."

Jesus Martyrdom in the Theology of Jon Sobrino

Sobrino defines the Jesus martyrs as those "who follow Jesus in the things that matter, live in dedication to the cause of Jesus, and die for the same reasons that Jesus died."[28] In short, the Jesus martyrs live and die *like Jesus*. Further exploration of this concept of martyrdom requires a closer look at the connection between Jesus' life ministry and his death, which will help us answer two crucial questions pertinent to a theology which relates the death of the martyr to Jesus' own death as a martyr on the cross: Why did Jesus die? and Why do contemporary martyrs die? A correct theological understanding of contemporary martyrdom requires a theologically and historically sound interpretation of Jesus' own martyrdom.

Most liberation theologians reject the explanation of Jesus' death as the expiatory sacrifice required by God for the forgiveness of humanity's sins. For these theologians, God did not directly will the torture and crucifixion of Jesus. Boff, for example, argues that Jesus was killed, not because of a divine requirement for the atonement of sins, but precisely because of his message and his practice:

> Jesus' martyrdom has to be understood correctly. It was not a simple concordance with the will of God; historically it was the result of a rejection of his message and person by those who refused to be converted to the kingdom of God. If Jesus was to be faithful to himself

---

[28] Sobrino, *Witnesses to the Kingdom*, 122.

and to his mission, he had to accept persecution and martyrdom. God did not want so much the death of his Son as the fidelity implied, in the context of man's refusal to be converted, by his violent death.[29]

Sobrino similarly argues that, in order to preach the cross with truth, we must understand that Jesus "was executed as a political malefactor... because he disturbed all of the powers that made society an oppressor of the poor and weak."[30] For Sobrino, the essential dynamism of Jesus' life is what led to Jesus' death: "Putting it as simply as possible: (1) Jesus is murdered because he gets in the way; (2) Jesus gets in the way because he attacks the oppressors; (3) Jesus attacks the oppressors in order to defend the poor; and (4) Jesus defends the poor—to the end—because he loves them."[31] Those who follow Jesus also follow this essential dynamism of his life, which is a dynamism rooted in and propelled by love. As a result, they face the possibility of being killed for the same reasons as Jesus: for getting in the way, attacking oppressors, defending and loving those who are impoverished and oppressed.

The Jesus martyrs, then, "are not, strictly speaking, those who die *for* Christ or *because of* Christ, but those who die *like* Jesus and *for the cause of* Jesus."[32] Their affinity with Jesus' life and death and their effective following of Jesus is what gives rise to their martyrdom. As such, they are killed not explicitly out of *odium fidei* so much as *odium iustitiae* and *odium misericordiae*, which brings us back to an earlier point. These martyrs can be found both inside and outside the church—wherever the struggle for justice is carried

---

[29] Boff, "Martyrdom," 13.

[30] Jon Sobrino, "Holy Week in El Salvador: The Cross of a Crucified People," in *We Make the Road by Walking: Central America, Mexico and the Caribbean in the New Millennium*, ed. Ann Butwell et al. (Washington, DC: EPICA, 1998), 194.

[31] Sobrino, *Witnesses to the Kingdom*, 124.

[32] Sobrino, "Our World: Cruelty and Compassion," 19.

out with compassion for the least among us. They are not strictly martyrs of the *church*, but rather martyrs of the reign of God, martyrs of solidarity with the poor and oppressed, and martyrs of humanity. As we will soon see, in the case of ecomartyrdom, they are also martyrs of solidarity with the earth, our common home.

According to Sobrino, the Jesus martyrs are a sign of the times in which God is present and active and in which the crucified and risen Christ is made manifest in history. He thus argues that the reality of martyrdom should be given precedence in the Christian faith and way of life. As a central reality for the faith and discipleship, then, the Jesus martyrs call Christians to embody a spirituality of persecution and martyrdom. Sobrino considers this spirituality, characterized by a readiness to sacrifice one's own self-interest and suffer for the sake of justice and liberation, to be a necessary element of Christian life for two reasons. First, a spirituality of martyrdom is necessary a priori, for the New Testament tells us that those who are faithful to Christ will suffer the same fate as Christ.[33] As we saw earlier, however, Jesus' own fate was not decided in a historical vacuum. He was killed because he confronted the forces of sin and evil as they were wielded historically by the arrogant and powerful. Second, a spirituality of martyrdom is necessary a posteriori because the oppression and persecution of people living in poverty and their allies is a historical fact.[34] Where the *anti-reino* manifests itself, those who promote the reign of God and defend the poor and oppressed will represent a threat to the oppressors and will suffer persecution as a result.

Saint Óscar Romero gave clear testimony to this reality and the necessity of a spirituality of martyrdom in both his words and actions:

---

[33] Jon Sobrino, *Liberación con Espíritu* (San Salvador: UCA Editores, 1985), 112. See also Matt 10:24; John 15:20; 1 Thes 2:14; 3:2.

[34] Sobrino, *Liberación con Espíritu*, 111.

> Christ invites us not to be afraid of persecution because,
> believe it brothers and sisters, to commit oneself to the
> poor means to suffer the same fate as the poor. And in El
> Salvador we know what the fate of the poor means: to be
> captured, disappeared, tortured, and found dead.[35]

It is important to remember here, however, that God does not want death. God wants life. Nor do martyrs want to die—they want to live! In following the will of God as revealed in Jesus' ministry, Romero and other martyrs of solidarity in twentieth century Latin America did not seek death, but life for the impoverished and oppressed and for all of humanity. In a context of historical sin, injustice, and violence, though, doing the will of God inevitably carries with it the risk and reality of martyrdom. This is the historical reason why a spirit of self-sacrifice and readiness for suffering are essential elements of the Christian faith. This is the spirituality that the Jesus martyrs challenge us to embody in our everyday lives.

Jesus Martyrdom in Light of Ecomartyrdom

The "Jesus martyrs" of late-twentieth-century Latin America, whose witness has informed so much of Latin American liberation theology, were killed for their denunciation of injustice, oppression, and violence, on the one hand, and annunciation of justice, liberation, and peace, on the other. They were targeted specifically for their solidarity with social movements aimed at securing workers' rights, land reform, national sovereignty, and freedom from the political and economic tyranny of old landowning aristocracies and newer corporate oligarchies. Many such martyrs were inspired by what Matthew Whelan calls a "politics of common use," which "prioritizes the access of all people to the gift of Creation." This politics is

---

[35] Archbishop Óscar Romero, February 17, 1980, Homily, in *Homilias, Tomo VI* (San Salvador: UCA Editores, 2009).

grounded in a "theological grammar of Creation as common gift" that recognizes what the Catholic social tradition understands as the "universal destination of created goods."[36]

According to Whelan, calls for land reform and solidarity with landless workers in the Latin American church and in Catholic social teaching more broadly are concrete expressions of the politics of common use. Saint Óscar Romero is a paradigmatic embodiment of this politics, which in his context and in many contexts today is a risky endeavor that Whelan characterizes as "cruciform."

> In Romero's El Salvador, those who spoke out against or otherwise opposed the ubiquity of the concentration of land and who advocated for the landless and land-poor to have access to land to cultivate suffered enormously as a consequence. This suffering points to how, under the conditions of sin and violence, the politics of common use can lead to the cross. In other words, those who hunger and thirst for others to have access to what is theirs in justice often risk laying down their lives in charity.[37]

I would only amend this to say that such a risk is run first and foremost by landless and land-poor peoples when they *themselves* "hunger and thirst *for [their own communities]* to have access to what is theirs in justice." Jesus himself was a member of an oppressed and marginalized people, and his own ministry began from below, not from the heights of political or religious power. Highly visible martyrs like Romero often enter into solidarity with struggles for justice, liberation, and land rights not as the vanguard of these struggles, but as the rearguard, committed to accompanying and

---

[36] Matthew Philipp Whelan, *Blood in the Fields: Óscar Romero, Catholic Social Teaching, and Land Reform* (Washington, DC: Catholic University of America Press, 2020), 20.

[37] Whelan, 26.

defending popular movements in their own praxis of solidarity in their communal struggle for dignity and liberation.[38] Some murdered land defenders have come from a social location a lot like that of Jesus—marginalized and oppressed—whereas others have come from a social location in which they have benefited from existing power structures and have become like Jesus insofar as they subvert or renounce those benefits in favor of solidarity with the struggles of impoverished and oppressed peoples.

The martyrdom of land defenders is paradigmatic for twentieth-century Latin American liberation theologies of martyrdom. But the United Nations and human rights organizations like Global Witness also recognize land defenders as "environmental human rights defenders" because they are defending their communities' right to enjoy a safe environment in which they have access to clean and healthy life-sustaining resources. They are also environmental defenders because it is better for the environment (including the climate) when land use is managed by local communities (especially Indigenous communities) rather than profit-driven and extractivist landgrabbers, large landholders, and/or corporations. Even when local communities and individual farmers are not attentive to the most ecologically sustainable practices, the simple fact of preventing large-scale extractivist industries from destroying local landscapes and waterways also prevents large-scale contributions to deforestation, species loss, pollution, and climate change. Therefore, late-twentieth-century martyrs like Saint Óscar Romero and Blessed Rutilio Grande, who gave their lives in defense of *campesino* land rights and for the sake of agrarian

---

[38] See the argument for intellectuals as rearguard advanced by Boaventura de Sousa Santos, *The End of the Cognitive Empire: The Coming of Age of Epistemologies of the South* (Durham, NC: Duke University Press, 2018). Many thanks to Leonel Guardado for pointing me toward this language and resource for thinking about the relationship between the academy (and perhaps the institutional church) and popular movements.

reform, are, in some respects, ecomartyrs. To an even greater extent, martyrs like Father Josimo Tavares, who stood in solidarity with local communities in their struggle to defend their lands from loggers and ranchers in the Amazon, can be recognized as ecomartyrs. Their struggle was for continued and/or recovered access to land for subsistence farming, which is not only essential for people who need food, water, and shelter; it is far healthier than extractivism for the ecosystems in which human communities make our home. In this book, therefore, Fr. Josimo represents the connection between the twentieth-century Jesus martyrs who died in pursuit of justice and liberation, on the one hand, and contemporary martyrs of environmental human rights and ecological well-being, on the other.

Pope Francis has made this connection between the politics of common use and ecological well-being explicit in his solidarity with popular movements, his landmark encyclical *Laudato Si'*, and in his synodal commitment to ecological ministry in the Amazon region. Whelan points out that this connection is especially evident in Francis's addresses to the World Meeting of Popular Movements, in which Francis's appeal to the rights of *Tierra, Trabajo, y Techo* (Land, Labor, and Lodging) expresses a politics of common use grounded in the theological grammar of Creation as universal gift. In these addresses, Whelan argues, Francis

> extends and deepens reflection upon the politics of common use by underscoring its unavoidable ecological implications. "An economic system centered upon the deity of money," Francis observes in the first address, leads to a "throw-away culture" in which the excluded "are discarded, are 'leftovers.'" People without access to land, labor, and lodging are the result. But such a system, he continues, also "plunder[s] nature to sustain consumption at the frenetic level it needs." Throughout his pontificate, Francis has

pointed to the intimate relationship between the use this system makes of people and the use it makes of the earth itself—the devastation it does to whatever is fragile. The "invisible thread" that binds this devastation is a system that "has imposed the mentality of profit at any price, with no concern for social exclusion or the destruction of nature."[39]

Given that it is the same system that exploits people and destroys the planet, social justice and environmental justice are inextricably linked, and Francis rightly sheds light on how popular movements— grassroots movements of marginalized and oppressed peoples, along with their co-conspirators—are seeking the integration of these forms of justice in their everyday struggles for a more just and ecologically sustainable world.

Similarly, the primary insight at the heart of Pope Francis's articulation of integral ecology in *Laudato Si'* is that "everything is interconnected," such that the cry of the poor and the cry of the earth are deeply intertwined. Both cries are brought about by the same techno-economic system where

priority tends to be given to speculation and the pursuit of financial gain, which fail to take the context into account, let alone the effects on human dignity and the natural environment. Here we see how environmental deterioration and human and ethical degradation are closely linked. Many people will deny doing anything wrong because distractions constantly dull our consciousness of just how limited and finite our world really is. As a result, "whatever is fragile, like the environment, is defenceless before the interests of a deified market, which become the only rule."[40]

---

[39] Whelan, *Blood in the Fields*, 311.
[40] Pope Francis, Encyclical Letter, *Laudato Si': On Care for Our Common Home*, May 24, 2015, www.vatican.va, § 56. Henceforth cited as *LS*.

Because the cry of the poor and the cry of the earth are brought about by the same death-dealing systems, these cries can only be redressed by seeking social and environmental justice in tandem. Therefore, in his book *An Ecological Theology of Liberation*, Daniel Castillo argues that the integral liberation articulated for liberation theology by Gustavo Gutiérrez is extended, broadened, and corrected by a liberationist inclusion of the integral ecology that is championed by Pope Francis. Gutiérrez emphasizes the theological, cultural/psychological, and socio-structural dimensions of human liberation from sin, fatalism, and oppression, and according to Castillo, Francis's articulation of integral ecology upholds "the structure, dynamism, and ecclesial characteristic of Gutiérrez's integralism, while broadening its framework from love of God and neighbor, to love of God, neighbor, and non-human creation."[41]

Finally, the Synod for the Pan-Amazon Region was preceded by a process of dialogue and discernment that brought the global and local church into deeper relationships of encounter and collaboration with communities and ecosystems of the region of the world that many environmentalists pinpoint as among the most vital to preserve in the face of climate change. In his post-synodal apostolic exhortation *Querida Amazonia*, Francis integrates four dreams for the region: a social dream, a cultural dream, an ecological dream, and an ecclesial dream:

> I dream of an Amazon region that fights for the rights of the poor, the original peoples and the least of our brothers and sisters, where their voices can be heard and their dignity advanced.

> I dream of an Amazon region that can preserve its distinctive cultural riches, where the beauty of our humanity shines forth in so many varied ways.

---

[41] Daniel Castillo, *An Ecological Theology of Liberation: Salvation and Political Ecology* (Maryknoll, NY: Orbis Books, 2019), 52.

> I dream of an Amazon region that can jealously preserve
> its overwhelming natural beauty and the superabundant
> life teeming in its rivers and forests.
>
> I dream of Christian communities capable of generous
> commitment, incarnate in the Amazon region, and giving
> the Church new faces with Amazonian features.

Each chapter of the document addresses one of these dreams, with the
ecological chapter offering especially powerful articulations offered by
Amazonian peoples themselves during the synodal process. While the
ecclesial chapter introduces a certain disconnect with its omission of
local requests for women deacons, married priests, and an Amazonian
liturgical rite, the integration of the synod's four dreams offers a potent
expression of the dreams for which contemporary ecomartyrs have
given their lives, especially in the Pan-Amazon region.

Although *Querida Amazonia* does not highlight the reality of
ecomartyrdom in the Amazon per se, the bishops' Final Document
of the Synod mentions Amazonian martyrs four times, going so far
as to assert the folowing:

> One of the most glorious pages of the Amazon has been
> written by the martyrs. The participation of the followers
> of Jesus in his passion, death and glorious resurrection
> has accompanied the life of the Church to this day, espe-
> cially in the moments and places in which, for the sake of
> the Gospel of Jesus, Christians live in the midst of acute
> contradictions, such as those who struggle courageously
> in favour of integral ecology in the Amazon. This Synod
> admires and recognizes those who struggle, at great risk to
> their own lives, to defend the existence of this territory.[42]

---

[42] Synod of Bishops on the Pan-Amazon Region Final Document, "The
Amazon: New Paths for the Church and for an Integral Ecology," October 27,
2019, www.vaticannews.va.

Beyond this presence of the martyrs in the bishops' final document, the meeting of the synod of bishops at the Vatican in October 2019 was deeply marked by images of martyrs carried by attendees and supporters, as well as by The Way of the Cross of the Martyrs of the Amazon that was prayed outside the Vatican during the synod.[43] Here we see very clearly in not only sacred rhetoric but also art and liturgy that murdered land and environmental defenders embody and bear witness to the integration of social and ecological liberation in our world today.

Fr. Josimo Taveres, Chico Mendes, Fr. Alcides Jiménez, and Sr. Dorothy Stang—four ecomartyrs whose stories we contemplated in chapter 4—were all included in The Way of the Cross of the Martyrs of the Amazon outside the Vatican during the synod.[44] Whereas Fr. Josimo represents the martyrial bridge between land defenders and environmental defenders, Chico Mendes represents the move to integrate socioeconomic analysis and human liberation with environmental justice analysis and concern for the continued existence and ecological health of the Amazon forest itself. His martyrdom represents a definitive ecological turn in popular movements of Latin America at the end of the twentieth century, bearing witness to a politics of common use that recognizes the inextricable link between human well-being and the well-being of the natural world. The issues at stake in these movements therefore expand from the question of who owns and/or has access to the land to the question of how those who live on the land, relate to it, and make use of it in more or less sustainable ways. Therefore, popular struggles for justice and liberation in Latin America increasingly have begun to incorporate ecological concerns and defense of ecological integrity into their prophetic praxis. Furthermore, a transformation in popular movements' understanding of land rights has been

---

[43] See "Amazonian 'Way of the Cross' Prayed during Vatican's Amazon Synod," *Catholic News Agency,* October 20, 2019, www.catholicnewsagency.com.

[44] Interestingly, so was Archbishop Óscar Romero!

taking place over the course of these past four decades since Chico's death. Whereas late-twentieth-century struggles for land reform often concentrated on the possession of land as private property, it has become more and more common for these struggles to seek structures of communal land usage, under the guidance of Indigenous wisdom that "the land does not belong to us; we belong to the land." While communal land usage—i.e., the age-old practice of "commoning" discussed in chapter 5—is not necessarily an ecological panacea, it is a particularly effective means of integrating and embodying social and environmental justice.

Whereas Chico Mendes represents this transition from martyrdom for social and economic justice to martyrdom for an integrated praxis of environmental justice and ecological well-being, it is important to note that Indigenous communities have been integrating human and more-than-human well-being for millennia. Western Christian concepts of justice, human rights, and liberation do not translate on a one-to-one basis to Indigenous concepts and cosmovisions. However, the interconnectedness of human and ecological well-being articulated in Francis's integral ecology has already been expressed and embodied, albeit in very different ways, in the ancient cultural and ecological wisdom of Native peoples. We have discussed in chapter 5 that this wisdom should not be romanticized or commodified, but it should be recognized and honored, especially in the case of Indigenous peoples who have been killed for their resistance to the intertwined terrors of land-theft, genocide, and ecocide. Different Indigenous communities may or may not appreciate such mass murders being theologized under the rubric of ecomartyrdom, but it is important to recognize once again here that violence against Indigenous land and environmental defenders has been perpetrated by colonial and neocolonial regimes for over five centuries now. The reality of ecomartyrdom—whether we call it by this name or not—is sadly nothing new.

Christian Theology in Light of Ecomartyrdom[45]

One of Sobrino's most significant contributions to liberation theology is his insistence that the Jesus martyrs must be given precedence, not only in Christian faith and praxis, but in critical reflection on that faith and praxis as well: they are "*ipso facto* a central reality for faith, for the church and for theology."[46] In fact, as embodied manifestations of the divine presence in history, the martyrs are of fundamental and universal importance to the faith and must be taken into account in *all* theology, not just so-called "contextual theologies."[47] Sobrino therefore laments the fact that the reality of martyrdom is so neglected in the discipline today and asks whether paradigm shifts have made the martyrs "obsolete ... a theme for historical research and piety, but not for theoretical reflection, as if theology had more important things with which to busy itself than martyrs and crucified peoples."[48] Insofar as the martyrs resemble Jesus, though, they give theology a "Jesus-like" specificity which, according to Sobrino, is of utmost importance because when Christian theology "distances itself from Jesus of Nazareth and, above all, from his cross, it becomes bourgeois."[49] In light of this study of extractivism and ecomartyrdom, I would add that, insofar as the comforts of bourgeois existence depend on extractivist industries and the violences that they perpetrate, a bourgeois theology lacking in Jesus-like specificity is dangerously complicit in the crucifixion of the poor and the planet alike.

Sobrino maintains that the Jesus martyrs interrupt bourgeois existence to give theology a "Jesus-like" specificity because they are a historical and theologal sign of the times in which the crucified

---

[45] Parts of this section are revised versions of text from Gandolfo, "Women and Martyrdom."

[46] Sobrino, "Our World: Cruelty and Compassion," 20.

[47] Sobrino, "Los mártires jesuánicos en el tercer mundo," 248

[48] Sobrino, "Los mártires jesuánicos en el tercer mundo," 247.

[49] Sobrino, "Los mártires jesuánicos en el tercer mundo," 252.

and risen Jesus is present. For him, the martyrs "not only refer us to the theological concepts of God and Christ, but rather, and above all else, they *make these concepts present*."[50] In his view, their affinity with the fundamental dynamism of Jesus' life and death makes their martyrdom important to theology because their martyrdom becomes "a hermeneutical principle, a mystagogy for understanding the martyrdom of Jesus."[51] The martyrs thus provide an epistemological perspective that better illuminates Jesus' liberating person and work and the mystery of the "God of the poor" who wills that people whose lives are threatened and cut short by poverty and oppression have liberation and life in abundance.[52] This epistemological advantage also operates negatively insofar as the martyrs witness against historical idols—the *anti-reino* gods of injustice and death that opposed Jesus' proclamation of God's reign and continue to oppose the martyrs' participation in that proclamation.[53] The same theologal dynamic and epistemological advantage is true for ecomartyrs, who are killed for their opposition to these same idols, with an even deeper and more complex understanding of how extensively these idols demand the sacrifice of not only human lives but the life and integrity of more-than-human Creation as well.

Because martyrdom illuminates the content of theology by making that content present in history, Sobrino argues that centering martyrdom also serves to infuse the entire theological task with some fundamental dispositions. Doing theological reflection in light of ecomartyrdom can extend, deepen, and guide these dispositions along prophetic paths of not only integral human liberation but ecological conversion, intersectional liberation, and interreligious dialogue as well.

---

[50] Sobrino, "Los mártires jesuánicos en el tercer mundo," 248. Emphasis in the original.

[51] Sobrino, "Our World: Cruelty and Compassion," 20.

[52] Sobrino, "Los mártires jesuánicos en el tercer mundo," 250–252.

[53] Sobrino, "Los mártires jesuánicos en el tercer mundo," 251–252.

A Theologal Disposition

First and foremost, Sobrino avers that remembering martyrdom cultivates a "theologal disposition" that places theology not in the realm of abstract categories and concepts but in the embodied realm of "that which, for human beings, is ultimate: life and death."[54] In Sobrino's theology, which draws on the work of his martyred Jesuit friend and colleague Ignacio Ellacuría, speaking of reality as "theologal" refers to the incarnate presence of God in the fleshy, material realities of Creation. The sacramental imagination of many ecomartyrs bears witness to the reality of God's life-giving creativity present in the beauty and abundance of Creation and to the presence of divine pathos and solidarity in the realities of death and destruction. In fact, these martyrs are embodied, incarnate manifestations of divine creativity, compassion, and solidarity. They themselves are sacraments of divine solidarity with Creation. In light of their witness, theology cannot avoid grappling with ultimate questions about suffering and sin, or about hope for resurrection, God's reign, and its accompanying justice for the poor, the planet, and even the cosmos as a whole. Ecomartyrdom in particular puts Christian praxis and theology in embodied, social, and ecological contact with these questions, requiring Christian discipleship and theological reflection that not only reflects cognitively on concepts like "deep incarnation" but also—indeed, primarily—seeks paths of contemplative and liberative participation in the deep incarnation of the divine in our corner of Creation, our common home.

A Dialectical Disposition

Second, Sobrino maintains that the martyrs bring to theology a "dialectical disposition" that challenges the discipline to not only announce the good news of God's grace, justice, truth, and life, but

---

[54] Sobrino, "Los mártires jesuánicos en el tercer mundo," 249.

also to denounce the historical realities of sin, injustice, falsehood, and death. As the first several chapters of this book attest, ecomartyrdom is a stark revelation of how the anti-ecological imaginary of extractivism is a violent manifestation of sin in our world today. This dialectical disposition opens up Christian theology in general and liberation and ecotheologies in particular to self-examination and critique in light of the witness of land and environmental defenders who have incorporated not only liberationist and ecological but also intersectional, feminist, and decolonial analyses into their struggles for environmental justice. Centering ecomartyrdom certainly corroborates ecological critiques of Christian anthropocentrism, a flaw that has plagued not only conservative Christianity but also many liberation theologies centered exclusively on human liberation as well. On the other hand, ecomartyrs bear witness to a robust commitment to the well-being of human communities and the earth in tandem, as opposed to the misanthropic commitments characteristic of certain expressions of Deep Ecology. By and large, land and environmental defenders are being murdered not for a purely conservationist approach to environmentalism, but for their commitment to the integration of human and ecological well-being that we discussed above.

This integral commitment has led many land and environmental defenders to deepen and extend their understanding of how the coloniality of the current world system is designed to privilege an elite minority at the cost of the colonized and the earth itself. Remembering the analysis and praxis of Berta Cáceres, for example, reminds us that the *anti-reino* that the ecomartyrs stand against as dialectical witnesses is not only structured by capitalism (a fact that Sobrino would readily admit), but by the colonial ravages of racism and patriarchy. Christian liberation theologies and ecotheologies alike would do well to take these critiques into account as we attempt to formulate our dialectical understanding of how the sinful dynamics of anti-social and anti-ecological imaginaries operate in complex, interconnected webs of violence and oppression. Just as the life-giving elements and energies of the cosmos are all interconnected, so too are the human systems that produce the cries of the earth and of the poor. These cries intersect with the cries of Indigenous and Afro-descendent peoples, of women (especially women of color), of immigrants and refugees, of LGBTQ+ folks, of the disabled, of the elderly, and of all those whom society disregards as disposable. Pope Francis's integral ecology gestures toward these intersections but requires significant correction with regard to its omission of an explicit analysis of racism and its reassertion of binary and essentialist thinking around gender and sexuality.[55]

One other dimension of the dialectical disposition that remembering ecomartyrdom can cultivate in Christian theology pertains to the dangers of Christian supremacy and the need for cultivating a culture of interreligious encounter characterized by humility and solidarity. The murder of land and environmental defenders is a worldwide phenomenon claiming the lives of far more non-Christians than Christians. Indigenous peoples, many or most of whom hold their own cosmovisions and practice their own forms of ancestral spirituality, are particularly vulnerable to violent persecution for their resistance to extractivist projects. Remembering that ecomartyrdom encompasses and transcends many religious and spiritual traditions can challenge Christian theology to internal critique of the barriers to meeting non-Christian communities with a dialogical spirit of genuine respect and collaboration. Given the history and ongoing legacy of Christian complicity with the extractivist coloniality of capitalism, racism, and patriarchy, Christians certainly have much to learn from such dialogue.

---

[55] See *LS*, § 155.

A Soteriological Disposition

Finally, Sobrino posits that centering martyrdom also lends a "soteriological disposition" to theology because the martyrs "support—or can support—the hope that in Jesus' cross (along with his life and resurrection) there is salvation."[56] The love that leads to the crosses of Jesus martyrs and ecomartyrs in history is what "verifies" for Christians today the saving power of God's love made manifest on Jesus' cross two thousand years ago. What does Jesus martyrdom in general and ecomartyrdom in particular teach us about that saving power? Or rather, what, if anything, can be called salvific in the suffering and deaths of the martyrs? Juan Hernández Pico argues that the deaths of martyrs are not initially productive of salvific fruits, but rather bring about frustration, horror, anger, fear, and discouragement:

> [Their martyrdom] represents primarily the triumph of powerful criminal violence, of state terrorism, which silences a prophet's voice forever, brutally interrupts a reformer's project, mercilessly cuts short the life of a researcher, permanently extinguishes the thoughts of a genius, or humiliates and rapes the dignity of a community.[57]

A broadcast by Radio Progreso in Honduras made this same point in a reflection offered on the fourth anniversary of the assassination of Berta Cáceres:

> A person whom we confess to be a martyr was above all a victim of a cruel assassination, a person whose body we saw broken, who suffered wounds of the flesh in their body, who endured and suffered the horrors of death. Before being confessed as a martyr, the person was horrifically

---

[56] Sobrino, "Los mártires jesuánicos en el tercer mundo," 249.

[57] Juan Hernández Pico, "The Hope Born of the Martyrs' Love," in Okure et al., eds., *Rethinking Martyrdom*, 130.

> assassinated, and we saw their body broken and shattered,
> in the midst of a trail of blood, with their face disfigured,
> with the grimace of an ungracious death. No confession
> of martyrdom can make this bloody reality of violent
> death disappear.[58]

These reminders warn us against the dangers of romanticizing redemptive suffering already discussed above. The soteriological disposition that centering martyrdom lends to Christian theology must first and foremost denounce the assassination of the martyrs and never lose sight of the violence and injustice of their deaths. At first glance, then, it appears that there is nothing of salvation, light, or hope to be found in the horrific death of a martyr. Brutality and murder contain nothing of goodness in them. Violent death, in and of itself, is purely negative. But this is not the end of the story.

Liberation theologians and ecclesial base communities in the church of the poor in Latin America have been insisting for fifty years now that there is something of God's saving power at work in martyrdom. First and foremost, the Jesus martyrs' and ecomartyrs' unconditional solidarity with the oppressed, coupled with the stark reality of their murders, unmasks the idols of death that require sacrifices—of human life and labor, of the earth and its goods—to survive.[59] Furthermore, the legacy of the martyrs calls the church to conversion, challenging all Christians to become *real* human beings, incarnate in *reality*, as opposed to remaining within the illusions of unreality. Ecomartyrs in particular call us to compassion for the marginalized and oppressed—including the earth and its more-than-human creatures—and they encourage us to take upon ourselves the burden of reality, even if such action comes at

---

[58] "Berta y el Martirio," Radio Progreso Broadcast, March 5, 2020, https://radioprogresohn.net/enfoque/berta-y-el-martirio/.

[59] Sobrino, *Witnesses to the Kingdom*, 114.

a cost to our own comfort and security.[60] Their unceasing love and fidelity invite us to live with freedom from selfishness, in joy over sorrow, and in hope against resignation. According to Sobrino, "In this freedom, joy and hope there is already a sort of reverberation of resurrection."[61] The legacy of the martyrs thus demonstrates that death does not have the last word, and their memory invites us to live as a resurrected people, actively confident in the promise of the coming of God's reign, the advent of a new heaven and a new earth. They reveal the face of a God who is love, solidarity, and justice, just as they show us that "it is possible to live with great love in this world and to place all of our capabilities at the service of love."[62] Ecomartyrs in particular witness to the ecological face of this love and the inextricable link between ecology, liberation, and salvation. The reverberation of resurrection that can be felt in their witness calls us to actively hope for justice and reconciliation between human beings and our common home, and for the renewal of our earth community. Ultimately, their sacrifice becomes salvific when we take up their cause, which is the cause of Jesus, the cause of human and ecological liberation, the cause of the reign of God.

Points of Light

The landscape of extractivism in the Americas and beyond is bleak, and it is hard to see a way forward in the midst of the violence and fear that plague marginalized human communities and the vulnerable ecosystems of our common home. For those of us far removed from sites of extractivist industries, these realities of environmental injustice and ecological degradation are either invisible or so over-

---

[60] Jon Sobrino, "Martyrs: An Appeal to the Church," in Okure et al., eds., *Rethinking Martyrdom*, 141–144.

[61] Sobrino, "Martyrs," 148.

[62] Sobrino, *El Principio Misericordia* (San Salvador: UCA Editores, 1992), 263.

whelming that hope is hard to come by. Added to this hopelessness in the face of extractivism is the growing sense of despair, especially among young people, with regard to the enormous challenges of the climate crisis and the intractability of the systems and institutions with the power to mitigate global warming and its catastrophic effects on human beings and the entire earth community. The persecution of communities and the murder of individuals on the front lines of these struggles for environmental and climate justice can certainly add to this milieu of hopelessness. And yet communities across Latin America have experienced resurrection hope in the memory of their ecomartyrs, interpreting their witness as

> *Points of light*
> *in the darkness of fear*
> *shining with courage*
> *forging peace*
> *there on the horizon*
> *the greater flame*
> *the justice of God's reign*
> *Resurrection*[63]

---

[63] These are selected lyrics from a song featured in the video "Mártires da Caminhada," cited in note 1 of this chapter. Portuguese text written by Cireneu Kuhn, SVD, and English translation adapted from that of Pedro Andrés Sánchez.

Conclusion

RESPONDING TO THE WITNESS

Honoring Ecomartyrs with Our Lives

At the sixth national meeting of the ecclesial base communities of Brazil in 1986, participants affirmed: "*Nós queremos nossos mártires vivos e não mortos.*" We want our martyrs alive, not dead! Witnessing to the sacred interconnectedness of human life and the life of our earth community, our common home, should not lead to unjust and early death. It should not provoke persecution, criminalization, defamation, torture, or imprisonment. It should not lead to death threats, nor should it end in the violent theft of human lives. To be a witness to the integrity of Creation and to human dignity, justice, and peace is an option for life, albeit in the face of death. Indeed, in the words of Marcelo Barros:

> The journey of the popular church and its immersion in struggles for liberation teach us that martyrdom is not only a way of dying; it is above all a way of living. We [in the popular church] are witnesses that there is redemption in this world and that, despite all the forces of evil, we will continue on this journey."[1]

---

[1]   Marcelo Barros, "Queremos nossos mártires vivos," Brasil de Fato Website, March 25, 2019, https://www.brasildefatope.com.br/2019/03/25/queremos-nossos-martires-vivos#.

Similarly, all land and environmental defenders in the Americas and around the world continue on this journey of life, witnessing to their own particular wellsprings of love for humanity and the earth as one interconnected community. In their continued struggle, their persistent praxis of ecological love and liberation, they make present and honor the resurrection and legacy of those witnesses who have fallen. They continue to bear witness to the realities for which the ecomartyrs have died, refusing to be silent in the face of extractivist violence and continuing to build an alternative world in which many worlds are free to coexist, a world that resembles, at least in part, the reality named by Christians as the reign of God.

How should Christians and people of good will respond to the witness of land and environmental defenders? How might we enter into solidarity with their commitment to and struggle for environmental human rights and ecological flourishing for all of Creation? How might we participate in the resurrection of those who have fallen in this struggle? Michael Lee's framework for responding to the martyrdom of the "revolutionary saint" Óscar Romero can be helpful for framing our own response to ecomartyrdom today. Lee bases his analysis on Romero's own response to martyrdom in his context, and on the three-fold approach to poverty taken by the Latin American bishops at their landmark meeting in Medellín in 1968.

Listening to the Martyrs of Reality

First, just as the Latin American bishops advocated denunciation of material poverty as a sinful injustice that cries out to the heavens, Lee argues that our response to martyrdom should before all else be grounded in an understanding of violent death today as the catastrophic and sinful martyrdom of reality itself. The violent pillage of our common home, the displacement of human beings from their homelands and territories, and the exploitation of human bodies to do the work of extractivist labor—these are all realities of violent death that witness to the world as it really is. Borrowing the language of Ignacio Ellacuría, Lee reminds us that the crucified people reveal that which needs to be resisted, denounced, and opposed in the world. Ellacuría, Romero, and Lee all privilege the human victims of history when they name the crucified people as "martyrs of reality," but we can add to their number the untold ecological "martyrs" of extractivist violence—forests, rivers, wetlands, entire mountaintops, and the millions of species that are being wiped from the planet in the midst of this sixth great extinction. Lee tells us that Romero's own theological response to the martyrs of reality is "listening to the voice of blood":

> They testify to reality. Without valorizing their suffering, one can acknowledge their testimony as something that cannot be ignored. Theirs is the cry of Abel's blood. Theirs are the moans of the slaves in Egypt. Any people that wishes to hear the voice of God must hear it in these cries. The testimony of these victims is like that of Lazarus in the bosom of Abraham. They demand justice; they call for transformation.[2]

Listening to the voice of the blood that has been extracted from the "open veins" of the Americas will require humble listening to and learning from the voices—the cries and the wisdom—of the earth itself and those on the front lines of environmental and climate justice movements.

We should all make our way to those front lines, but right now it is the world's most oppressed and marginalized communities who are leading the way in resisting ecological degradation and climate breakdown. They are experiencing the death-dealing effects of

---

[2]   Michael E. Lee, *Revolutionary Saint: The Theological Vision of Óscar Romero* (Maryknoll, NY: Orbis Books, 2018), 171.

extractivism and climate chaos now, and they are responding with resistance and resilience in their struggles to defend our common home and its inhabitants from harm. This book has only scratched the surface of these struggles. Our response to the witness that has been laid forth all too briefly in these pages should be to continually educate ourselves and others about how the intersecting nodes of capitalism, racism, and patriarchy conspire to produce death and destruction for people and the planet alike. To name and denounce these unjust systems for the sinful and violent realities that they are, we must understand them, and to understand them, we must listen to and learn from those who are most affected by them—poor communities, Indigenous, and Afro-descendent peoples, women who must provide for their families from the fruits of the earth, trees that depend on one another to communicate and survive, rivers that beckon to their people to swim in their waters, and ecosystems that require reciprocity and equilibrium to flourish. Listening to and learning from the martyrs of reality should be our first response.

Cultivating Ecological Conversion

The second dimension of Lee's framework for responding to martyrdom parallels the Latin American bishops' understanding of spiritual poverty and draws on Romero's own spirituality of martyrdom. Our response to martyrdom, Lee argues, should involve "the utter devotion and dependence on God" that mark the calling to spiritual martyrdom shared by all Christians. Though not all Christians will face a martyr's death, and the language of "spiritual martyrdom" runs the risk of pietistic escapism, Lee helps us understand that Romero "saw spiritual martyrdom as a recognition of one's duty to live for others that comes from the insight of dependence on God."[3] But placing this call to dependence on God in conversation

---

[3]   Lee, 198.

with Pope Francis's call to ecological conversion can bear great fruit for cultivating a life-giving, hope-filled response to ecomartyrdom and the continued struggles of land and environmental defenders today.

In *Laudato Si'*, Francis draws on the rich heritage of the Christian tradition to advocate a spiritual renewal in humanity capable of transforming our relationship with our common home and motivating "a more passionate concern for the protection of our world."[4] This conversion is not an individualistic pursuit of self-improvement, but a communal cultivation of certain embodied dispositions, such as gratitude and gratuitousness, a willingness to give of oneself for the sake of others, "and a loving awareness that we are not disconnected from the rest of creatures, but joined in a splendid universal communion."[5] This final disposition reveals that Francis's call to ecological conversion is not a call to self-abnegation or unhealthy asceticism based on the assumption of scarcity. Rather, it calls us to a robust spirituality of abundant life!

Indeed, Francis muses that Christian spirituality is capable of cultivating ecological conversion insofar as it

> proposes an alternative understanding of the quality of life, and encourages a prophetic and contemplative lifestyle, one capable of deep enjoyment free of the obsession with consumption. We need to take up an ancient lesson, found in different religious traditions and also in the Bible. It is the conviction that "less is more." A constant flood of new consumer goods can baffle the heart and prevent us from cherishing each thing and each moment. To be serenely present to each reality, however small it may be, opens us to much greater horizons of understanding

---

[4] Pope Francis, Encyclical Letter, *Laudato Si': On Care for Our Common Home*, May 24, 2015, www.vatican.va, § 216. Henceforth cited as *LS*.

[5] *LS*, § 220.

and personal fulfilment. Christian spirituality proposes a growth marked by moderation and the capacity to be happy with little. It is a return to that simplicity which allows us to stop and appreciate the small things, to be grateful for the opportunities which life affords us, to be spiritually detached from what we possess, and not to succumb to sadness for what we lack. This implies avoiding the dynamic of dominion and the mere accumulation of pleasures. Such sobriety, when lived freely and consciously, is liberating. It is not a lesser life or one lived with less intensity. On the contrary, it is a way of living life to the full.[6]

People who knew and loved ecomartyrs like those whose stories we have contemplated in this book often remark that they were vibrant human beings who lived life to the fullest—who appreciated and cared for their own embodiment in the created world and their dependence on the divine and the earth for existence and sustenance, who encountered and celebrated the sacred presence of the divine in themselves and other people and the planet, who lamented the defilement of God's good Creation, who sang and danced and wrote poetry and music, who sought not greater wealth or possessions for themselves but equity in the distribution of the abundant goods of Creation for all to enjoy.

Many ecomartyrs drew on the biblical and contemplative wellsprings of their Christian faith to cultivate such fullness of life, but many others drew on other wellsprings of their own traditions. Their witness calls us all to "drink from our own wells"—from the spiritual aquifers that nourish the roots of our own ancestral, cultural, and religious traditions and from the ecological aquifers that nourish the roots of our material existence in this world. As we drink from these wells and tend to the roots of our spiritualities,

---

[6] *LS*, §§222–223.

we too might experience, embody, and bear prophetic witness to the reality of our dependence on the sacred interdependence of all reality for our existence and well-being.

Standing in Solidarity

Third and finally, Lee echoes the Latin American bishops' call to voluntary poverty in his account of how "martyrs of solidarity" like Romero (and the ecomartyrs highlighted in this book) are persecuted because they make a choice to stand in solidarity with the martyrs of reality. "They die because their witness induces a hatred from those principalities and powers that feed on victims. The martyrs of solidarity are those who bear the brunt of this hatred because of their love for their fellow human beings."[7] As this book's account of extractivism and ecomartyrdom has demonstrated, it is often the martyrs of reality themselves who make this choice to remain in solidarity with their people, stay on their land, and protect the ecosystems in which they make their home, all the while standing fast in the face of danger. With his account of these "martyrs of solidarity," Lee ties all three senses of martyrdom together:

> [T]he martyrs of solidarity respond to the testimony given by the martyrs of reality and in doing so inspire others to concretize the disposition of spiritual martyrdom in our world today. It may not be in dramatic fashion. It might even be, as Jesse Jackson used to say, simply declaring to a dehumanizing system, "I am somebody." However, the martyrs of solidarity invite everyone to be honest with reality.[8]

Moreover, martyrs of solidarity like Romero and the ecomartyrs featured in this book should challenge, inspire, and empower us all to enter into committed solidarity with the causes for which

---

7   Lee, 172.
8   Lee, 173.

they lived and died. In the case of ecomartyrs, this means entering into active solidarity with the contemporary struggles of land and environmental defenders. In fact, Lee refers to Romero's legacy as "a well from which all people can draw sustenance and nourishment" for participation in these revolutionary struggles to cast the mighty from their thrones and lift up the lowly. So too, the legacy of ecomartyrs—of Josimo, Chico, Alcides, Dorothy, Marcelo, Berta, and so many more—is a wellspring that offers lifegiving waters of courage, hope, and solidarity.

What does concrete action in solidarity with this legacy of ecomartyrdom look like? How might those of us who benefit from privileges conferred by the realities of extractivism and ecomartyrdom enter into concrete solidarity with contemporary land and environmental defenders? There is not one unambiguous answer to this question, of course. Each of us must discern what form solidarity takes in our own lives and contexts. However, it is important to conduct our discernment and enter into relationships of solidarity with *local* and *global* consciousness aimed at *personal*, *cultural*, and *political* transformation. Each of these elements are intertwined with the others, and the struggles of local land and environmental defenders often take all of them into account as they form global networks of personal and communal support and political action. First Nations and Native American water protectors from the Tar Sands of North America, for example, have entered into relationships of solidarity with the original peoples of Abya Yala to resist global networks of fossil fuel extraction and promote clean energy alternatives. Solidarity for readers of this book might look like partnering with local environmental justice organizations fighting the environmental racism of coal ash contamination or hog farm pollution, while making personal decisions about consumer purchases that avoid undue reliance on metallic mining to produce endlessly replaceable electronic devices. It might look like divesting one's own investment portfolio from extractivist industries and/or advocating for one's religious community or university to divest from such investments as well. Solidarity for Christians will also require putting pressure on our churches and governments, locally and globally, to publicly denounce and divest from the violence of extractivist industries that criminalize, persecute, and murder land and environmental defenders in the Americas and beyond. Readers can find just a few resources for taking action on the companion website to this book at www.ecomartyrdom.net. But the possibilities are endless. This can feel overwhelming and may even contribute to the sense of hopelessness and despair so prevalent in our world today. But in the words of a prayer mysteriously attributed to Saint Óscar Romero but penned by Fr. Ken Untener, "we cannot do everything," but we can do something and "do it very well":

> It helps, now and then, to step back and take a
>   long view.
> The kingdom is not only beyond our efforts, it is even
>   beyond our vision.
> We accomplish in our lifetime only a tiny fraction of
>   the magnificent enterprise that is God's work.
> Nothing we do is complete, which is a way of saying
>   that the Kingdom always lies beyond us.
> No statement says all that could be said.
> No prayer fully expresses our faith.
> No confession brings perfection.
> No pastoral visit brings wholeness.
> No program accomplishes the church's mission.
> No set of goals and objectives includes everything.
>
> This is what we are about.
> We plant the seeds that one day will grow.
> We water seeds already planted, knowing that they
>   hold future promise.

We lay foundations that will need further development.
We provide yeast that produces far beyond our
*   capabilities.*
We cannot do everything, and there is a sense of
*   liberation in realizing that.*
This enables us to do something, and to do it
*   very well.*
It may be incomplete, but it is a beginning, a step
*   along the way,*
An opportunity for the Lord's grace to enter and
*   do the rest.*

We may never see the end results, but that is the
*   difference between the master builder*
*   and the worker.*

We are workers, not master builders; ministers,
*   not messiahs.*

We are prophets of a future not our own.[9]

Let us honor the ecomartyrs with our lives by planting seeds of solidarity with those who carry on their legacy in defense of our common home and all of its inhabitants. Let us join them in their prophetic struggle for a future that is not our own.

---

[9] This prayer is often erroneously and rather mysteriously attributed to Archbishop Romero, and it is sometimes even titled "The Romero Prayer." However, according to the United States Conference of Catholic Bishops website, it "was first presented by Cardinal Dearden in 1979 and quoted by Pope Francis in 2015. This reflection is an excerpt from a homily written for Cardinal Dearden by then-Fr. Ken Untener on the occasion of the Mass for Deceased Priests, October 25, 1979. Pope Francis quoted Cardinal Dearden in his remarks to the Roman Curia on December 21, 2015. Fr. Untener was named bishop of Saginaw, Michigan, in 1980." See "Prophets of a Future Not Our Own," USCCB Website, https://www.usccb.org/prayer-and-worship/prayers-and-devotions/prayers/prophets-of-a-future-not-our-own.

Appendix A

Study Guide

This study guide is designed for use in classrooms, book clubs, community study groups, nonprofit organizations, and/or religious education programs. Here you will find English-language resources for deepening your understanding of the topics presented in this book, along with questions for reflection and discussion. Additional resources, including audiovisual materials, are available on this book's companion website www.ecomartyrdom.net.

Chapter One

The Pillage of Our Common Home:
Ecomartyrdom and Extractivism in the Americas

Resources for Further Study
Reading Materials

- Roxanne Dunbar-Ortiz. *An Indigenous People's History of the United States.* Boston: Beacon Press, 2014.
- Eduardo Galeano. *Open Veins of Latin America: Five Centuries of the Pillage of a Continent*, 25th Anniversary Edition. New York: Monthly Review Press, 1997.
- Dina Gilio-Whitaker. *As Long as Grass Grows: The Indigenous Fight for Environmental Justice, from Colonization to Standing Rock.* Boston: Beacon Press, 2020.

Documentary Films

- *Exterminate All the Brutes.* Directed by Raoul Peck, 2021.
- *The Condor and the Eagle.* Directed by Sophie Guerra and Clément Guerra, 2019.

Questions for Reflection and Discussion

- How does the history of Indigenous environmental history presented in this chapter and/or in the resources suggested above compare with your previous assumptions about how Indigenous peoples made use of the lands that are now known as the Americas?
- How does the account of European conquest and colonization of the Americas presented in this chapter and/or in the resources suggested above compare with your previous knowledge of these historical processes?
- What does Atahualpa Yupanquí mean when he sings that there is something more important than God in this world: "that no one should have to spit out blood so that others can live a more comfortable life"?
- Identify two or three concrete examples of extractivism in which the earth and marginalized human beings have been or are compelled to literally or figuratively "spit out blood" so that others can live with greater comforts and conveniences.
- How does the anti-social and anti-ecological imaginary of extractivism operate in your own life and community?

Chapter Two

Fighting for Our Common Home:
Extractivism and the Struggle for Environmental
Justice in the Americas

Resources for Further Study
Reading Materials

- "Pacha: Defending the Land." Collaborative report presented by the Group of International Relations and Global South and the Federal University of the State of Rio de Janeiro. Available online at http://www.grisulunirio.com/wp-content/uploads/2019/01/Cartilha_Final_Ingl%C3%AAs_Web.pdf.
- Ayana Elizabeth Johnson and Katherine K. Wilkinson. *All We Can Save: Truth, Courage, and Solutions for the Climate Crisis.* New York: One World Books, 2020.

Documentary Films

- *Zapatista.* Directed by Big Noise Films, 1999.
- *Last Mountain.* Directed by Bill Haney, 2011.
- *The New Conquistadors.* Presented by the Pulitzer Center on Crisis Reporting and the Canadian Broadcasting Corporation, 2012.
- *Raising Resistance.* Directed by David Bernet and Bettina Borgfeld, 2013.
- *First Daughter and the Black Snake.* Directed by Keri Pickett, 2017.
- *LN3: Seven Teachings of the Anishinaabe in Resistance.* Directed by Suez Taylor, 2020. A discussion guide for this film is available at https://www.stopline3.org/the-study-guide.

- Multiple documentaries on environmental racism are available to stream online via the Global Environmental Justice Observatory of the University of California, Santa Cruz, at https://globalenvironmentaljustice.sites.ucsc.edu/resources-2/united-states-environmental-justice/films-and-documentaries/.

Questions for Reflection and Discussion

- Why do many members of local communities resist extractivist projects, even when they promise "jobs" or "development"?
- How is extractivism related to patriarchy and racism?
- How is extractivism related to climate breakdown?
- What is the relationship between your own community and extractivism? Does your community benefit from the privileges it provides? And/or does it suffer from the violence it does to human beings and the earth?
- How are environmental justice movements resisting extractivism throughout the Americas?
- What are some of the alternatives to extractivism that environmental justice movements seek to embody in the daily lives of their communities?

Chapter Three

Dying for Our Common Home:
The Criminalization and Assassination of
Environmental Defenders

Resources for Further Study

- United Nations Declaration on the Rights of Indigenous Peoples, https://www.un.org/development/desa/indigenouspeoples/wp-content/uploads/sites/19/2018/11/UNDRIP_E_web.pdf.

- "Escazú Agreement for Young People" is a document produced by UNICEF that lays out the contours of the agreement in an accessible way. https://www.unicef.org/lac/media/19326/file/escazu-agreement.pdf.
- The website for Global Witness houses an archive of annual reports on threats against and assassinations of environmental defenders, along with helpful resources for visualizing the data. Explore the website and read the latest report here: https://www.globalwitness.org/en/campaigns/environmental-activists/.

Questions for Reflection and Discussion

- How do you depend on the goods of the natural world for your everyday existence and flourishing?
- Does your family and community enjoy and/or lack access to a safe, clean, healthy, and sustainable environment? What structures facilitate and/or impede that access?
- How are environmental defenders in the Americas being persecuted for their work on behalf of social and environmental justice?

Chapter Four

Narrating the Witness:
In Memory of Murdered Land and Environmental Defenders

Resources for Further Study
Fr. Josimo Tavares

- Binka Le Breton. *A Land to Die For.* Atlanta: Clarity Press, 1997.

Chico Mendes

- Chico Mendes and Tony Gross. *Fight for the Forest: Chico Mendes in His Own Words*. London: Latin America Bureau Research and Action, 1989.

- Andrew Revkin. *The Burning Season: The Murder of Chico Mendes and the Fight for the Amazon Rain Forest*. New York: Houghton Mifflin, 1990.
- *The Burning Season*. Feature film, directed by John Frankenheimer, 1994.

Fr. Alcides Jiménez

- "La Vida por La Amazonía-Capítulo 5-Padre Alcides Jiménez-Semillas del Putumayo." Short film produced by SIGNIS ALC for the Red Ecclesial Panamazonica (REPAM). Available via YouTube at https://youtu.be/kzDhvC9vZfo.

Sr. Dorothy Stang

- Roseanne Murphy. *Martyr of the Amazon: The Life of Sister Dorothy Stang*. Maryknoll, NY: Orbis Books, 2007.
- Binka Le Breton. *The Greatest Gift: The Courageous Life and Martyrdom of Sister Dorothy Stang*. New York: Doubleday, 2008.
- Michele Murdock. *A Journey of Courage: The Amazing Story of Sister Dorothy Stang*. Cincinnati: Sisters of Notre Dame de Namur, 2009.
- *They Killed Sister Dorothy*. Documentary film directed by Daniel Junge. First Run Features, 2008.

Marcelo Rivera

- Robin Broad and John Cavanaugh. *The Water Defenders: How Ordinary People Saved a Country from Corporate Greed*. Boston: Beacon Press, 2021.
- "The Mysterious Death of Marcelo Rivera," an excerpt from *Return to El Salvador*. Documentary film directed by Jaime Moffett. Available via YouTube at https://youtu.be/yvXm52BhSHQ.

Berta Cáceres

- Nina Lakhani. *Who Killed Berta Cáceres? Dams, Death Squads, and an Indigenous Defender's Battle for the Planet.* New York: Verso, 2020.
- "Las Semillas de Berta Cáceres." Documentary film, produced by the Entre Pueblos journalism project, 2021. Available via YouTube at https://youtu.be/gBC5I16oKO4.
- "Guardiana de los Ríos." Documentary film, produced by Campaña Madre Tierra and distributed by Radio Progreso, 2016. Available via YouTube at https://youtu.be/Lwwe4MOGfmo.

Questions for Reflection and Discussion

- How do the stories of moral exemplars function in your own life and/or community?
- How were the individuals featured in this chapter part of larger communities that formed and supported them in their environmental justice work?
- How are the individuals featured in this chapter ordinary people? How or why did they become extraordinary?
- What were the difficult decisions that the individuals featured in this chapter had to confront as part of their work for environmental justice? What do you think guided them in their decision-making?
- Why do those responsible for the murder of land and environmental defenders enjoy impunity for their crimes?
- Why are so many murdered land and environmental defenders invisible to the international community?

Chapter Five

Wellsprings of the Witness:
The Ecological Imaginations of Land and
Environmental Defenders

Resources for Further Study
On Integral Ecology

- Pope Francis. *Laudato Si': On Care for Our Common Home.*
  www.vatican.va. Many helpful commentaries and study
  guides have been published to assist popular readings of
  this encyclical.

On Latin American "Good Living"

- Néstor Medina. "Embracing a Millennia-Old Cosmovision." *Sojourners.* January 2021. https://sojo.net/magazine/
  january-2021/embracing-millennia-old-cosmovision.

On Traditions of Commoning

- David Bollier. *Thinking Like a Commoner: A Short Introduction to the Life of the Commons.* Gabriola Island, BC:
  New Society Publishers, 2014.

On Decolonial Feminism

- Melisa Pagán. "Extractive Zones and the Nexus of the
  Coloniality of Being/Coloniality of Gender: Towards a
  Decolonial Feminist Integral Ecology." *Journal of Hispanic/
  Latino Theology* 22, no. 1 (Spring 2020).

On Indigenous Cosmovisions

- Robin Wall Kimmerer. *Braiding Sweetgrass: Indigenous
  Wisdom, Scientific Knowledge, and the Teachings of Plants.*
  Minnneapolis: Milkweed Editions, 2011.

- George E. "Tink" Tinker. *American Indian Liberation: A Theology of Sovereignty*. Maryknoll, NY: Orbis Books, 2008.

On African-Heritage Religions

- Melanie L. Harris. *Ecowomanism: African American Women and Earth-Honoring Faiths*. Maryknoll, NY: Orbis Books, 2017.
- "Black Agrarian Wisdom—Young Farmers Conference 2019." Stone Barns Center for Food and Agriculture. Workshop led by Leah Penniman of Soul Fire Farm. Available via YouTube at https://youtu.be/nEQOqCxKHXY.
- Valdina Oliveira Pinto and Rachel E. Harding. "Afro-Brazilian Religion, Resistance and Environmental Ethics." In *Ecowomanism, Religion, and Ecology*. Edited by Melanie L. Harris. Leiden: Brill, 2017.

On the Sacramental Imagination of Postconciliar Catholicism

- Mary Catherine Hilkert. *Naming Grace: Preaching and the Sacramental Imagination*. New York: Continuum, 1997.
- Maria Clara Bingemer. *Latin American Theology: Roots and Branches*. Maryknoll, NY: Orbis Books, 2016.
- Matthew Fox. *Creation Spirituality: Liberating Gifts for the Peoples of the Earth*. New York: Harper Collins, 1991.

Questions for Reflection and Discussion

- Where do you think the inspiration to stand up for environmental human rights comes from? What is the source of such courage?
- What are your own wellsprings of strength and courage in the face of injustice, oppression, and violence? Where does your own inspiration to fight for environmental justice come from?

- What should be some guidelines for practicing interreligious dialogue and cooperation in the face of environmental injustice and climate breakdown? How might we come together across traditions without watering down our various traditions and/or culturally appropriating the traditions of others?

Chapter Six

Remembering the Witness:
Ecomartyrdom in Christian Theological Perspective

Resources for Further Study

- Jon Sobrino. *Witnesses to the Kingdom: The Martyrs of El Salvador and the Crucified Peoples.* Maryknoll, NY: Orbis Books, 2003.
- Michael Lee. *Revolutionary Saint: The Theological Vision of Óscar Romero.* Maryknoll, NY: Orbis Books, 2018.
- In this book, Appendix B makes available an English translation of the transcript of "Berta and Martyrdom," a March 2020 broadcast by Radio Progreso in Honduras that lays out an argument for calling Berta Cáceres a martyr.

Questions for Reflection and Discussion

- What does it mean to be a Christian martyr? A Jesus martyr? An ecomartyr?
- What are the dangers of interpreting the murders of land and environmental defenders in terms of martyrdom?
- Is it possible to recognize non-Christians as martyrs?
- What are the challenges that martyrs of solidarity in general and ecomartyrs in particular pose to Christian theology and praxis?

Conclusion

Responding to the Witness:
Honoring Ecomartyrs with Our Lives

Questions for Reflection and Discussion

- What are the three dimensions of Saint Óscar Romero's response to martyrdom in his own context that might help us discern paths for honoring and responding to ecomartyrdom today?
- How might you incorporate these responses into your own life and the life of your family and community?
- What is one action that you can take to stand in solidarity with land and environmental defenders today?

Appendix B
"Berta and Martyrdom"

A Broadcast of Radio Progreso, Honduras
March 5, 2020[*]

When we confess or proclaim someone to be a martyr, before all else we are talking about a person who did good for others, who was generous and gave themselves over to a cause that was not centered on themselves. A martyr is someone who before we call them that, we can identify in their life a commitment to a cause that was greater than their own personal or familial interests. We are talking about a person who was ethically committed to a social cause external to their own particular needs. They were a person in whom we can see a life lived for others.

A person whom we popularly proclaim to be a martyr has been, above all, a person made of flesh and bones, with virtues but also with flaws, with strengths but also with weaknesses. They are a person whom we have known to be immersed, down to the marrow of their bones, in the reality of daily life, and, in the midst of daily life, they knew how to find the strength to see beyond the ordinary, beyond appearances and superficiality.

A person whom we proclaim to be a martyr is one who knows themself to be a part of the people, who has been immersed in the life of the people and, from there, has transcended that life

---

[*] https://radioprogresohn.net/enfoque/berta-y-el-martirio/.

to encounter the dynamism of transformation. They are someone who, for defending or championing a cause, is well-loved by humble, grace-filled, and ethically committed people. And for the same reasons, they are frowned upon, discredited, questioned, discriminated, mistreated, denounced, and judged, condemned by the sector of people who are well-off and wary of change in society.

A person whom we proclaim to be a martyr is one who died violently as a consequence of their struggle, assassinated for their ideas, for the testimony of their lives, and because they did not submit to the bribes or compromises offered to them by the powerful. They are a person who would not be bought by money, or praise, or vanity. The market could not control them. A martyr is one who during their life was the cause of joy and respect for many humble and humiliated people, as well as a hindrance and discomfort for the wealthy and privileged elite of society.

A person whom we proclaim to be a martyr is someone who, above all, is misunderstood, at times not only by the elites and the powerful, but also by other individuals and groups among the people, and even by people who are close to them or from their own family. Before being persecuted, captured, or assassinated, a martyr was first slandered with false testimonies aimed at discrediting and disparaging them as a person.

Long before they were persecuted and assassinated, a person whom we proclaim to be a martyr was already the victim of attacks by the corporate media, and they were stigmatized even by the church as a bad example that should be nipped in the bud. Their personality and their struggles were distorted and presented as unbalanced or maladjusted.

A person whom we proclaim to be a martyr is one who, before being assassinated, risked their life to the end, did not act in a calculated way, broke out of the ordinary molds of circumspection, and gave their life for others, for what they believed, and gave testimony with their life that protecting their own life was not as important as protecting the lives and dignity of other people, communities, oppressed humanity, and the rights of the whole people.

A person whom we confess to be a martyr was above all a victim of a cruel assassination, a person whose body we saw broken, who suffered wounds of the flesh in their body, who endured and suffered the horrors of death. Before being confessed as a martyr, the person was horrifically assassinated, and we saw their body broken and shattered, in the midst of a trail of blood, with their face disfigured, with the grimace of an ungracious death. No confession of martyrdom can make this bloody reality of violent death disappear.

Confession of a person as a martyr is preceded by the pain and frustration that their death has provoked in many people. People have wept and anguished over the assassination of the person whom we call a martyr later on. But once we have seen their lifeless body or we have found out about their assassination, a personal, communal, and social process of interiorizing this stolen life begins immediately.

Once we have wept and experienced the absence of this person whose life was violently ripped from our side, we begin the process of transforming our tears into recognition of their life as an offering and an oblation, and we even interiorize the fact that this person was assassinated for defending our cause, that they died for us. And so we babble and stammer at first, until we are able to convert into complete sentences and testimonies that this person was assassinated for their commitment and that their death cannot remain mired in horror or in pain. Their death acquires meaning for our lives and, from the loss, frustration, and failure, we begin to experience strength for our own journey from the death of a person like this.

When we experience the bloody death of a person so courageous as one whom we proclaim to be a martyr, that person's death cannot be in vain, nor should it be forgotten. And so we begin to experience a personal and communal strength that guides us to discover that there is no other way but to attempt to make our own lives look a little more like that person who is no longer with us, and that what we do should be in keeping with the cause and the values for which that person was assassinated and for which they gave their lives. Then we become convinced that life has meaning and that, if we are faithful to those who shed their blood for us, they will live on insofar as we make them present in our actions and testimony.

We offer these reflections with the face, the voice, and the life of Berta Cáceres in mind. Is it not the case that she is a model of martyrdom in our time? Berta Cáceres was a woman who made people uncomfortable. No one could buy her off or tame her because her identity was always intertwined with the people. She made the wealthy and powerful very uncomfortable.

Who else compares to Berta Cáceres in their capacity to make the powerful uncomfortable? With whom can we compare her? Certainly with Jesús the uncomfortable one of Nazareth who made the established powers of his time uncomfortable and confronted the religious authorities of his time with his prophetic word. Those authorities not only failed to understand him; they called him a blasphemer, glutton, drunkard, and friend of sinners. And they handed him over to the Roman empire. That's how uncomfortable Berta Cáceres made people.

Although it may seem blasphemous to some of the curia and their staff, Berta reminds us of María, the mother of Jesús, with her proclamation of the Magnificat. It was she who anticipated the mission of Jesús when she proclaims the Magnificat. It was she who anticipated the mission of Jesús when, in the first chapter of the Gospel of Luke, she cries out with joy because God her savior looked upon her humility and because, from then on, generations upon generations would call her blessed. María proclaims that the Lord shows mercy to all those who decide to live in God's presence, because the Lord destroys the proud, casts the mighty from their thrones and exalts the humble, fills the hungry with good things and sends the rich empty away.

That is María, the mother of Jesús. Is this not what Berta Cáceres said and did? Berta is also our Monseñor Romero in our Honduras, although again, it may sound blasphemous to certain clergy who are well-situated. And if it doesn't seem that way to them, then we are saying it wrong because Jesús was assassinated with the approval of those who were religiously well-situated in his time. Berta always broke out of the traditional and formal molds of the system.

Berta Cáceres is the dignification of women, of those who struggle for life. She is the dignification of Indigenous people, and the exemplary popular leader. She is the dignification of the common goods of nature. She is the model of martyrdom of our time and for our times, whose words in defense of mother earth, wounded by human beings, have never ceased to shake up our lives: "*Wake up, wake up, humanity. We are out of time.*"

Permissions

Every effort has been made to identify the owners and obtain permission for all reproduced content in this book. We would be grateful to be notified of any inadvertent errors or omissions.

Permissions to reproduce the following poems and songs are on file with the author:

"Como Tú," by Roque Dalton. Used by permission of Juan José Dalton.

"A Morte Anunciada de Josimo Tavares" by Pedro Tierra. Used by permission of Pedro Tierra (Hamilton Pereira da Silva).

"Alcides" by Libardo Valdés. Used by permission of Libardo Valdés and the producer, SIGNIS, ALC.

"To Be a Priest," by Josimo Tavares, trans. by Binka Le Breton. Used by permission of Binka Le Breton

"Mártires da Caminhada," by Cireneu Kuhn, SVD. Used by permission of Cireneu Kuhn.

"Cuando Los Angeles Lloran." Words and music by Jose Fernando and Emilio Olvera Sierra. Copyright © 2010 Tulum Music (ASCAP). All Rights Administered by WC Music Corp. All Rights Reserved. Used by permission of Alfred Music.

"Latinoamerica," by Rene Perez, Eduardo Cabra and Rafael Arcaute. Copyright © 2010 Warner-Tamerlane Publishing Corp. (BMI), Residente Music Publisher (BMI), WC Music Corp. (ASCAP), Visitante Music Publishing (ASCAP), and EMI Blackwood Music

Inc. (BMI). All rights on behalf of itself and Residente Music Publisher administered by Warner-Tamerlane Publishing Corp. All rights on behalf of itself and Visitante Music Publishing administered by WC Music Corp. All Rights Reserved. Used by permission of Alfred Music.

The visual art in Chapter 4 was created by and used by permission of Grace McMullen.

Cover art: "Ecomartirio, voz de la tierra—fuerza de vida," by Alexander Serpas. Used by permission of Alexander Serpas.

INDEX

239